TRUE SONS OF THE REPUBLIC

**Recent Titles in
Reflections on the Civil War Era**

Decision in the Heartland: The Civil War in the West
Steven E. Woodworth

TRUE SONS OF THE REPUBLIC

EUROPEAN IMMIGRANTS IN THE UNION ARMY

MARTIN W. ÖFELE

Reflections on the Civil War Era
John David Smith, Series Editor

Westport, Connecticut
London

Library of Congress Cataloging-in-Publication Data

Öfele, Martin, 1968–
   True sons of the Republic : European immigrants in the Union Army / Martin W. Öfele.
      p.   cm. — (Reflections on the Civil War era, ISSN 1939–649X)
   Includes bibliographical references and index.
   ISBN 978–0–275–98422–9 (alk. paper)
      1. United States—History—Civil War, 1861–1865—Participation, Foreign.
2. United States. Army—History—Civil War, 1861–1865.   3. United
States—History—Civil War, 1861–1865—Social aspects.   4. Immigrants—United
States—History—19th century.   I. Title.
   E540.F6O44   2008
   973.7′1—dc22   2007044133

British Library Cataloguing in Publication Data is available.

Library of Congress Catalog Card Number: 2007044133
ISBN: 978–0–275–98422–9
ISSN: 1939–649X

First published in 2008

Praeger Publishers, 88 Post Road West, Westport, CT 06881
An imprint of Greenwood Publishing Group, Inc.
www.praeger.com

Printed in the United States of America

The paper used in this book complies with the
Permanent Paper Standard issued by the National
Information Standards Organization (Z39.48–1984).

10 9 8 7 6 5 4 3 2 1

On the front cover: Michael Corcoran (1827–1863), an American Army Officer of
The Nineteenth Century (American Lithograph).

A native of Donegal, Ireland, Michael Corcoran served in the British revenue service until he
sided with the Irish nationalist patriots and eventually emigrated in 1849. Taking up residence
in New York City, Corcoran joined the ethnic Irish 69th New York Militia and soon rose
to colonel. When in 1860 the Prince of Wales visited the city, the Irish rebel stood by his
national principles and refused to parade the regiment in honor of the representative of the
oppressive English government. Corcoran faced court-martial charges for insubordination, but
at the outbreak of the Civil War was acquitted to reorganize his unit into federal service.
Leading the 69th in the first battle of Bull Run, Colonel Corcoran was wounded and taken
prisoner. After his exchange a year later, the national hero was made brigadier general and
raised a predominantly Irish brigade from New York, called the "Corcoran Legion." While
riding through winter quarters in Virginia with his friend Thomas Francis Meagher, shortly
before Christmas 1863, the popular officer was killed when his horse slipped and fell.

"Stand by the Union;
Fight for the Union;
Die for the Union!"
(*Boston Pilot*, January 12, 1861)

CONTENTS

Series Foreword   ix

Preface and Acknowledgments   xi

Chapter One: Nineteenth-Century European Emigration: Poverty
and Revolutions   1

Chapter Two: Immigrants in American Society, 1840–1860   17

Chapter Three: The Coming of the War   33

Chapter Four: Serving Their Adopted Country   69

Chapter Five: Ethnic Visibility in the Early War   87

Chapter Six: To Fredericksburg: Slaughter and Glory   113

Chapter Seven: Chancellorsville to Missionary Ridge: Humiliation
and Triumph   137

Epilogue: The Aftermath of War   157
Notes   163
Bibliographical Essay   183
Index   189

SERIES FOREWORD

"Like Ol' Man River," the distinguished Civil War historian Peter J. Parish wrote in 1998, "Civil War historiography just keeps rolling along. It changes course occasionally, leaving behind bayous of stagnant argument, while it carves out new lines of inquiry and debate."

Since Confederate General Robert E. Lee's men stacked their guns at Appomattox Court House in April 1865, historians and partisans have been fighting a war of words over the causes, battles, results, and broad meaning of the internecine conflict that cost more than 620,000 American lives. Writers have contributed between 50,000 and 60,000 books and pamphlets on the topic. Viewed in terms of defining American freedom and nationalism, Western expansion and economic development, the Civil War quite literally launched modern America. "The Civil War," Kentucky poet, novelist, and literary critic Robert Penn Warren explained, "is for the American imagination, the great single event of our history. Without too much wrenching, it may, in fact, be said to *be* American history."

The books in Praeger's *Reflections on the Civil War Era* series examine pivotal aspects of the American Civil War. Topics range from examinations of military campaigns and local conditions, to analyses of institutional, intellectual, and social history. Questions of class, gender, and race run through each volume in the series. Authors, veteran experts in their respective fields, provide concise, informed, and readable syntheses—fresh looks at familiar topics with new source material and original arguments.

"Like all great conflicts," Parish noted in 1999, "the American Civil War reflected the society and the age in which it was fought." Books in *Reflections on the Civil War Era* series interpret the war as a salient event in the hammering out and understanding of American identity before, during, and after the secession crisis of 1860–1861. Readers will find the volumes valuable guides as they chart the troubled waters of mid-nineteenth-century American life.

John David Smith
Charles H. Stone Distinguished Professor of American History
The University of North Carolina at Charlotte

PREFACE AND ACKNOWLEDGMENTS

Times of war and upheaval have always been times of migration and social change. During the Napoleonic Wars that shook the European continent between 1793 and 1814, soldiers in the vast peoples' armies experienced a whole new sense of mobility. For the first time in European history, not mercenaries and professional soldiers but citizens constituted the majority of national armies. Volunteers and draftees, single men and family men left their homes and covered unprecedented distances to battlefields as far apart as southern Italy and Spain, Moscow and eastern Prussia, Austria, Belgium, Saxony, and even Egypt. A few decades later in America, Union and Confederate soldiers also found themselves marching across their continent engaging in a large-scale Civil War, often far away from their homes. To urban New Englanders stationed on the South Carolina Sea Islands the environment seemed as foreign and strange as it did to Louisiana farmers who for the first time in their lives saw the rolling Shenandoah Valley.

By the time the Civil War started, the United States had become the favorite destination for millions of Europeans who left their home countries in a mass emigration movement starting in the 1830s. In the twenty years before the war more than 4.2 million immigrants, mostly from northern and central Europe, including the eastern provinces of the Kingdom of Prussia, the Slavic and Hungarian parts of the Habsburg Empire, and the Italian states, came to America. In 1860, one out of nine white Americans was foreign-born, and in the northern states of the Union, almost one-fourth of the white population numbering 21 million had come from Europe.[1]

While immigration waned after the outbreak of the war, it never stopped and the numbers of newcomers from some countries, Sweden for example, even increased between 1860 and 1865. After the occupation of New Orleans in April 1862, the North controlled all major immigration ports and therefore could draw on an unabated stream of potential recruits from abroad, adding to its already superior manpower pool. Eventually, soldiers from over twenty different nationalities served in the Union army. Some 25 percent of the more than 2 million white Union soldiers had been born in Europe, among them some 145,000 Irish, 54,000 English, 21,000 Swedes, and up to 4,000 Poles from the various Russian and Prussian Polish provinces.[2] The number of German soldiers has been the subject of debates ever since the first exhaustive work on the Germans in the Civil War by Wilhelm Kaufmann appeared in 1911.[3] In the pan-Germanic spirit of the time, Kaufmann included several thousand Swiss, Danes, ethnic Poles, and even the 800 Hungarians into his compiled number of 216,000 German soldiers. Four decades later, Ella Lonn in her seminal work on foreigners in the Union army and navy defined ethnic groups with more precision and qualified Kaufmann's inflated statistic, arriving at little more than 200,000 German-American Union soldiers.[4]

Although a portion of all these immigrants served in the various ethnic German, Irish, or other ethnic regiments, by far the majority enlisted in mixed and predominantly American units. Because many of them possessed military education and experience from their service in the European armies, these soldiers contributed eminently to molding masses of raw recruits into effective fighting forces. One indication of the value of immigrants for the Union army is the number of foreign-born officers who eventually rose to generalships. Of the 583 generals wearing the northern uniform, forty had come from Europe, among them twelve from Germany and Prussia. The same number had been born in Ireland, five in Britain, three in France, and two each in Hungary and Poland. In addition, one general each came from Russia, Spain, Sweden, and Switzerland.[5]

Like many of their fellow immigrants, several of these ethnic commanders had already fought for independent and democratic nation states in Europe in several uprisings and revolutions between 1830 and 1849. To them, the American Civil War finally linked European and American struggles for national unity and universal civil rights. Exiled revolutionaries like Thomas Francis Meagher, Franz Sigel, and Julius Stahel saw participation in the war as the logical continuation of their own cause as much as proof of their loyalty to the American republic. As Heinrich Börnstein, one of the revolutionaries of 1848, called out in his St. Louis newspaper upon the outbreak of the war,

> The present revolution of the people is greater and far more momentous than the one of 1776. In its victory rest all hopes of the free people in America and the whole world.... Should this republic perish, a gigantic cry of despair and anger would resound

throughout mankind; a cry of despair over the God of History and a cry of anger over the cowardly race, over us, who have dropped the holy banner of freedom into the dust.[6]

Drawing on the multiple research done in the field of ethnic participation in the Civil War over the last decades, this book attempts to portray the various immigrant experiences in that crucial American conflict that not only destroyed slavery but also forged a new multicultural society. A short survey of the background to European emigration and the ethnic factor in society and politics before the Civil War will provide some necessary information on why so many immigrants had come to America, where they settled, and how their influence on society developed on the road to war. The motivations and wartime participation of those immigrants who entered the Union army will make up the main body of the book, while the ethnic civilian experience and ongoing political struggles on the home front have been largely left out as a concession to space and simplicity. Too limited in scope to encompass all immigrant groups present in the Civil War, the book will focus on those ethnic groups that made up the vast majority of immigrants during that time and minor groups that figured prominently in the northern Civil War armies. Corresponding to their numbers and importance to European immigration in the mid-nineteenth century, Irish and German immigrants will thus receive the most attention, as their combined numbers constituted almost three-quarters of all immigrants coming to America in the twenty years before the Civil War. Other immigrants will appear in due course and will make their voices heard whenever they contribute to the overall picture of the ethnic side of the Civil War. From the multitude of sources, I have selected a few exemplary protagonists who in letters, diaries, and memoirs explained their motivations, battle experiences, and their relations with Americans and other ethnic groups. Because immigrant participation was confined largely to the Union, the "tens of thousands" of Confederate foreign-born soldiers, according to historian Ella Lonn, have not been attended to.[7] Finally, while not every ethnic group or key person will receive adequate attention, I have not purposely neglected any of the ethnic groups that made up Civil War America.

Several friends and colleagues have been extremely helpful in the creation of this book and have rendered immensely valuable assistance. Professor John David Smith was instrumental in conceiving the whole project and time and again has tried to keep me on the right path. Esteemed colleague and profound specialist on the German-American war experience, Chris Keller has contributed priceless suggestions and more than once prevented me from drawing false conclusions. My good and old friends, Malcolm Richardson and Mike Musick, spent much time smoothing out the recurring bumps in my prose. Last but not least, I am most grateful, as usual, to my family and close friends who never lost their patience with me and offered guidance throughout.

ONE

NINETEENTH-CENTURY EUROPEAN EMIGRATION: POVERTY AND REVOLUTIONS

The nineteenth century was a century of migrations in Europe, both within continental boundaries and to overseas destinations. In the decades following the Napoleonic Wars, newfound geographical mobility, together with improved education, provided an outlet for countless Europeans longing for a better life and improved living conditions. By the mid-nineteenth century, emigration affected every European country and people in every occupation and social class. North America soon became the favorite destination for those leaving their home countries, and in the decades preceding the American Civil War, an unparalleled stream of emigrants crossed the Atlantic Ocean. It was mostly economic motivations in the wake of the Industrial Revolution that fueled European emigration. The pan-European phenomenon (in the first half of the nineteenth century) of an unmatched population upsurge began in Britain in the late eighteenth century and by 1850 had spread through the Nordic countries into all of central and Eastern Europe. Within a hundred years, the European population almost doubled from 145 million to 265 million, and that figure takes into account the estimated 15 to 20 million emigrants who left Europe during that time. Reforms and revolutionary inventions in the fields of agriculture, medicine, and hygiene allowed for this explosive growth in population. Ironically, thanks to this progress ever more people survived during the nineteenth century "only to go hungry all their lives."[1]

Mainly affecting rural areas and lower social classes, population growth promoted and accelerated social change. Farms had to support growing numbers of tenants, and plots could only be divided so many times before they became too small to support their occupants. More and more landless migrants moved to the cities in search of employment in the thriving industrial trades. At the same time, the transition from agrarian to industrial societies in most countries created an overabundance of urban labor that in turn enabled factory owners to lower wages and dictate employment practices. However, for people in highly secluded and destitute rural areas such as the Scottish Highlands or Skåne in southern Sweden, industrial jobs often seemed available only in America. Thus, emigration to a country that promised land and work for everyone became a tempting alternative for countless Europeans who felt that they did not have much to lose anyway. Eventually, some 85 percent of the European population would become immersed in a vast migration movement throughout the nineteenth century, of which overseas emigration—as immensely as it affected Europe and America—constituted only a fraction.

Yet, while industrialization and its side effects undoubtedly played a major role in this unprecedented movement, other factors influenced migration as well. In his seminal 1985 study of immigrants in American cities, John Bodnar argued that the "movement to America of millions of immigrants in the century after the 1820s was not simply a flight of impoverished peasants abandoning underdeveloped, backward regions for the riches and unlimited opportunities offered by the American economy."[2] Two most important push factors stand out in their singular effects on European migration history, propelling mass emigration to new levels in the 1840s and 1850s. First, the devastating harvest failures during the "hungry forties" are best known for bringing the Great Famine to Ireland, but also had severe effects on other countries as well. Second, the national revolutions of 1848 and 1849 with their reactionary aftermaths worsened social and political conditions in several European countries and caused emigrants to seek a better and more secure life elsewhere.[3]

OVERPOPULATION AND HARDSHIP: EMIGRATION FROM NORTHERN EUROPE

For most Irishmen, the decision to emigrate was not an easy one, although living standards deteriorated for many of them during the first half of the nineteenth century. The English Crown had converted farmland into grazing territory to increase agricultural exports. Angered and impoverished, Irish peasants faced unemployment, ever diminishing amounts of land to cultivate, rising rents, and a haughty and distanced government that cared little about their condition. Still, until the 1840s the proverbial ties to their native soil prevented most Irish from packing up and leaving. The cultivation of potatoes still provided meager subsistence. But its rapid population growth in the preceding decades had turned Ireland into the most densely settled area in Europe and emigration became increasingly attractive. Education played an important role in spreading the early migration movement. Similar to Britain and much of continental Europe, the literacy rate in Ireland had begun to rise enormously with the introduction of public schools in the 1820s. Now even peasants were able to read newspapers, guidebooks, and letters from emigrants and thus gain knowledge about America. Encouraged by these sources of news a wave of emigrants, mostly single men in their twenties, left Ireland in search of better opportunities. Then beginning in 1845, the *hungry forties* with their catastrophic harvest failures provided a new incentive for emigration. The potato blight had hit farmers on a regular basis for years, but its severity in that decade together with the dependence of most Irish peasants on one single crop made consequences intolerable. Within months people were starving by the thousands and now emigration to America, where some of their fellow citizens had already found new homes, became the desperate hope of those escaping near-certain death. Overall, in the wake of the Great Famine, up to 1.8 million emigrants boarded ships to North America yearning for a better future. The famine also served as a catalytic force in the political radicalization of both Irish and Irish Americans. When revolutions hit continental Europe in 1848, rebellious Irishmen calling themselves the "Young Ireland" staged a revolt against English hegemony. Their movement collapsed, however, and several leaders were convicted and banished to the Australian island of Tasmania. Thomas Francis Meagher and John Mitchel were among those who eventually escaped to America, where they reunited in 1853.[4]

Poverty and deteriorating living conditions also sparked emigration from Britain to America. In the first twenty years of the nineteenth century alone, the combined population of England, Wales, and Scotland grew by almost 40 percent from 10.9 million to 14.6 million. The resulting demographic pressure was most severe in Scotland whose populace increased by three-fourths between 1800 and 1850. Large-scale migration from Scotland and Wales began in the 1820s and had similar causes as prefamine Irish emigration. Overpopulation in rural and underdeveloped areas combined with rising rents and the displacement of tenants by capitalist landlords to create widespread impoverishment. Simultaneously, the advent of the Industrial Revolution replaced the traditional guilds of professions such as carpenters, shoemakers, or metal and wood workers. Thrown out of their businesses, many unemployed craftsmen had to compete with farmers and unskilled laborers for factory jobs. By the middle of the century, Britain had developed into the first urban and industrial nation with only one-fifth of its working population still engaged in agriculture or related fields of work. As industrialization also gained momentum in the United States, the nation's hunger for coal and steel grew insatiable. With unemployment high in Britain, thousands of miners and ironworkers joined the emigrant movement and introduced professional mining in America. Additionally, the repeal of the protectionist Corn Laws in 1846 resulted in free trade and falling grain prices and prompted a large number of British farmers to emigrate.[5]

More than in England and Wales, the emigration movement in Scotland took on a decidedly vital character for many impoverished peasants. In 1851, almost one in every three British emigrants to the United States came from Scotland, more than double the Scottish share of the whole population. Scotland lost more of its population to emigration than most other European countries in the nineteenth century, and during the 1850s its proportion of emigrants to overseas destinations was second only to Ireland. Nineteenth-century Scotland was economically and socially divided into its Highland and Lowland regions. Since the late eighteenth century, the Highlands had been seriously overpopulated and could hardly support its tenants. Resulting economic hardship had already driven some Highlanders to Ireland and to colonial America in the seventeenth and eighteenth centuries, but most Highlanders resisted emigration longer than their Lowland neighbors. Then in the early nineteenth century the infamous Highland Clearances did much to depopulate whole regions of northern Scotland when English landlords—often forcibly—evicted small tenants to make room for sheep farms. To many Highlanders the situation became unbearable when in 1846 the *hungry forties* spread to Scotland and the potato crop failed with similarly destructive effects as in Ireland. The time had come when even the proud Scottish Highlanders severed their traditionally strong ties to home and hearth and set out in search of a better future in the United States.

Unlike the Irish famine emigration, it were not usually the poorest who left Britain but instead those who had enough money to pay for their own and their families' journeys, and those who could profit economically in the expanding United States' economy. Additionally, a number of British emigrants left their home country for ideological and political reasons. For many, coming to the United States meant escaping the petrified British class system to join a more egalitarian society. Other emigrants hoped to exchange a remote and centralist government for a republican democracy in which everybody could participate. Like the Society of Friends, or Quakers, who had already founded American communities in the eighteenth century, Welsh Calvinist Methodists emigrated because they saw their traditional religious and ethical values threatened by ruthless commercialization in Britain. In all, a little more than 690,000 English, Welsh, and Scottish emigrants came to the United States during the 1840s and 1850s. Together with the Irish and Germans, they accounted for 90 percent of all newcomers in this period.[6]

Overpopulation in the Nordic states of Sweden, Finland, and Norway caused the same problems as in Britain, and may have been exacerbated because these countries lagged behind in industrialization and urbanization. Because there was no industrial sector in any of these countries to absorb the growing labor force, population pressure was enormous and economic motivations dominated emigration. Only few emigrants left in search of religious freedom and fewer still for political reasons. Leading the movement, Norwegians began emigrating as organized groups in 1836. Over the next fifteen years some 18,000 emigrants departed for America, the vast majority from the isolated interior mountain regions. Swedish emigration to America began in 1846 when a deviant religious sect led by self-proclaimed minister Eric Jansson fled religious dogmatism. Several Mormon and Baptist groups followed, but the majority consisted of small farmers and artisans emigrating with their families. In the 1850s, almost 21,000 Swedes came to the United States. The former Swedish province of Finland saw only 1,000 of its people come to America during the prewar decades. In 1860, 94 percent of the Finnish population was still employed in agriculture and urbanization had actually decreased in the preceding decade. Most Finnish emigrants preferred Norway as a destination, where they could find work as fishermen or miners. Although the Danish population had also increased substantially by the mid-century, an era of political reform and educational improvement had relieved social and demographic pressure there. Thus, overpopulation did not affect Denmark as much as other European countries. Only slightly over 4,000 Danes emigrated in the 1840s and 1850s, half of them Baptist and Mormon converts who followed their brethrens' call to the United States. Interestingly, none of the Scandinavian countries and Finland experienced serious revolutions, although in Denmark and Norway farmers and laborers demanded more rights, and in the Swedish capital violent demonstrations in 1848 ended in bloody clashes with the armed forces.[7]

A CONTINENT IN UPROAR: THE REVOLUTIONS OF 1848

It seems only natural today that population growth and widespread poverty would eventually lead to demands for personal liberty, political participation, and national unity in most of Europe. Political unrest had found its first radical expression in the French Revolution of 1789. That momentous upheaval made people in Europe aware of universal social and political problems. It also demonstrated that there was no divine order that had predestined social and economic castes. Instead, even the lower classes could successfully rebel and overthrow unjust social structures. This notion gained momentum when allied European citizen armies defeated Napoleon Bonaparte's forces three decades later and ended over twenty years of warfare in Europe. A new age dawned and liberal thinkers like German Friedrich List called for substantial national and democratic reforms in Europe. They envisioned a continent free from autocracy whose nation states would recognize their citizens' civil rights. National contracts modeled on the American Constitution should guarantee such liberties for every individual. However, in 1815 the Congress of Vienna shattered these expectations. Politicians ignored the reformers' pleas, and the three principal monarchies returned to control the continent. Prussia ruled over most of the small and middle German states, while the Austrian Habsburg Empire had a firm grip over southern Europe including Hungary and much of Italy. In addition to his vast Russian territory, Czar Nicholas presided over the eastern provinces of Poland.[8]

It was too late, however, to put an end to the drive for liberty and nationalism. Tensions mounted, and the second French Revolution in July 1830 sparked two tumultuous decades in Europe. French laborers revolted in Lyon and Paris, and in Great Britain a new workers' party began to spread contagious ideas of equality and democracy. Triggered by events in France, revolts broke out in Belgium, Poland, Italy, and several German states, leading to rudimentary political and social reforms. German students, together with Polish and French democrats, challenged the authority of the state at the Hambach Festival in the Palatinate in 1832, and rebellious Giuseppe Mazzini called for national independence of the scattered Italian microstates ruled by Austria. Overpopulation and pauperism in the wake of industrialization led Silesian weavers to revolt and fueled a movement that would eventually become known as communism. In 1844, a censored booklet of nationalist poems by exiled poet Heinrich Heine smuggled into the homes of many Germans described the volatile situation:

> A newer song, a better song,
> My friends, let's bring to birth now!
> We shall proceed right here to build
> The Kingdom of Heaven on earth now.
> We wish to be happy here on earth,
> All want eradicated;
> The idler's belly shall not consume
> What toilers' hands have created.[9]

Triggered further by epidemic outbreaks of hunger and starvation during the hungry forties popular unrest finally culminated in two years of violent upheaval all over Europe. The revolutions began in January 1848, when Italians in the Habsburg kingdom of Sicily and Naples revolted against King Ferdinand II and proclaimed a provisional government in Palermo. In France, social unrest led to the third revolution within sixty years and the swift overthrow of the monarchy in February. The new provisional government included socialists, and for the first time in Europe civil rights such as the right to work and universal male suffrage were guaranteed. But in April the inexperienced voters expelled the socialists from the government and installed a conservative government, provoking bloody street fights between workers and republican troops in Paris. The rebellion subsided after several weeks and 3,000 casualties. Over 10,000 revolutionaries were exiled, some of them eventually emigrating to the United States. The revolution soon spread to southern Germany. News about the French Revolution reached the Grand Duchy of Baden in late February and demands for a unified German republic rose. Nationalist leader Gustav Struve publicly called for an all-German parliament and his fellow revolutionary Friedrich Hecker planned to march a people's army against the Badenese capital of Karlsruhe. Yet Hecker only succeeded in gathering some 1,000 troops, his campaign failed, and many revolutionaries faced jail sentences or exile. A frustrated Hecker escaped to

Switzerland and later emigrated to America—as would many of his fellow so-called "forty-eighters."[10]

Then in March, another revolution exploded in Hungary. Radical nationalist Lajos Kossuth, a lawyer by profession and a charismatic journalist, openly defied Austrian authority over his homeland and demanded Hungarian autonomy under a parliamentary government. Together with members of the ethnic Magyar intellectual elite and nobility, Kossuth called for a free press, civil and religious rights, and a national army. Intimidated, Ferdinand II partially gave in to the Hungarian requirements, but politicians in Vienna refused to cede authority and rejected Kossuth's claims. At the same time, social unrest broke out among students and other dissatisfied citizens in the Austrian capital, forcing the government to declare the city under a state of siege. To make things worse for the Habsburg rulers, enraged Venetians freed political prisoners and declared a republic in the Italian lagoon city. Reacting to the Vienna and Venice uprisings, the Milanese also revolted and took up arms against Austria. Soon the Habsburg regime found itself under pressure in every corner of its empire.

Meanwhile, Karl Marx and Friedrich Engels had published highly subversive thoughts in their *Communist Manifesto*. "The modern bourgeois society," they argued, "that has sprouted from the ruins of feudal society has not done away with class antagonisms. It has but established new classes, new conditions of oppression, new forms of struggle in place of the old ones." Therefore the communists called on all "Proletarians of all countries," to unite in the struggle against economic and social oppression. Translated into several languages, such radical pleas set off violent social protest among European workers. By mid-March, the revolution reached tightly ruled Prussia. In the capital of Berlin insurgents erected barricades and for several days fought royal troops to a standstill. Incensed by the Hungarian uprising, dissatisfied Polish citizens in the Prussian province of Posen also demanded their political recognition as an autonomous ethnic group. Like another nationalist insurgence two years before, the revolt was quickly and brutally suppressed. Sympathizing with their fellow revolutionaries, a few Prussian citizens liberated captive Polish freedom fighters from a Berlin prison. At the same time, Prussia sent armed forces against Denmark, which had annexed the German Dukedom of Schleswig in March. From everywhere in Germany nationalists joined the campaign to "liberate" the northernmost German state that had formed a union with its southern neighbor Holstein since the fifteenth century.

In Baden, where Friedrich Hecker's military plans had come to naught, Bavarian troops occupied the city of Mannheim to quell turmoil and restore order. Still, many reform-minded Germans became optimistic when on May 18 the first publicly elected German national parliament convened in St. Paul's Church in Hessian Frankfurt. Four days later a Prussian national parliament came to session in Berlin. Composed strongly of doctors, lawyers, professors, and other middle-class professionals, high hopes rested with the delegates of each body to establish constitutional nation states.

Meanwhile, a separate Slavic Congress convened in Prague where Czech nationalists from Bohemia, together with Moravians and ethnic Germans from Silesia, labored toward the creation of a separate Slavic state within the Austrian empire.

While politicians debated and angry citizens rebelled, the most imminent peril to conservative Europe was mounting in its southeast, where Lajos Kossuth had recruited a national "Honved" army. The Hungarians beat back loyal Croatian troops and marched to the Danube River, openly threatening the Austrian heartland. When juvenile Emperor Franz Joseph ascended the throne following his father's abdication, the mutinous Hungarians refused to acknowledge his authority and instead declared their independence. At this point social protest in Austria and the Hungarian national uprising confluenced. As the government turned the army against its own citizens and besieged Vienna, the Honved troops attempted to aid their revolutionary allies but eventually lacked the power to relieve the city. Finally, after three weeks' heavy fighting the Viennese rebels surrendered on October 31. Setting out against Kossuth's troops, the imperial army in early January occupied the principal Hungarian cities of Pest and Buda.

In Baden, a second revolutionary attempt by Gustav Struve had already failed in September and the end of the revolutionary year made it clear that all over Europe reactionary forces would prevail. On December 1, Prussian King Friedrich Wilhelm IV dissolved the ineffective Berlin parliament and imposed a constitution that placated many Prussians' demands for a constitutional order, while relieving fears of further social unrest. Although the national parliament in Frankfurt continued its work and agreed on basic civil rights, the conservative middle and upper class delegates were afraid of losing their economic and political privileges and thus prevented far-reaching democratic reforms. Swiss-born Hermann Lieb, a participant in the April barricade fights in Paris, would later concur with many of his contemporaries when he judged that the futile revolution "gave evidence, that the German people at that time had no sense and mind for the republic."[11]

The dawn of 1849 brought the final demise of revolutionary experiments in Europe. Emperor Franz Joseph dissolved the parliament and reestablished authoritarian rule in Austria, while the Frankfurt parliament in a desperate shot for a German nation sacrificed its republican ideals and elected Friedrich Wilhelm IV as emperor. The Prussian monarch, however, refused to accept the crown because it was afflicted with the "stench of revolution" and thus delivered the fatal blow to the national idea. Crippled by the departure of many disappointed delegates, the parliament tried to reconvene in Stuttgart in Württemberg, but royal troops soon broke up the meeting and eradicated what was left of republican politics. Prussian troops met little resistance when they set out to crush renewed uprisings and restore monarchical authority in Saxony, the Prussian Rhineland, and once more in Baden. In the meantime, the newly elected French president Louis Napoleon sent troops to occupy Rome where the citizens had dethroned Pope Pius and declared a republic. Two of the most influential Italian revolutionaries had to go into exile—Giuseppe Mazzini continued his fight for a unified Italy from Switzerland and romantic freedom fighter Giuseppe Garibaldi found temporary homes in England and later in New York.

Finally, the longest and most radical European revolution collapsed in August. The Honved army had won several impressing victories against the Austrians, culminating in the liberation of Pest and Buda in May. But these military successes, together with Kossuth's bold declaration of independence, spooked a mighty neighbor. Czar Nicholas feared the rebellion would infest Russia and sent 200,000 troops against the Hungarians. Realizing that no European nation would recognize his Hungarian state and that the allied Russian and Austrian armies badly outnumbered his men, Kossuth fled to Bulgaria. Harsh retribution in the wake of the Hungarian surrender in August forced numerous revolutionaries into exile. Exiled German poet Heinrich Heine, always a champion of civil rights, lamented that with Austrian victory the last citadel of freedom had fallen in Europe: "Freedom's last trench was overmatched, And Hungary is at death's door."[12] By the fall of 1849, the European revolutionary fervor had passed without yielding major results. Two years later, even France returned to monarchical rule when Louis Napoleon declared himself emperor.

The American people had followed the European revolutions sympathetically and diplomats had even raised Hungarian hopes of formal recognition. Indeed, President Zachary Taylor's administration considered recognizing the Hungarian Republic in 1849. In the following year, serious clashes occurred between the United States and Austria over Hungarian exiles who had escaped to America. Similarly, Irish nationalists following Meagher and Mitchel found sympathizers in America. In 1852, a resolution in the Senate even called on England to pardon the Irish exiles in Australia. The European belief in the United States as a haven of freedom and opportunity swelled considerably in the years following the failed revolutions, hastened by political frustration and economic distress created when the conservative powers tightened their hold on the continent.[13]

Of all the nations and peoples affected by the European Revolutions of 1848–1849, the Hungarians had led the most unified and successful struggle for national identity and independence. They had fought not only against their Austrian rulers, but also against Russians, Croats, Serbs, and other ethnic groups, strengthening their own ethnic consciousness. In addition, due to their persistent defiance the Hungarians suffered most from reactionary retribution following Kossuth's defeat. Thus, it is no wonder that emigration from Hungary in the 1850s included the highest proportion of political exiles in Europe. Among them were numerous veterans of the Honved army and several of Kossuth's closest friends and relatives who fled persecution. Although their total number probably did not exceed a few hundred, ex-revolutionaries and active supporters of the national cause constituted the intellectual ethnic leadership of Hungarian emigrants to the United States before 1860. As in Hungary, political refugees left the Prussian and Russian Polish provinces after the revolutions.[14] Passionate anti-imperialist and nationalist sentiments among Poles forged their image of the United States as an ideal society embodying Polish dreams of a liberal nation state.

Wladimir Krzyzanowski was born in 1824 in Roznow (in Prussian Poland) as a farmer's son. His family, including cousin Frederic Chopin, had strong nationalist convictions and had supported the Polish revolution of 1830. Engaged in the Polish national cause himself, Krzyzanowski had to flee Prussian prosecution at age twenty-two and emigrated to America. Musing over his motivations to leave Europe, the exiled nationalist later wrote that he had emigrated "So that I could seek my fortune, as well as liberty. So that I could drink my fill from the fountain of liberty, so that I could build my strength in a country that was built by the nobles as well as by the dregs of Europe. A country that was able to unite these opposites into a union of tolerance, equality, and brotherhood."[15] After 1849, a renewed wave of emigrants, especially from Prussian Silesia, left for America, among them many small farmers, peasants, and craftsmen. One of their most influential leaders was Stanislas Kiolbassa. A prosperous Silesian farmer, Kiolbassa had been an elected member of the Berlin Parliament. In 1854, Kiolbassa led his family and other Polish emigrants to America where they founded Panna Maria, the first ethnic Silesian settlement in Texas.

Crop failures had already sparked the emigration movement among Polish and Bohemian peasants during the hungry forties. Following the European Revolutions, Czech emigration rose dramatically, and in the 1850s 23,000 Czechs left their homes for the United States. Although Czech Bohemians and Moravians had defended their ethnicity, as emigrants they often mingled with Germans and Austrians. Persons counted as Austrians in passenger lists or immigration records could as well be Germans or Czechs from Bohemia, Transylvanian Saxons, or members of other groups from the multiethnic Habsburg Empire. Austria proper did not supply significant numbers to the migration movement in the decades preceding the American Civil War; there were some participants of the Vienna uprisings who fled prosecution as well as few farmers and craftsmen who went to America in search of economic improvement. The most prominent Austrian émigré probably was Heinrich Börnstein. Born in Hamburg, Börnstein had served in the Austrian Army before taking part in the Paris and Vienna uprisings. In 1848, he fled to the United States with his wife and three Vienna-born sons, all of whom would later fight in the Civil War.[16]

Unrest in France had, as in Austria, concentrated largely in its capital city of Paris. Through several reforms, France had developed into a modern bourgeois and technologically advanced state by the middle of the nineteenth century. In addition, France and Austria had experienced no similar population growth to other European countries. Thus only a few dissidents and revolutionaries went to the United States, along with a small number of other emigrants who left the country for economic reasons. Hermann Lieb had come from Switzerland to Paris in 1845 at age nineteen and served in the republican *Garde Mobile* during the April uprising. When this organization was disbanded after the election of Louis Napoleon, Lieb decided to emigrate and seek new fortunes in America. Although not French by birth, Lieb probably serves as an example for most emigrants from France during this period. Fellow emigrant Gustave Paul Cluseret also had been a member of the *Garde Mobile*, but subsequently had resigned his commission. In the Italian wars of unification Cluseret joined the republican forces and led Giuseppe Garibaldi's French Legion before emigrating to America.[17]

Only 11,000 Italians, mainly from the Habsburg-ruled northern parts of Italy, came to the United States during the twenty years before the Civil War. Not surprisingly, the majority emigrated after 1848, during the era of conservative restoration, or *Risorgimento*, which suppressed the national movement until eventual Italian unification in 1859. Similarly, the small rural countries of Belgium and the Netherlands lost few citizens to emigration. A slow economic recovery after two hard depressions in the Netherlands, together with political reforms bringing forth a liberal constitution in 1848, stemmed Dutch emigration in the 1850s. In contrast, from the tiny mountainous country of Switzerland, 30,000 emigrants came to the United States between 1841 and 1860. Situated between France, southern Germany, and the Habsburg Empire, Switzerland had also witnessed some fighting in the revolutionary year of 1848. However, the Swiss Republic remained politically stable and even harbored a great many refugee forty-eighters. Swiss emigration was principally driven by economic and religious motivations. The most prominent Swiss emigrant was Johann August Sutter, who became famous after the discovery of gold on his California sawmill in 1848, thus providing an important magnet for many other European emigrants.[18]

Germans had come to America since colonial times, and after 1848 many had an additional reason to do so. German and Prussian emigration reached its peak years in the 1840s and 1850s, with close to 1.4 million leaving for the United States during these two decades. As in other countries, economic motivations clearly dominated German emigration among almost all social classes and religious denominations. Although it affected the German states later than Britain, industrialization created the same effects of internal and external migration, especially in the densely populated southern states of Württemberg, Baden, and the Palatine. At the same time, the literacy rate rose even faster than in many other European regions, and travel books and journals spread the "America fever." In addition, a number of young men fled conscription or jail, and several thousand Jews escaped economic and social discrimination. Importantly, the transition from an agrarian to an industrial society and sociopolitical change had the strongest impacts on the migration movement, just as it did in the rest of Europe.[19]

The early decades of European mass emigration brought to the United States a highly heterogeneous collection of ethnic, social, professional, and religious immigrant groups and individuals. Contrary to earlier emigration waves, more people left

Europe in organized groups triggered by steadily growing streams of trans-Atlantic information. Emigrants now journeyed in families, allowing ethnic groups to procreate and develop their own identities in the United States. This stream did not abate when the war started, although European immigration dropped from almost 154,000 in 1860 to 92,000 the following year. Including a larger percentage of single young men and outright adventurers hoping to profit from the war, an aggregated 800,000 Europeans arrived almost exclusively in the immigration ports of the North during the war years. A good portion of them moved on to the Midwestern states where they connected with fellow immigrants, while others entered the war industries along the East Coast. Together with those who had come with the intention to join the war or had been lured to the army right off the ships, a large number of these wartime immigrants eventually enlisted in the Union army.

THE FORTY-EIGHTERS: REBELS IN EXILE

In 1864, a Swiss-born immigrant who had seen some service in the Union army presented his military autobiography, revealing a most interesting professional and personal history. Ulysses Scheller-de Buol had graduated from the Italian Military Academy at Milan in 1834 and subsequently served in a regiment of Hungarian hussars and in the engineer corps. In 1848 then, Scheller had "joined the Hungarian revolutionary party, and after the defeat of the revolution I went to France, where I remained until the Hungarian refugees were ordered out of the Empire. From France I went to England for a short time, and then came to the United States in the year 1850." The forty-eighter told a story similar to that of numerous European soldiers and commissioned officers who had decided to join the revolutionary forces in 1848. Scheller never gave a reason for his decision to leave the regular Austrian army. It is possible that during his service with the Hungarian cavalry he had become acquainted with Kossuth's nationalist movement. Scheller himself told how his old regiment deserted upon the rebellion's outbreak and "cut its way through a large Country and outnumbering Enemis, and arrived at Hungary" to join the Honved Army.[20] Scheller's career was typical for that of many professional officers who had changed sides due to their affiliation with the rebellious nationalist causes. Among the best-known of these disloyal officers was Franz Sigel from Sinsheim in Baden, a graduate of the Karlsruhe Military Academy. He resigned his commission in 1847 for political reasons and identified strongly with the French revolutionary movement. At the head of a people's corps, Sigel joined Hecker in Baden in 1848 and fled to Switzerland after their defeat. Returning in 1849, Sigel again led revolutionary troops until the final collapse of the popular uprising. Escaping once more to Switzerland from where he was eventually expelled, Sigel went to England and in 1852 emigrated to New York, where he took up teaching.

While many forty-eighters had been officers in the regular armies before, others had joined the uprisings from civil life like Gottfried Kinkel, a professor at the University of Bonn who was instrumental in turning many students against their government. When Kinkel was imprisoned in the fortress of Rastatt, one of his students participated in his forcible liberation. Carl Schurz would subsequently rise to become the most famous forty-eighter and German American politician in the nineteenth century. Born in Munich in 1805, Gustav von Struve had studied law and during his studies had embraced radical democratic opinions resulting in the abandonment of his noble title. Arguing against censorship, Struve faced criminal charges in 1845. Friedrich Hecker defended his friend in court but could not prevent conviction. In 1848 and 1849 then, Struve and Hecker led revolutionary forces in Baden before they had to emigrate. Several forty-eighters had joined the revolutions as mere youngsters. Among these juvenile insurgents was Ladislas Zsulavszky, a cousin of Lajos Kossuth, whose military career "commenced almost at my boyhood—having carried a musket in 1849 at the age of 13."[21] Zsulavszky would later rise to regimental command in the Civil War, just like his compatriot Frederick Knefler who had joined Kossuth's forces when only fifteen years old. Carl Gottfried Freudenberg, later commander of a German infantry regiment from New York, had been the same age when he participated in the Baden revolution.[22]

Exiled after what they viewed as a temporary defeat in their universal struggle, the majority of the forty-eighters first escaped to neutral or relatively safe countries like Switzerland, France, and England. Most of them at that time did not intend to leave Europe but return to continue their struggle in due time. In time, however, most of them became fugitives like Struve who later recalled that "I had to flee, because I faced certain death had I remained. Expelled from Switzerland, under police surveillance in France, without secure means of income in England, I had to decide to emigrate to America. I did that with utmost reluctance, only yielding to inexorable necessity."[23]

An estimated 5,000 to 6,000 participants in the pan-European revolutionary movements eventually emigrated to America. Only a few of these European refugees have made it into the history books as charismatic military leaders, shrewd ethnic politicians, or successful publishers. There were numerous lesser known forty-eighter emigrants who also continued to serve ethnic and national causes in America. Stanislas Kiolbassa's Polish settlement of Panna Maria would become a center of antislavery sentiment in Texas and provided several Union soldiers during the Civil War. Alexander Asboth and Charles Zagonyi served as officers under Kossuth before they fled Austrian retaliation and found refuge in the United States. Together with other Hungarian immigrants they became active in ethnic Hungarian communities and eventually served in the Union army. Influenced by the subversive ideas of Marx and Engels, former Prussian artillery officer Joseph Weydemeyer had turned communist and became an influential leader of the German labor movement in America. Julius Reichhelm, on the other hand, was a devout Catholic. As his biographer has noted, Reichhelm's "fight for religious freedom naturally led him into the revolutionary movement, which culminated in 1848. He became a member of a revolutionary organization in Cologne, and its president. His speeches and contributions to liberal newspapers soon made him a marked man, so that in the fall of 1848, when the revolution was suppressed, his arrest for treason was ordered." Via Brussels and Bremen Reichhelm eventually fled to New York.[24]

The forty-eighters came from all professions, social classes, and confessions. Among the several thousand Jews who left Europe for America in the 1850s, many, like Frederick Knefler, had participated in revolutionary movements. August Bondi had been a member of the student revolutionary movement in Vienna and with his family emigrated to St. Louis late in 1848. Bondi's idealism eventually led him to Kansas where he participated in the fight against slavery and teamed up with radical John Brown. One of only few Jewish officers in the Prussian army, Leopold Blumenberg from Brandenburg joined his fellow officers who changed sides in 1848. Together with many other Jews, Blumenberg fled an increasingly anti-Semitic atmosphere in the reactionary backlash after the revolutions. Among the most prominent of Jewish forty-eighters were the brothers Salomon from Magdeburg in Prussia. Emigrating to Wisconsin in 1848, Friedrich and Carl Eberhard Salomon eventually rose to important field commands during the Civil War, while Eduard Salomon was elected governor of Wisconsin.[25]

Regardless of their backgrounds, the common fight for universal civil and human rights had made this band of international activists the first true Europeans. Bavarian Catholics, Polish Jews, French communists, and Bohemian freethinkers fought side by side against arbitrary oppression. As a matter of fact, many revolutionary troops included international brigades, like the Polish and Bohemian battalions that fought with Sigel and Hecker in Baden. August Willich, another Prussian officer turned communist and revolutionary leader, commanded a "Workers' Legion" with several Frenchmen in its ranks. Some veterans later fought with Garibaldi when he campaigned for Italian unity in the 1850s. While many of them had already earlier looked to the United States as a country of democratic and republican principles, leaving Europe for most of the forty-eighters was not a voluntary decision. Irish revolutionaries John Mitchel and Thomas Francis Meagher—traditionally omitted from the group defined as forty-eighters—even escaped banishment in Tasmania to the United States. The members of the "Young Ireland" movement had fought for the same national ideals as their fellow revolutionaries, and ultimately had to endure the same fate. Strongly influenced by the French revolution of 1848, the Young Irelanders can be placed in close intellectual proximity to the revolutionary movements on the continent. Defeated, captured, and banned from their homeland, Mitchel and

Meagher (together with other Irish freedom fighters) found new homes in America. Far from broken, these Irish forty-eighters were determined to continue their struggle and eventually return to their cause. Like most of the other forty-eighters, they eventually made their homes in America and fought for their own and their country's cause in the Civil War.

TWO

IMMIGRANTS IN AMERICAN SOCIETY, 1840–1860

In the two decades preceding the Civil War the foreign-born element rose to 20 percent of the Union's white population. German and Irish immigrants were the most numerous. From 1820 to 1860, Irish immigrants never constituted less than one-third of all immigrants, while every fourth immigrant came from Germany.[1] By 1860, the Irish and Germans together constituted 70 percent of all foreign-born Americans, becoming especially visible in the growing cities of the East Coast and in the rapidly developing urban Midwest, where they contributed to the urbanization of the United States and mingled with the native-born. Arguably the most visible ethnic group in the decades before the Civil War were the immigrants from Prussia and the smaller German states. Germans spread over the whole country, from Texas to New York, and the "German triangle" between St. Louis, Cincinnati, and Milwaukee became well known as a center of "deutsche Kultur." Urban Germans occupied every professional and social niche; they were Catholics, Protestants, Jews, and freethinkers, and argued over every political and clerical topic. Their different regional, religious, and social backgrounds ultimately made it impossible for the various German fractions to share a common national identity that would unite them as an ethnic group in the United States.

Irish immigrants in the 1840s and 1850s on the whole were unskilled young laborers. They hoped for employment in the growing industries of the Northern cities and anywhere else where labor was in demand, making them the most urbanized European immigrants. In 1850, for example, Irishmen made up one third of Boston's working population, even outnumbering Massachusetts natives. Unlike the German experience, however, many Irish Americans found unity in a common cause that gave them a sense of national identity. Irish clubs and militia companies formed under the auspices of the Fenian Brotherhood aimed at the forcible overthrow of English rule over their homeland. When celebrated rebels Thomas Francis Meagher and John Mitchel came to the United States in the early 1850s they, too, began to promote the Irish national cause and thus strengthened ethnic identity. Saluting Meagher's arrival, the *Boston Pilot* wrote jubilantly, "In him the Irish in America will find a chief to unite and guide them."[2] Soon an acclaimed speaker, Meagher worked throughout the nation toward the assimilation of Irish into American society as well as their unification in the common struggle against England.

Thanks to the publicity of Lajos Kossuth and despite their relatively small number, Hungarians became another visible group in some cities like New York and St. Louis. When the famed revolutionary leader visited the United States for several months in 1852, an enthusiastic American public welcomed him as one of the true heroes of the European democratic revolutions. The year of the Irish leaders' arrival and Kossuth's acclaimed visit also saw the visit of German forty-eighter Gottfried Kinkel. Like Kossuth, Kinkel received favorable attention, although he did not catch on with the American public as well as the Hungarian champion. Carl Schurz, who arrived in the same year, realized (unlike many of his fellow forty-eighters) that forming a pan-German identity like the Irish or Hungarians would be very difficult.

In many cases the urban areas became the battleground for ethnic predominance in American society. The struggle for supremacy and social influence was most noticeable as immigrant groups tried to preserve their ethnic identity through the formation of self-help organizations, foreign-language newspapers, and exclusive social clubs. This ethnic rivalry surfaced most prominently in labor competition. Lacking other job opportunities, Irish immigrants frequently had to accept the lowest and least-paying jobs, more often than not leading to a shameless exploitation of Irish labor. As a mainly unskilled work force, Irish immigrants in the North frequently saw themselves in direct competition with free black workers. It is no wonder then that Irish and African-Americans never became societal allies. To make themselves less vulnerable to abuse and discrimination, Irish immigrants formed powerful labor unions and other ethnic aid organizations that were instrumental in building an Irish ethnic identity stronger than that of any other prewar immigrant group. Their collective membership in the Catholic Church provided another source of ethnic consciousness as well as a way of gaining influence in that organization.[3]

German immigrants, on the other hand, were present in nearly all occupations from skilled workers to trained craftsmen, from white-collar professionals to farmers and artists. Only a small percentage were unskilled laborers who entered into labor competition with the Irish or free blacks. Urban Germans organized early on in unions and fought for workers' rights. The vigor of the German-American intellectual leadership also became apparent; in 1860 some 250 journals and newspapers made the German-language press by far the most influential of all ethnic presses.[4]

The close proximity of conflicting ethnic interests in the American cities frequently led to fights, especially between Germans and Irish. As a gateway to the Upper Midwest, for example, St. Louis had mushroomed in the 1830s and 1840s and boasted a population that was one third German and almost one-fifth Irish-born by 1850. Ethnic tensions were ubiquitous, and forty-eighter Heinrich Börnstein in his biased way lamented the frequent brawls between Germans and "the Irish and American mob."[5] The high visibility of urban immigrants also led to antiforeign sentiment among many Anglo-Americans who perceived everything foreign as alien and threatening. In the age of Social Darwinism, most Americans believed in inherited racial characteristics when confronted with unfamiliar cultures, languages, and religious beliefs. Stereotyping and prejudice bloomed, especially in cities where immigrants gathered in visible ethnic neighborhoods like "Over the Rhine" in Cincinnati, or New York City's notorious Five Points district. Many Americans could not easily accept the fact that mass immigration was transforming their more or less homogeneous white Anglo-Saxon Protestant society into a multicultural one and reacted with prejudice and discrimination. Germans in particular developed what American puritans saw as a hedonistic counterculture. Instead of reserving Sundays for silent worship and rest, Germans rowdily gathered at beer gardens and frequently ended up in fights with "the fellow 'from the Green Isle'" or other immigrants.[6] Thus Anglo-Americans often perceived the stereotypes of beer drinking and gluttonous Germans as outweighing the benefits of their unquestionable achievements in publishing or the fine arts and sciences. When Bohemians, Austrians, or Poles spent their Sundays in an equally unholy fashion, they soon became "German" in the eyes of many Americans. Another outward sign of alleged German unwillingness to assimilate was their membership in ethnic organizations like shooting clubs, singing and theater societies, and *Turnvereins*. Founded in the wake of the 1848 Revolution in Germany and in America, these gymnastic clubs not only promoted physical fitness, but also performed regular rifle drills with the original intent of preparing for the final battle against autocracy and monarchy. Membership in the United States grew rapidly and by 1851 *Turnvereins* existed in cities all over the Union. Similar in its goals and activities to the Irish Fenian Brotherhood, the German Turner movement behaved less secretly. With their public conventions, parades, and festivities, the *Turnvereins* contributed to the high visibility of German culture. Irish immigrants had to confront even worse prejudice and open discrimination. Generally poor and deprived of social upward mobility, this ethnic group earned the stereotypical labels of violent criminality and drunkenness. Native-born Americans scoffed at the Hibernian immigrants' alleged lack of hygiene and disregard of reliability and punctuality. Caricatures and derogatory rhetoric often compared an alleged Irish racial inferiority to that of African-Americans. As Catholics, Irish-Americans faced additional charges that they would rather obey the Vatican than a democratic government.[7]

Most other urban immigrants remained largely invisible and therefore usually avoided nativist trouble. Those from Italy, for example, had not yet evolved into a viable ethnic group in the United States by the mid-nineteenth century. Some 11,000 Italians lived scattered across the nation in 1860, most of them shopkeepers or craftsmen in cities like New Orleans or New York City. Their lack of language proficiency and Catholic faith made assimilation difficult for these urban dwellers who often cultivated friendships with their Catholic Irish neighbors. In New York, a few influential immigrants struggled to uphold Italian ethnic identity. One of them, Francesco Secchi de Casale, was instrumental in the publication of the Italian newspaper *L'Europee-Americano*. Most French immigrants shared the Italians' linguistic and denominational barriers to assimilation. Professional skills and training, however, enabled many Frenchmen to succeed economically. Similar to the Italians, French Americans did not develop a strong ethnic identity. With the notable exception of the French colony in Louisiana and especially in New Orleans, they preferred assimilation and melting "into the mass of American life" over gravitating toward fellow immigrants.[8] Also too few in number to form ethnic organizations, Danes simply blended in with neighboring Germans and the urban population in general. Swedes, however, became the most visible of all the Scandinavians and often coalesced in ethnic neighborhoods in cities like Chicago or St. Paul. True to their Protestant principles, Swedish immigrants combined education and spiritual welfare with hard work. Universities like Augustana College in Sioux Falls, South Dakota, or Gustavus Adolphus College in St. Peter, Minnesota, soon gained high reputations. Swedish newspapers like the Chicago *Hemlandet* served both religious needs and promoted ethnic and linguistic identity. Founded by Tufve Nilsson Hasselquist, the puritanical journal vehemently condemned Germans desecrating the Sabbath with their beer gardens and jolly music. Although preferring to settle in ethnic environments, Swedes usually did not reject assimilation. On the contrary, many of them expressed their happiness with American egalitarianism. As one immigrant wrote, here everybody was "alike, the farmer, the minister, and the judge. One does not need to go and bow and nod, hat in hand. . . . No count in Sweden lives better."[9]

Aptly called the "invisible immigrants" by Charlotte Erickson, Britons encountered the fewest difficulties when it came to integrating into American society. Even though diplomatic relations between their nations still suffered from two previous wars, most Englishmen and Americans perceived themselves as sharing the same Anglo-Saxon background. Coming from the most advanced industrial nation, English working-class immigrants provided a greatly diversified labor force with valuable skills badly needed in America's growing iron and steel industries, as well as in textile mills and coal mining. Moreover, the shared language opened respectable white-collar professions more easily to English than to other immigrants. Similarly, the Welsh and Scots found it relatively easy to assimilate into American society. Although some of them privately adhered to their Gaelic language, they tended to assimilate quickly and found ready employment in mining, industry, and farming. Scots, like English, represented all occupational levels and settled all over the United States, even as far south as Texas.[10]

Outside the big cities, there was less pressure for assimilation and usually less tension between immigrant groups. Many ethnic settlements dotted the rural country from Minnesota to Texas, where Stanislas Kiolbassa had founded Panna Maria and German culture flourished in the towns of Fredericksburg and New Braunfels. Most rural settlements sprang up in the Midwest, like the Swiss town of Highland in Illinois, or the numerous German settlements in the fertile farmlands of the Mississippi, Ohio, and Missouri river valleys. As an ethnic enclave, Eric Jansson's Illinois colony Bishop Hill attracted newcomers from Scandinavia and established successful economic ties with surrounding settlements. Another influential Swedish immigrant was Hans Mattson. Lured by the promises of a free country with immeasurable natural resources, the former soldier came to Chicago in 1851. Later he went on to Minnesota where he founded the Swedish settlement of Vasa near St. Paul and became an influential Swedish American leader. Fewer in number than their Scandinavian cousins, Norwegians nevertheless founded scattered ethnic settlements in Wisconsin, Iowa, and southern Minnesota where they engaged mainly in farming, lead mining, and lumber work. Like their Swedish neighbors, Norwegians upheld a strong ethnic identity through schools, churches, and newspapers, like the *Emigranten* in Madison, Wisconsin. Scandinavian immigrants soon won the sympathy of Anglo-Americans through their Protestant work ethic and their willingness to adapt to American society. Describing a trek of Swedish settlers heading west in 1851, the Washington, DC, *National Intelligencer* appreciated the fact that "In the first wagon was displayed the American flag." Approvingly, the paper added, "The whole company had a remarkable comfortable and respectable look." The Buffalo *Commercial* spied another group en route to Bishop Hill and expressed its hope that these Swedish newcomers "like most of their countrymen who have preceded them, will make industrious and useful citizens."[11] In contrast, through their more exclusive behavior many Germans rejected assimilation. As a German woman from Jefferson City in Missouri told her brother, "we withdraw, carry on our business, read newspapers, and wish for a bit more social activity." Geographically distant from the cultural centers of "educated Germans," Jette Bruns longed for more socializing but preferably not with Americans.[12]

ETHNIC POLITICS AND THE ROAD TO WAR

Mass immigration to the United States in the mid-nineteenth century coincided with the intensified struggle over territorial expansion and the problem of slavery. Most immigrants found it impossible to evade these pressing political questions that threatened to split their new home country. The existence and expansion of unfree labor, one of the crucial conflicts that eventually led to war, greatly affected foreign-born Americans. The leading Welsh newspaper *Y Drych* claimed in 1851 that "we, although foreigners through birth, are Americans and Republicans in sentiment; and have made Washington's country our adopted land; and [we] appreciate the Freedom and Conveniences that we are allowed to enjoy."[13] Resounding among Englishmen and Scots, this argument for universal freedom led numerous British immigrants to support not only the containment of slavery, but also full emancipation. Most German Americans condemned slavery as well, especially the forty-eighters and other prominent spokesmen. One of the most influential was Gustav Körner. A member of the earlier generation of political refugees from the 1830s, Körner eventually rose to become lieutenant governor of Illinois as well as a personal friend of Abraham Lincoln. At the forefront of ethnic American liberalism, German newspapers like the Milwaukee *Corsär*, the Pittsburgh *Freiheitsfreund und Courier*, or the Baltimore *Wecker* ("alarm clock") early argued for the abolition of slavery and other social reforms.

The majority of immigrants in the North had long tried to avoid the subject. Lacking direct confrontation with slavery, most immigrants were primarily concerned with their own economic and political interests. Some Catholics and conservative Lutherans even found biblical justification for slavery, and, as members of the Democratic Party, were much less likely to press for abolition. Dietrich Gerstein, a farmer from Westfalia and former sympathizer with the 1848 revolution, sneered at those ultra-religious immigrants who were "entangled in the Bible which tells them that the negroes are the descendants of Ham . . . and for this have to suffer today in American slavery."[14] Because of their general dislike for blacks, Irish Catholics remained neutral at best when it came to the question of emancipation. Until the firing on Fort Sumter, Thomas Francis Meagher, for instance, argued in favor of southern states' rights and never condemned slavery. John Mitchel even moved to Tennessee, because, as he declared, "Not only does America content me, the South especially delights me."[15]

Immigrants in the slaveholding South largely adapted to their environment and tolerated the existence of slavery around them. Although the almost 250,000 foreign-born southerners in the eleven states that formed the Confederacy did not exceed 5 percent of the white population, they comprised as many nationalities and classes as the immigrant populace in the North. The Texas hill country had its share of Latin Farmers of whom many disagreed with the system of unfree labor. On the whole, German and the few Scandinavian immigrants outside the urban areas usually adhered to their traditional methods of small-scale farming without competing with the plantation system. Their majority did not openly oppose slavery. Besides British and French immigrants, Germans also figured prominently in southern cities like Charleston, Richmond, and New Orleans, where many of them worked as artisans and skilled workers, or ran stores. However, Irish laborers outnumbered Germans in these urban centers, as well as in Savannah and Mobile, where they even composed

14 and 11 percent of the population totals. Immigrants, and especially Irish, dominated the unskilled labor force in many southern cities, constituting the majority of river men and dockworkers, as well as railroad, canal, and turpentine workers. Often competing with free black workers, these immigrants would only rarely condemn surrounding slavery.

Those immigrants who settled in southern cities as merchants, cotton brokers, or tradesmen even profited from the existing economic system and therefore had less inclination to oppose it. Although the majority of ethnic Americans in the South did not overtly agree with the "Peculiar Institution," immigrants in several cases owned slaves themselves if they could afford it. Writing from a Swedish Texas colony that included several slaveholders, Svante Palm told the *Hemlandet* in 1855: "We live in a slave state, are in daily contact with both masters and slaves, and find that the slaves are provided with better food, accorded better treatment, and are better cared for than the working classes of Sweden. A few of us own slaves and all of us aspire to own slaves when we are in position to purchase them." Promptly, Swedes all over the country flooded the paper with protest letters stating that they did not advocate slavery at all.[16] To be sure, there were immigrants in the South who vehemently spoke out against slavery. Together with other German, Bohemian, and Polish immigrants in Texas, the Panna Marians became highly visible for their free labor attitude. When a small radical group of Texas Germans from San Antonio published an antislavery pamphlet in 1854, they bore immediate criticism by fellow immigrants and Texans.

The yeoman ideal of free labor on free land had traditionally aligned most immigrants with the Democratic Party. The party of Jefferson and Jackson with its egalitarian attitude and its welcoming reception of foreign-born voters attracted Catholics and Jews as well as traditional Protestants and freethinkers. However, liberal-minded immigrants always criticized the northern Democrats for not taking a clear stand against slavery. When the antebellum reform movement gave birth to the Republican Party, these immigrants regarded the new party as an alternative because it promoted the restriction of slavery as well as the free right for settlers to purchase and cultivate land of their choice. Yet many immigrants in turn were unhappy when they discovered that the "free-soil" Republicans also called for highly unpopular reforms such as temperance and the strict enforcement of Sunday laws. One did not have to be a festive German or a hard-drinking Irishman to reject such proposals, all the more because factions of the Republican Party showed clear anti-immigrant tendencies. Highly organized in urban political organizations, Irish immigrants remained Democratic almost to a man in most cities, with the sole exception of Philadelphia, where Irish were well represented among the Republicans. Irish Americans felt strongly about competition with free blacks on the labor market and opposed the Republicans' antislavery agenda. In addition, they had suffered too much from nativist attacks and anti-Catholic intolerance to turn their backs on the Democratic Party, which had tried to defend them. Other Catholic groups agreed. One of the most combative conservative newspapers, the Milwaukee *Seebote* told its German readers that the Republicans consisted of "temperance men, abolitionists, haters of foreigners, sacrilegious despoilers of churches [and] Catholic killers."[17]

Among those immigrants who reacted favorably to the Republican message were many British and Scandinavians unaffected by prior prejudice and German forty-eighters who believed in reform more than they feared nativism. Swedes and Norwegians, whose Lutheran religion and puritanical principles conformed easily to the party's moral credo, were the first ethnic groups to solidly support the Republicans in the early 1850s. Firmly backing the reform movement, Missouri Norwegians even fired pastors who defended slavery. Hans Mattson successfully campaigned for the Republicans among the Swedes in Vasa and surrounding rural Minnesota, while Norwegian leader Hans Christian Heg did the same for his ethnic group. Gustav Körner, Carl Schurz, and several other German political refugees tried to win over their compatriots, while simultaneously campaigning against the party's anti-immigrant tendencies. In a widely published letter to the Republican State Central Committee of Illinois, Körner stated that he would only support the party further if it agreed that "all American citizens without distinction of birth and religion should be entitled 'to rule America.' "[18] More and more immigrants also began to view the slavery question as both a political and a moral problem. As Carl Schurz told his friend Gottfried Kinkel, he had gathered and analyzed every argument defending slavery "except the biblical ones," and finally reached the conclusion that "the question of freedom is one indivisible." Not only had philanthropic sentiments convinced Schurz, but also, as he claimed, "this system's indirect and direct impacts on the whole organism of the United States, the aristocratic character of the southern society," and "the demoralizing influence of the slave power on the northern politicians."[19] Having escaped European states that denied freedom to their citizens, numerous immigrants joined the radical abolitionist movement and engaged in the Underground Railroad, guiding fugitive slaves to safety in the North and Canada. When authorities captured and jailed a refugee slave in Racine, Wisconsin, local Britons joined the public protest against the Fugitive Slave Laws. In Wisconsin, New York, and other states, British immigrants actively aided escaping slaves.[20]

In 1854, the nativist American Party, a third party poised to replace the decaying Whigs, infuriated Democratic and Whiggish immigrants alike when it tried to introduce office-holding and voting right restrictions for Catholics and foreign-born Americans in the Kansas-Nebraska Bill. This bill became a watershed in ethnic politics because it made even apolitical immigrants aware of the civil rights they had begun to take for granted but now found jeopardized. Always a keen observer of the political scene in Missouri, Jette Bruns wrote in September that "one party, which is called the Know-Nothings, is more in favor with the Americans. These are native Americans who deny the immigrants and Catholics many of their rights."[21] As a result, protest meetings united immigrants in opposition to this threat and sometimes created unlikely alliances across ethnic boundaries. On July 4, Chicago Germans demonstrated their opposition to the bill in a parade together with the Irish Hibernian Society and the Scandinavian Union. To many, the attempt to introduce Kansas as a slave state to the Union represented a vital danger to free labor. The ensuing guerrilla war in Kansas and Missouri made it clear how deeply the country was split already, and immigrants soon learned that they could not stay clear from the coming conflict. Thomas Edwards from Bristol involuntarily became involved in the border war when he wanted to settle in Kansas. As soon as local citizens learned that he was against slavery, however, they forcibly prevented him from entering the territory and Edwards had to return to Illinois. A Swedish farmer who also wanted to settle in that state dreaded the influx of slavery when he wrote in 1856, "I hope that Kansas will be a free state so that we can remain and make it our home."[22]

When John Brown gathered his force to strike against slavery in Kansas, at least four immigrants from Poland, Bohemia, Bavaria, and Austria joined his band. August Bondi, a Jew from Vienna who had participated in the 1848 uprising, was highly devoted to the grim hater of slavery, who "prepared a handful of young men for the work of laying the foundation of a free Commonwealth."[23] Another radical abolitionist who joined Brown's band was Charles Kaiser, a Bavarian who had fought in the Hungarian Revolution. Kaiser was captured and probably killed when Brown and his men defended the town of Osawatomie against a southern attack. The struggle over "Bleeding Kansas" not only foreshadowed the terrible guerrilla war in the border state that would continue for years, but it also pitted immigrants against immigrants. Not all foreign-born settlers were antislavery men, and in the infamous Pottawatomie Massacre a Polish Jewish immigrant from Brown's band assisted in hacking to death William Sherman, a prosouthern immigrant from Oldenburg in Germany. After his death, Brown became a martyr for many Republican immigrants such as John Dieden, who had emigrated in 1848 from the Palatinate and settled in Chicago. Dieden told his cousin that Brown "died with the most heroic defiance of death and said on his way to the scaffold that through his death he would accomplish more than if they had let him live; his words have been confirmed by what has happened since."[24] A successful and educated merchant, Dieden was one of many Catholic Germans in Chicago who backed the Republicans. A higher education and frequent contact with Anglo-Americans often led open-minded Catholics to support the libertarian and free-soil program of the Republicans, while the majority of German as well as Irish Catholics would have strongly disagreed with Dieden's judgment on Brown. Full of derisive sarcasm, Dietrich Gerstein told his brother in February 1860 that "the old man Brown has been hanged, as you surely know. The 350,000 slaveholders triumph in their victory over one old man with his 20 comrades and the preserving of their 'Divine Institution.' "[25]

The struggle for Kansas considerably radicalized the political climate in the United States. Ethnic free-soil and antislavery propaganda was increasingly successful and in 1856 the Republicans put immigrant voting to its first national test when they introduced John C. Frémont as their presidential candidate. Running against Democrat James Buchanan, Frémont stood for the abolition of slavery and against southern demands for state sovereignty. Scandinavians readily voted Republican because, as one Swede wrote, "If Frémont is elected, then Kansas will be free. If Buchanan wins, we must continue to fight for freedom."[26] To Carl Schurz the Republican platform "sounded like a bugle call of freedom, and the name of Frémont, the Pathfinder, surrounded by an aura of daring bravery, mightily roused our imagination. Now we would fight for the old cause of human freedom on the soil of the New World."[27] Despite strong efforts to gather Republican support, the Germans remained split along political and religious lines. Many of the "Greys," as those immigrants who arrived before the late 1840s came to be called, did not care about politics at all. To the dismay of Körner and activist "Greens" like Schurz, Struve, and Hecker, it was generally easier to rally protest meetings against temperance laws or the closing of beer halls on Sundays than to interest many of these Germans in national politics.

Predictably, the Irish vote remained firmly Democratic, thanks in large part to united ethnic leadership. John Mitchel summed up the attitudes of many of his countrymen in his newspaper, *The Citizen*: "He would be a bad Irishman who voted for principles which jeopardized the present freedom of a nation of white men, for the vague forlorn hope of elevating blacks to a level for which it is at least problematical whether God and nature ever intended them."[28] Mitchel's friend, Meagher, likewise supported the Democratic Party and actively campaigned for James Buchanan through his own ethnic journal, the New York *Irish News*. But Frémont's defeat in the national elections only strengthened the ethnic Republicans' zeal. In November, Schurz told a friend that "we have to shake up the German population over the next four years and feed them into the fire of the election campaign in 1860 in great masses."[29]

In 1856 and again in 1860, German Republicans allied with Scandinavians in the race for ethnic votes. Such coalitions show how many immigrants had gradually changed their ethnic consciousness in America. While old ethnic boundaries often vanished or altered, immigrants created new identities that sometimes brought forth uncommon loyalties as well as new enemies. Many Magyar Hungarians in the United States, for example, cultivated an aversion to Slavic immigrants from Hungary because Croats and Russians had helped suppress their revolution in Europe. However, Polish immigrants developed harmonious relations with Germans in the United States, even though Poles had fought Prussian domination for decades. Having lived in America for some time when the first Polish immigrants arrived, Germans often assisted the newcomers in settling down and provided a familiar cultural environment. Irish immigrants seemingly were at odds with everybody: Irish workers competed with blacks and other minorities, Irish Catholics fought German and French Catholics over language domination in the Church, and the rebellious Fenian Brotherhood utilized Anglo-American conflicts such as the Oregon dispute to torpedo British immigrants' interests.

Whatever their alliances, immigrants had come to accept political involvement in a democratic society as a means to actively campaign for their own interests, something most had not been able to do in Europe. By 1860 then, the stage was set for an election that would decide the fate of their new home country. When the nation went to the polls in unprecedented numbers on November 6, few immigrants did not exert their right to vote. Many of them had become involved in the struggle about the expansion of slavery and the threat to free soil and free labor. The way immigrants had participated in the political debates and struggles in the decades before the Civil War also predestined their loyalties and their individual decisions in the coming conflict.

One day after the election on November 7, 1860, Carl Schurz wrote to his wife that "The election is over, the battle is fought, victory is ours."[30] Lincoln had won the presidency, and the Illinois *Belleviller Zeitung* rejoiced triumphantly, "The anti-slavery principle has triumphed over the reign of the slaveholders and Southern aristocracy."[31] In perfect accord with the divided nature of German political affiliation, however, in another heavily German Illinois community the local paper expressed a different opinion. Employing similarly strong language, the Freeport *Deutscher Anzeiger* lamented that "The so-called Republicans seem to have been victorious in all Northern States and the Democrats are totally beaten, but not dead and buried." Defiantly, the *Anzeiger* predicted that "The time will come when the people of the United States will again gather around the banner of democracy and hold on to the principle of self-government, because this principle alone wants the rights of all citizens in the Union to be respected and protected."[32]

Such fundamentally opposed opinions rang out all over the North and reflected the unabated gap between German-American political allegiances shortly before the outbreak of the war. Writing from the Democratic stronghold of Jefferson City, Jette Bruns told her brother back in Germany that it was not easy to uphold Republican sympathies. In her letter, she expressed anxiety over what was going to become of them after the election. "The election of Mr. Lincoln to the presidency has caused a great uproar in our slave party," she said, "and one can hear all kinds of threats." Still, her husband pursued his political activity for the Republicans, because he "has always favored this party."[33] Ever true to both his Catholic faith and the Republicans, John Dieden wrote to his cousin in late November that "Lincoln, the man of liberty, the fighter against slavery, the champion of equal rights, has been elected to the presidency for four years." Still, Dieden added, the impending secession cast "dark clouds over the political skies."[34] Another member of that minority within a minority proudly stated that "We Republicans have worked faithfully since the Chicago convention and elected our candidates. For that the German element deserves the honor." With little sympathy for the conservative members of his denomination the writer added that "the arch-Catholics were against us. Now they are on the side of the disunionists."[35] As usual, not even German Catholics could agree.

The Scandinavians, on the other hand, had overwhelmingly voted for Lincoln and consequently expressed unreserved joy over the election and confidence in Republican politics. The Chicago *Hemlandet* rejoiced, "There is still hope for freedom, uprightness, and purity. Let fears and mistrust be banished. Let every friend of the fatherland fan the flames that now rise from freedom's altar in his fatherland. Let people cry with joy, the battle is fought and victory won."[36] In another example of united ethnic partisanship, the ethnic Irish vote had almost exclusively gone to Democratic candidate Stephen Douglas. As the *Boston Pilot* sneered, the enemy Republicans stood for nothing else than "hatred and prejudice and injustice to the Irish particularly."[37] Another Irish paper reminded its readers that under Lincoln's presidency they would have to "compete with the labor of four million emancipated slaves."[38] Suspecting a radical turn in society, Irish leaders also doubted Lincoln's intellectual qualifications for the presidency in contrast to the more experienced senator Douglas.

Most other immigrants did not vote in ethnic blocs, mainly because the lack of ethnic spokespersons or interest groups who could unilaterally rally political consciousness. Casting their ballot according to religious and moral convictions, Hungarian immigrants opted for a strong central government that opposed the further spread of slavery. Scottish, English, and Welsh immigrants also voted against slavery—and for a president whose humble origins reminded them of their own. Eventually, except for the Irish, a majority of foreign-born voters in the North decided on Lincoln as a free-soil man who opposed the expansion of slavery and strictly stood by an indivisible Union.[39] Many immigrants might have agreed with a Welsh reverend's son who wrote to his parents that "the factions of Douglas, Bell, and Breckenridge united against the worker's man and all the friends of freedom throughout the world." Combining Welsh workers' pride with his own religious conviction, the immigrant went on, "although the powers of darkness were unleashed against the lovers of freedom . . . to the glory of the King of Kings the workmen have won with hundreds of thousands majority for Lincoln. Lincoln is the man we have needed for many a day." In consequence, he told his parents, "Some of the Southern states are leaving the Union to form a new government." However, the young Welshman was sadly mistaken when he added that "this is not very important."[40] In December South Carolina declared the dissolution of the Union, followed by six more southern states in the coming two months.

THE FORTY-EIGHTERS: ETHNIC LEADERSHIP IN THE UNITED STATES

Entering the United States in the 1850s, the forty-eighters encountered a society that had already accommodated several generations of Germans. Describing his fellow immigrants in Milwaukee, Carl Schurz later called them "good-natured, calm and industrious citizens among whom were men of extraordinary capabilities contributing much to the growth of their community, and who conversed in their simple, merry way." Then came the Greens: "The forty-eighters brought something like a flood of spring sunshine into this life. These were for the most part enthusiastic, fiery young men filled with pure ideals which they had not been able to realize in the Old World . . . Some were scholars educated at the German universities, some where artists or men of literature." Active in singing and theater societies, rifle clubs, and other social organizations, the forty-eighters "began immediately to enliven society with artistic enterprises."[41] Most German Americans at that time would have agreed with Schurz that the forty-eighters did not take long to make themselves visible within the ethnic communities, but few would have concurred with his overtly positive assertion of these newcomers. As down-to-earth farmers, craftsmen, and merchants, old immigrants for the most part did not share the ideological and intellectual ambitions of these so-called Greens. The forty-eighters were naïve utopians, a Cincinnati German mocked, who "knew how the Romans had dressed and what kinds of shoes they had worn," but were not capable of doing regular work "to acquire new clothes to replace their threadbare coats and shabby trousers."[42] The Democratic *Wisconsin Banner* from Milwaukee ridiculed them as "bankrupt merchants, lawyers without offices, dismissed civil servants, craftsmen without clients, drunken workers and the like."[43]

Representing a minority among the postrevolutionary newcomers, with their military or academic backgrounds many forty-eighters were atypical immigrants lacking practical knowledge. Some, like Franz Sigel, could take up teaching, and others, such as Heinrich Börnstein and Gustav Struve, went into publishing. The less fortunate ones often tried to make a living as simple laborers, as porters, painters, or waiters. A typical case was that of Charles Zagonyi. The trained soldier had been a cavalry commander under Kossuth and after his banishment to America, via Turkey and England, eked out a living taking on different jobs. Among others, Zagonyi worked as house painter, a farmhand, and a tailor until he became a riding instructor in Boston. Stranded in New York City with his family in December 1848, Julius Reichhelm shared Zagonyi's fate. Originally a lawyer by profession, Reichhelm had to accept various jobs, from common laborer to cigar maker, before he was lucky enough to find employment as a clerk at the German *New Yorker Staats Zeitung*. Also a trained lawyer, Friedrich Hecker settled near Belleville in eastern Illinois close to St. Louis. Joining other Germans who tried their luck in agriculture, Hecker soon became known as one of the "Latin Farmers" who could recite classical literature while tilling the land.[44]

Many of these émigrés soon found the United States not the perfect society they had envisioned. In addition to the existence of slavery, for example, Ulysses Scheller equally detested American evils such as "all kinds of bawdiness" and hypocritical religious affection. Most of all, the immigrant loathed American newspapers that only contained "tales of murders and robberies, huge swindles and impudent frauds, and grossly inflated steam boat & railroad accidents." Overall, Scheller's picture of the American republic in 1859 was not a very favorable one. "I have been treated roughly in this praised country of freedom," the disillusioned forty-eighter wrote to a friend in Switzerland, "and I would very much like to return to Europe if I could... and frankly, I could just the same live in a tyrant's state as in this lawless republic where they not only sell & buy black slaves, no, where a father will sell his own children."[45] While Scheller restricted his criticism to private communication with his family and friends in Europe, other forty-eighters openly criticized political and social conditions in the Union, condemning slavery and moral hypocrisy as well as nativist sentiment, inhuman industrial working conditions, and political corruption.

Like many of his fellow exiles Carl Schurz did not feel at ease with American society at first. Eventually, however, he, along with the majority of forty-eighters gave up hopes of returning to Europe and accommodated to his new environment. By 1852 Schurz had already decided to "make the United States my permanent home."[46] Not content with private life in what they viewed as an imperfect society, several forty-eighters took up their cause for equal rights and a better democracy in their new home country. A gifted orator and soon a master of the English language, Schurz tackled political issues as well as matters of ethnic interest. After his arrival in New York in 1851, fellow revolutionary Joseph Weydemeyer set out to educate immigrant workers and became an important leader of the German labor movement. Like Schurz, the Marxist recognized the moral wrong of slavery as well as the need for universal workers' rights, connecting labor issues with the call for emancipation. Reform-minded Karl Heinzen and Heinrich Börnstein soon were among the most influential and controversial German newspaper editors. Heinzen first settled in Louisville, Kentucky, where he published the radical abolitionist *Herold des Westens*, alienating both southerners and German Americans who accepted the institution of slavery. Later he would move to St. Louis and, finding himself too radical for even the strongly Republican German community there, finally ended up in Boston. Heinrich Börnstein was one of the most picturesque characters among the forty-eighters. Settling in Illinois after his arrival, Börnstein later went to St. Louis where he became known as theater manager, political author, and editor of the prestigious *Anzeiger des Westens*, the city's oldest German-language newspaper. The Austrian forty-eighter's outspoken abolitionism caused irritations similar to Heinzen's. In his memoirs, Börnstein graphically described the inhumanity of slavery, and describing regular slave auctions just south of St. Louis, told his readers, "The German Americans witnessed with horror, how human beings like themselves, with the only difference lying in their dark skin, under blue skies were... offered for sale just like livestock."[47]

These radicals' blunt criticism of societal evils and shortcomings alienated fellow immigrants and Anglo-Americans alike and polarized the German-American community throughout the country. Identifying more with his new home country than with his German compatriots, an immigrant New Yorker bitterly complained that to "these German apostles of freedom our republic is little or not good at all."[48] In addition, their radical political activities provoked fierce reactions among those parts of the German American population still loyal to the Democrats. In her memoirs, a German Jewish immigrant illustrated how physical these differences could get recalling an incident in Cincinnati. "I remember vividly," Emily Seasongood wrote, "when Karl Schurtz came over to America and gave, or tried to give, a political stump speech [in the city's German district] Over the Rhine. It was customary on those days to go to a wine or beer garden like the custom in Europe, and families would sit gemüthlich [*sociably*] together, eating and drinking. I do not remember the circumstance, but recall that Karl Schurtz was pelted with stones while on the stand, and was almost mobbed."[49] Democratic German-language newspapers issued fiery editorials against Schurtz and the forty-eighters. Immediately preceding the 1860 election, the *Cincinnati Volksfreund* warned its readers: "Emigrant Germans, have we come into this land of freedom in order to meet here the same evils which we tried to run away from over there? . . . Do you want the [forty-eighter] demagogues who ruined things in Germany to have the government turned over to them?"[50] In the end it was exactly this polarizing power that made the forty-eighters so visible and important for ethnic America. Through their public campaigns they contributed to political awareness and ethnic identity building among immigrants. While the Irish revolutionary veterans remained dedicated Democrats and appealed to Irish nationalism, the large majority of Hungarian, Polish, and German forty-eighters supported the Republican cause. When the national crisis escalated in the election of 1860, it was to a major extent their achievement that a large part of the ethnic vote went for Lincoln.

When it finally came to choosing sides, the forty-eighters were Union men. Along with Julius Reichhelm and a small number of other revolutionary veterans clinging to the Democratic Party, all of them realized and condemned the peril of disunion. When the southern states carried out their threat and broke up the nation, the forty-eighters rallied behind the Union with few exceptions. Even Ulysses Scheller, despite all his contempt for America, volunteered for the Union army against "this southern Negro Rebellion," and subsequently rose to command an African-American artillery regiment.[51]

THREE

THE COMING OF THE WAR

With secession a fact by December 1860, immigrants and Anglo-Americans in the northern states reacted in similar ways. A vast majority of all ethnic and societal groups condemned the destruction of the Union and far more citizens than had actually voted for Lincoln expressed their firm belief that the republic should be restored with force if necessary. The more real the danger to the country became and the more probable an armed conflict over its restoration seemed, the louder became the calls among all ethnic groups to end political partisanship and rally behind the cause of the Union. Swiss and Scandinavian Midwestern farmers expressed their love for the adopted home country as decidedly as urban Milwaukee Germans, St. Louis Hungarians, and Irish-Americans in New York City, or Polish immigrants in Cincinnati. Likewise, Italians, Scots, English, and members of all other immigrant groups either individually or in public manifests demonstrated their devotion to the Union.

Everywhere in the north, ethnic newspapers pointed out the debt immigrants and refugees owed the Union. The *Emigranten* reminded Scandinavians that "we must defend the land just as much as our native-born fellow-citizens, that we in each relation meet the same privileges as they, and that we therefore also have the same duty to protect the land against inner and outer enemies."[1] The German-language *Washingtoner Intelligenzblatt* had already several months earlier urged its readers that "We immigrant citizens have the holy duty to throw ourselves into the breach and to preserve the Union and the Constitution, these great legacies of the Revolution, for the future." Indeed, the paper added, German immigrants who had fought for national unity before were better suited to defend the country's integrity than Anglo-Americans who "are demoralized physically and spiritually. Love, true attachment for this land is entirely lacking. They are unworthy of the freedom, the inheritance of their fathers. They do not understand free institutions, because to them the difference between freedom and despotism is unknown. To us immigrants it is reserved to save this land from destruction. And we will do it!"[2]

Surprisingly to many Irish immigrants, ethnic newspapers that had passionately campaigned against Lincoln rushed to the defense of the Union after the first southern states had seceded. "Stand by the Union; fight for the Union; die for the Union," the *Boston Pilot* called boldly in January 1861.[3] With such unexpectedly clear calls for support of the Republican government, Irish editors and spokesmen often confused their staunchly Democratic fellow immigrants. Thomas Meagher, long since one of the most influential Irish-Americans, explained in one of his charismatic speeches that while he had been "a revolutionist in Ireland, I am a conservative in America."[4] Like many other ethnic leaders, Meagher retained his loyalty to the Democratic Party and an unconcealed sympathy for the South, but he perceived republican principles and an indissoluble Union as a higher cause worth fighting for. Many Irish leaders and editors fell in with Meagher and urged their fellow immigrants to stand loyally by the country that had sheltered them. Through their loyalty, they hoped, Irish immigrants would prove their worth as American citizens. As one paper argued, Irish immigrants had to defend the Union that had "made you its citizens," but most of all "the Constitution that has made you free."[5]

Meagher's old friend, John Mitchel, on the other side, likened the cause of southern independence to the European national movements and actively fought for freedom of the Confederacy against northern oppression. Many of his compatriots felt similarly. As a member of the 2nd U.S. Infantry told the *Illinois Staats Zeitung*, most of his regiment's German and American soldiers remained loyal to the "legal government," while many Irish favored secession. Although eventually a great number of Irishmen would fight in the northern armies, volunteers from the Green Isle provided the largest proportion of foreign-born troops in the Confederate forces as well. The Irish remained the only ethnic group to offer substantial support both sides in the war, and the *Tipperary Advocate* was probably not far off when it presumed that Irish loyalty to the North or South "is a mere question of locality."[6]

However, among most northern immigrants political discord and belligerent debates had become obsolete when southern batteries in Charleston harbor attacked their adopted country on April 12, causing four more states to leave the Union. The *Belleviller Zeitung* had already on the previous day uttered the hope that "Finally the miserable time of uncertainty, whether or not our government would act manly and honorably, seems to have come to an end."[7] The president's call for 75,000 volunteers two days later sustained these hopes and further buttressed the ethnic front. In his memoirs, Carl Schurz recalled the excited atmosphere in New York City:

> I found the population in New York incensed with the highest patriotic fervor after the fall of Fort Sumter and the president's call for volunteers. . . . Party spirits ceased amidst this enthusiasm. Men who until yesterday had chided every Republican as a lowly abolitionist and had called every abolitionist a traitor to the country, and had loudly sworn to prevent any armed force to march through the city of New York, now hurried to arms themselves . . . It was a veritable people's rising full of the noblest passion. A true spirit of equality and brotherliness came to bear in this great and universal effort to save the republic.[8]

What seemed most important to Schurz was the fact that "the immigrant citizen did not stand behind the native American in its devotion to fight for the Union."[9] Ethnic papers lauded Lincoln's step to prepare for war and did their best to round up support. The *Belleviller Zeitung* mobilized its readers, calling them "To arms! We finally have a government again!"[10] In St. Louis, the *Anzeiger des Westens* finally saw the opportunity for immigrants to prove their patriotism: "No longer will words decide— but weapons. . . . Every doubt, every reservation is now inappropriate. The country calls—we are ready."[11] The Madison *Emigranten* called out in Norwegian on the day Lincoln called for troops: "Landet er I Fare! Krig! Krig! Till Vaaben, till Vaaben!" [*The Country is in Danger! War! War! To Arms! To Arms!*]. In a glowing editorial a week later, the steadfast Republican paper exclaimed: "Countrymen! Almost before we know it, we are plunged into the midst of the most significant war that has ever been waged in any land. The rebels have not permitted themselves to hold back because of the patience and forbearance of the Union."[12] The editor effectively fostered Scandinavian immigrants' fears for their religious and worldly freedom in America. Drawing on the Scandinavian spirit of liberty and Enlightenment, the *Emigranten* held that "It is the country's safety, preservation of our popular form of government, preservation of our civic and religious freedom and in consequence also our temporal welfare that is at stake. Every enlightened man in the North feels that, and everyone with a heart in the right place knows also what his duty is."[13]

Likewise referring to the libertarian tradition, German forty-eighters kept with their radical activist tradition. They aligned the beginning conflict ideologically with the American and French Revolutions, as well as the European wars of liberation against Napoleon. Nobody made this clearer than idealistic Heinrich Börnstein, who explained in his *Westliche Post* that now the second and ultimate revolution had begun. While the forty-eighters now had the chance to continue their abortive fight, in their eyes Americans had the duty to complete their unfinished first revolution that had not created one country, but two conflicting systems: "Just as the American Revolution of 1776 preceded the French one of 1789 only by a few years, the logic of history has now ruled that our Second Revolution as a confirmation of the old one shall in very short time lead to the European Revolution. . . . Thus . . . everyone to the sacred fight for the restoration of freedom, of the republic, of humanity's unshakeable rock of hope."[14]

Universal patriotic enthusiasm often bridged old gaps and interethnic animosities. English and Irish immigrants united in their support for their new home country, as did traditional ethnic adversaries like Prussians and Silesians or Austrians and Hungarians. Already, the common cause of American national unity had begun to forge a new immigrant identity that stressed a common European background rather than religious or political regionalism imported from the old countries. Even intraethnic quarrels subsided. Irish members of the militant Fenian Brotherhood rallied in defense of the Union together with moderate immigrants who never had been politically active. Among the Germans, conservative Greys cheerfully joined the radical forty-eighter Greens in their support of the Union. As the German-language Washington *Tägliche Metropole* demanded, "Let us play down our previous political dissensions on the altar of the Union. Let us forget that we were Democrats or Republicans; let us be American citizens who love the happiness, the welfare, the greatness of this land and especially the foundations of all these blessings-the Constitution and Union."[15] Forty-eighter Gustav Tafel later even went as far as to completely disregard the differences of his fellow revolutionaries and their enemies. Praising German-American patriotism, Tafel later paid tribute to all those immigrants who in Germany had "fought behind the barricades, or had stormed them."[16]

In disregard of outdated loyalties, former enemies would even fight side by side in the Union army. Swedes like Baron Jakob Cederström, a late captain in the Danish war with Prussia, would serve the same cause as German revolutionary Peter Karberg from Schleswig and many of his fellow refugees who had rebelled against Denmark. Swedish nobleman Baron Ernst Mathias Peter von Vegesack had opposed German nationalists in the Danish-Prussian War, but found it most honorable to lead a regiment of German Turners in the American Civil War. A graduate from the Russian Military Academy in St. Petersburg, Ivan Vasilyevich Turchaninov had fought the Hungarian insurrectionists in 1849 as an Imperial officer. As John Basil Turchin, he rose from colonelcy of the 19th Illinois Infantry to brigadier general in the Civil War and fought for the same cause as his former Hungarian enemies from Kossuth's Honved Army. Gustave Paul Cluseret had helped suppress workers' uprisings of June 1848 in Paris. Like so many European officers he changed loyalties afterward and when he finally took command of the multiethnic 39th New York "Garibald Guard" in 1862, Cluseret fought side by side with French exiles who had participated in the revolution. These new comradeships posed a strange antagonism to the fact that at the same time many families and old friendships were ripped apart in a civil war that often enough pitted relatives and neighbors against each other.

It was no time for criticism or half-hearted unionism. As historian William Burton has pointed out, "Angry mobs in northern cities had little patience with either native-born Americans or immigrants whose loyalty was in doubt."[17] Across party lines and ethnic boundaries, most immigrants hurried to profess their loyalty and prove their patriotism. Still, there was prudent opposition to the ubiquitous anti-southern hysteria. The French *Courrier des États-Unis* from New York City agreed with most other ethnic newspapers that "The honor of the flag, irrevocably involved, makes war a necessity today; that we comprehend." In contrast to those editors who called their readers to arms against the disloyal South, however, the *Courrier* warned: "But we are among those who submit to it without approving it because, in our opinion, it was not inevitable; because, above all, the deplorable struggle which is beginning is fatally condemned to produce only bitter and sterile results."[18] Agreeing that the country faced a critical crisis, the German *Westbote* from Columbus nevertheless called for moderation and attacked old enemies for provoking nativism. The Ohio newspaper argued that "we do not know who gave this Carl Schurz the right to declare that all Germans are wiling to shoulder muskets and assist the Yankee fanatics in their crusade against the South. Yet we know that such a thoroughly imprudent and inappropriate language from the mouth of a German will easily revive the dormant Know-Nothing spirit in many."[19]

Like the *Westbote*, some Democratic newspapers kept up a fierce opposition to a war against the South albeit in the face of violent resistance from their own ethnic groups. As Carl Schurz wrote to his wife in April, "Last Monday people were so incensed here that they nearly destroyed the printing presses of the *News* and the [Milwaukee] *Seebote*."[20] Later, as military commander in the war, Schurz forbade circulation of the *Seebote* within his jurisdiction. Two other forty-eighters, Major Gustav Heinrichs of the 4th Missouri Cavalry and Colonel Fritz Anneke commanding the 34th Wisconsin Infantry, deemed the paper seditious and banned it because they feared detrimental effects on their soldiers' morale. The *New York Staats Zeitung* even continued to defend slavery, as did several Irish-American papers.[21]

In all their patriotic fervor, ethnic Americans often resorted to the same clichés as many Anglo-Americans when it came to identifying the causes of the conflict. Writing to her daughter in Germany from Baltimore in December 1861, Wilhelmine Schlüter explained the situation in elaborate, yet overtly simplistic terms. In her letter she explained that elections in America were held every four years, and "the one elected this time is a northerner who does not want the South to have so many slaves. And the South cannot exist without the Negroes, because a white man cannot work in their hot climate. . . . Now the southern states have left the Union and the North will not put up with that."[22] A German immigrant from Dubuque argued similarly that "only the southern states should be slave states, because of the unbearable heat. The other states shall and must remain free states so that we and our children will not be bereaved of our income and work through the horrendous multiplication of the slaves." With her opinion the writer not only revealed racist views about the allegedly unrestrained sexuality of African-Americans, but she also confirmed fear of economic competition with cheap slave labor as a typical motivation for many immigrants who opposed the expansion of slavery. Furthermore, the obviously Protestant immigrant expressed her deep-seated hatred of the southern "Catholic slave traders."[23]

Most immigrants named slavery as the cause of the war, certainly influenced by abolitionist rhetoric and the events in Kansas and Missouri. Hermann Bullenhaar put it bluntly in December 1861: "The cause for this war is the extermination of slavery."[24] Bullenhaar expressed what many idealistic immigrants hoped for—Germans as well as Scandinavians, Hungarians, Poles, and British. Like other forty-eighters, Minnesota farmer Theodore Bost elevated the conflict to the fundamental question of universal freedom. In a letter to his parents in Switzerland, Bost contemplated that more Americans should look beyond the political question "'whether our government is good for something,' that is, whether we can defeat the slave states." Instead, the immigrant was convinced that only full emancipation of the slaves as the ultimate goal of the war "would give us real dedication instead of mere excitement."[25] Others were more realistic in their judgment. Friedrich Martens had been a staunch Democrat before the war and had even predicted civil war if the Republicans won in 1860. However, like many Irish Democrats, he placed the Union above party politics and stood by the elected government. Blaming the South for starting the war, Martens explained that "the revolting states are slave states, and they want to expand slavery even further, which is against the will of the northern states, and alas! War is here."[26] Martens may not have hoped for the complete destruction of slavery before the war, but in any case he opposed its further expansion. A German farmer from Michigan reached a totally different conclusion when he lamented the falling prices for his produce and livestock after the war had begun. "Who is to blame," Josef Dünnebacke asked in a letter to his brother-in-law. "Unfortunately the abolitionists, among whom are many European forty-eighters."[27] Far removed from the question of slavery but directly exposed to the negative effects of the war on the home front, Dünnebacke and many other northern farmers would hardly have agreed with Bost or the idealistic forty-eighters about the causes of the war.

Depending on their views on slavery and the political and economic situation most often linked to their places of settlement, immigrants probably would have given similar explanations of why war had begun between North and South to those of most Anglo-Americans. Although Missouri had early become one of the focal points in the conflict of slavery, Johann Buegel from St. Louis did not engage in the often one-sided polemics about emancipation. Reflecting on the political situation, he wrote in his diary:

> slavery was involved only as far as the South wanted all remaining territories to become slave states. The South knew well enough that this would never happen, and so they thought they had a right to break away from the North. This was the main reason for

the war. The principal question, therefore, was the following: Whether one or several states had the right to separate from the Union or not. The South claimed this right, while the North disputed it. Therefore this great question could only be decided by force, and the victor would be right. The nigger was involved only to a minor extent or none at all.[28]

By that time, deciding "this great question" had already begun along the border between slave and free states where free-soil interests and slavery collided directly. The Kansas-Nebraska Bill had started a vindictive guerrilla war long before the firing on Fort Sumter, and the Kansas massacres of Pottawatomie and Osawatomie in 1856 showed clearly how far immigrants and Anglo-Americans alike were willing to go in their ferocity. Tensions continued to mount in the border states and more and more people realized the threat of disunion caused by impending secession. Surrounded by slavery and pro-southern sentiment, the *Tägliche Metropole* from Washington, DC, sanely argued in favor of national unity and pointed to the importance of the United States as a country of immigrants. "We Germans are no friends of slavery," the paper had urged on the eve of Lincoln's election, "but it by no means follows that we shall become sectional fanatics. What we are and what we have—our freedom, our existence as independent men and citizens—we owe to the Union; the future of our children depends on the Union; without the Union no more immigration!"[29]

Such language naturally reinforced the nativist attitudes of many southern sympathizers. In Missouri, Governor Claiborne Jackson openly promoted anti-immigrant measures such as the closing of saloons, beer halls, and theaters on Sundays. In response, immigrants pledged allegiance to the Union and entrenched in ethnic organizations such as rifle clubs and militia companies, or more peaceful singing societies. Even the St. Louis Irish publicly demonstrated their loyalty. When Jackson encouraged Missouri to leave the Union together with "her sister slave-holding States" in January, immigrants in St. Louis prepared to prevent this scheme, by force if necessary. Forty-eighter Adam Hammer, founder of the St. Louis Humboldt Institute, had already armed and drilled his medical students to guard the federal arsenal against a secessionist coup. On January 11, 1861, the city's leading German-language papers carried the following appeal: "As of today we have resolved to build an independent rifle company under the name of 'Independent black Rifle-Corps.'"[30] Every German loyal to the Union and willing to join this company was called to muster in and defend St. Louis and its immigrant community. Germans, together with loyal American citizens, Poles, Hungarians, and even a company of unionist Irishmen followed the call instantly, and during the following weeks several other ethnic militia organizations formed in the city.

Franz Sigel, the professional soldier and experienced revolutionary veteran, was already an ethnic idol in 1861 and had been the prime choice of St. Louis Germans and many Americans to command the first volunteer regiment to be mustered in from St. Louis. Prudently, however, the command of the 1st Missouri Volunteer Infantry went to Republican hero Francis P. Blair to prevent native Unionists from rejecting the battalion as too foreign. Eventually, Sigel and three other forty-eighters were appointed commanders of the following four regiments. Recruited primarily among the city's immigrants, these prestigious units accommodated many volunteers from the surrounding Latin Farmer settlements and even from neighboring states. Volunteers rushing to St. Louis to assist in the Union cause came from Indiana, Kentucky, Iowa, Kansas, Ohio, and even from far away Wisconsin and New York. Always on the forefront of radical action, Heinrich Börnstein had helped rally support for German Unionism through his newspaper and became colonel of the 2nd Infantry Regiment. Börnstein later proudly recalled that "my three sons and my son-in-law were with me in the same regiment, and all of them carried the musket as privates in the ranks except for my oldest son who had been elected my successor as captain of Company A."[31] Like Börnstein's sons, many immigrants made a point in serving as privates in a democratic army, just like the rebels of 1848. The initial Black Rifles formed the core of the 4th Missouri "Schwarze Jäger" under the command of Nikolaus Schüttner from Koblenz. A carpenter by profession, Schüttner had served in the Prussian army before he had taken part in the revolution. The Schwarze Jäger included a good portion of unionist Americans as well as a Bohemian company. Hammer, whose students made up one company of the 4th, became the regiment's lieutenant Colonel. Carl Eberhard Salomon, one of the three forty-eighter brothers from Magdeburg, took command of the 5th Missouri Volunteers. An able and popular commander, Salomon later commanded another German regiment and eventually rose to brigadier general.[32]

In April Jackson rejected Lincoln's call for volunteers and instead gathered state militia outside St. Louis to force secession. A member of Franz Sigel's 3rd Missouri Volunteers, Johann Buegel characterized the precarious situation with a delicate and undoubtedly exaggerated ethnic undertone. Jackson's "soldiers were recruited among refined American aristocrats," Buegel noted wryly, "some 500 men under the command of the southern general [Daniel Frost]. It was known to us all and an open secret that they wanted to take possession of the arsenal, seize all contraband there, and drown all of us damned Dutch in the Mississippi."[33] Buegel delicately pointed to the social difference between the working and middle-class German soldiers and their "aristocratic" antagonists. In Jefferson City, Jette Bruns sensed the difficulties ethnic citizens would have to endure in the months to come: "I wonder whether Missouri can stay neutral? We doubt it! And I fear that we shall side with the South. . . . In almost every county vigilante committees have been formed, and they direct their anger against Republicans and foreigners."[34]

In response to the secessionist threat, the city's military commander Captain Nathaniel Lyon received authority to uphold federal laws. Lyon mustered the ethnic regiments into federal service and on May 10 marched four of them to Camp Jackson, while the fifth (together with ethnic and mixed militia companies) guarded the city and the federal arsenal. The 3,400 Union forces surprised Jackson's 700 men, and

Buegel tells that "At 2 P.M. the rebel camp was surrounded from all four streets, the cannon loaded and manned by veteran German soldiers eager to have some fun. . . . When the rebels saw that escape was impossible and that the Dutch meant business after all, they surrendered unconditionally and laid down their weapons." Buegel's regiment remained as guard and cleared the camp the following day. "Thus came to an end the great American rebel reign over St. Louis," was his laconic resume of the Camp Jackson Affair that prevented St. Louis from falling into southern hands.[35]

Lyon's action caused violent protest among disapproving citizens when the soldiers escorted their prisoners to the city. As Jette Bruns reported, the soldiers "were fired upon from the crowd of onlookers. The Guards then reciprocated and several people from the mob fell, including some women!"[36] As unrest in St. Louis continued for the next couple of days, Bruns also feared retribution by vengeful southerners in Jefferson City and elsewhere. Still, she was proud that the ethnic troops had done more than merely saved St. Louis for the Union. German immigrants, she told her brother, had become "aware of their strength and their predominance. Now the Americans fear them, and later they will probably respect them more."[37]

However, Jette Bruns's fears were not unfounded and in the coming weeks anti-Union and anti-immigrant violence increased in Missouri. An anonymous writer from the pro-southern town of Lexington in the western part of the state told the *Westliche Post*: "Hatred around here is especially directed against these 'goddamned Dutch,' and none of the few Germans who are still here dare leave their houses after nightfall, because this gang of robbers have threatened to shoot down every 'goddamned Dutchman' out at night."[38] When Confederate General Sterling Price, whose troops included anti-immigrant guerrillas, occupied Lexington a few months later, many immigrants fled the state. Raids by regular and irregular southern troops plagued immigrant settlements along the border throughout the coming war, often enough without the slightest military necessity. These attacks were not restricted to German, Polish, or other visible immigrant groups. Even English and Scottish settlers were threatened when they voiced pro-Union sentiment.

Of course, immigrants tried to defend themselves wherever possible. Conrad Weinrich wrote from a German settlement in St. Charles County that "we had a regular fight here on Monday when the Americans fell like the French in the battle of Leibzig [sic]. But now we have to fear for our lives every minute . . . "[39] This beginning civil war in Missouri convinced many immigrants that joining militia companies and home guards was the only effective way of defending their homes and families.

THE ETHNIC REGIMENTS

While war was already raging in Missouri, the rest of the country prepared for a conflict most thought would be a matter of months, if not weeks. This naive perception caused great enthusiasm on both sides during the first months of recruitment and volunteering. Especially among ethnic Americans, Lincoln's call for volunteers fell on fertile ground already nourished by newspaper editorials and speeches, and immigrants often came forward more readily than Americans. While most Europeans were used to military service and standing armies as a part of society, Americans had traditionally distrusted the European system of conscription and professional soldiering. It had been, after all, the British troops of King George III who had suppressed American liberty until 1774. Therefore, the military profession did not enjoy high reputation, while for many immigrants it was an opportunity to earn steady wages and thus ensure economic status. Joseph Kugler had emigrated from Württemberg and, as a physician, had joined the United States Army in 1852. As he briefly summed up in his biography, "The loss of my parents brought me to this country, want of means into the Army."[40] Furthermore, for Europeans it was a significant difference to volunteer for an army protecting a democratic government instead of being drafted into an army serving a despotic monarch. In fact, Irish and German immigrants composed almost half of the enlisted troops in the American regular army before the Civil War.[41]

In reference to the minutemen who had started the American Revolution, militia units composed of volunteer citizens were much more popular in American society. Because several states excluded not yet naturalized foreigners from militia service, separate ethnic militia companies had formed over the years, in some cities like Milwaukee, even before the American ones. Besides underlining their claims to American citizenship through loyalty to the Union, immigrant militias served twofold purposes in the prewar years. First, they openly displayed ethnic defiance against nativist threats, which resulted in frequent brawls with Americans or other ethnic organizations. More importantly yet, these militias actually drilled and prepared for an armed conflict as many immigrants had not completely given up the hope of returning to Europe and continuing their revolutions. Among these were Fenian organizations like the 69th New York Militia, one of the best organized militia units from that city, serving under Michael Corcoran. A former revenue officer working for the English government in Ireland, Corcoran had changed sides after the Great Famine and joined the Irish rebels. Forced to emigrate in 1849, he joined the Fenian movement in New York and became active in Democratic politics. Corcoran finally won nationwide ethnic fame when he refused to parade his militia through the city honoring the visit of the Prince of Wales in 1860. Facing court-martial charges for insubordination, the rebellious Irishman indignantly stated that in "the Prince of Wales I recognized the representative of my country's oppressors." Speaking for many of his compatriots, Corcoran added that "in honoring that personage, I would be dishonoring the memories, and renouncing the principles of that land of patriots."[42] Thomas Meagher publicly defended Corcoran, who had "refused lawfully as a citizen, courageously as a soldier, indignantly as an Irishman"[43] After President Lincoln had issued his call for volunteers, over 500 Irishmen from New York rushed to join

Corcoran's militia within only eight days, making it the first Irish unit ready for duty.

Other Irish nationalist units, including the Philadelphia Meagher Guard or the Meagher Rifles in Boston, honored the most famous Irish freedom fighter. Irish militias repeatedly suffered from Know-Nothing nativism, as in the case of the Boston Columbian Artillery commanded by prominent Irish immigrant and active Democrat Captain Thomas Cass. In 1854 a fugitive slave was captured in Boston and returned to his owner according to the Fugitive Slave Law. Complying with the law, the militia escorted the slave to the harbor, while many native citizens protested against depriving the man of his freedom. Among Bostonians, a strange combination of abolitionist and anti-Irish sentiment led to harsh criticism of the Columbian Artillery that had acted in sharp contrast to many British immigrants helping escaped slaves to safety. Giving in to public pressure, the militia dissolved in the following year. Not plagued by anti-immigrant sentiment, Scottish militias like the New York Highlanders and the Highland Guards in Chicago upheld ethnic pride. The Swedish settlement of Galesburg, Illinois, had its own prestigious Galesburg Light Guards and the French Gardes (or Guards) Lafayette in New York celebrated the memory of their legendary general who had helped win American independence. German militias existed in every major city. In New York, the venerated 5th Militia counted Major Franz Sigel and other prominent exiles among its members. The Steuben Artillery in Evansville, Indiana, referred to a similarly strong national and ethnic symbol as the Gardes Lafayette.[44]

At the beginning of the war it was clear that the regular United States Army, numbering only 16,000 men and officers, could not wage a full-scale war against the South. Thus the state militias played an important role in forming the nucleus of the new volunteer army, just as the Missouri regiments had done. Ethnic visibility in the Union army was great from the beginning because immigrant militias, together with other ethnic organizations, were ready and willing to muster in. In every city, the members of the *Turnvereins*, physically fit and highly disciplined, followed Lincoln's appeal almost to a man. Eventually, the Turners would provide sixteen full regiments, among them the fighting 20th New York under forty-eighter Max Weber and the 17th Missouri, Franz Hassendeubel commanding.

Not all immigrant groups could resort to well-trained paramilitary organizations at the beginning of the war. Yet during the first waves of volunteering in 1861 and early 1862, ethnic visibility soon gained momentum through the formation of German, Irish, Scandinavian, French, and several mixed ethnic regiments. Quotas determined how many volunteer regiments each state had to raise according to their population, and immigrant leaders used their influence to fill these quotas with ethnic units. Charismatic public speakers called upon their fellow countrymen to come forward, especially in heavily immigrant cities like Cincinnati, Chicago, Milwaukee, St. Louis, and Boston. Italians had enthusiastically celebrated the unification of the old country in 1859 and at the beginning of the war promoted an all-Italian regiment in Garibaldi's honor. These efforts failed, but at least Francesco Casale succeeded in recruiting an Italian Legion in New York, later to become part of the multiethnic Garibaldi Guard. Scandinavian leaders proved highly successful in motivating their fellow immigrants. Hans Mattson appealed to all Scandinavians in the *Hemlandet*: "It is high time for us to rise as one people and defend our adopted country and the cause of freedom. We are here, profiting from the same rights as Native Americans. The road to honor and progress is open to us all just the same as for them, and we have sworn our allegiance to this land. Fellow citizens, rise! To arms, to arms!"[45] Swedes and Norwegians followed Mattson's call, partly for their rivalry with the Germans. Likewise, Norwegian Hans Christian Heg urged Scandinavian immigrants in Wisconsin to volunteer because Germans and Irishmen were already forming ethnic regiments.

Immigrant spokesmen had different motivations to set their ethnic group apart from others in their calls to come forward. Like Heg, most ethnic leaders fanned rivalry between the immigrant groups when it came to beating others in filling quotas. Norwegians and Swedes in the Midwest challenged German predominance as they stressed their own ethnic identity as Scandinavian-Americans. Especially Swedes called for the memory of their famed King Gustav Adolf who fell in the Thirty Years' War. Soon to be a famed artillery leader, Swedish Axel Silfversparre called out to his fellow Scandinavians in the *Hemlandet*: "Have you forgotten the heroes who for your religious freedom fought and fell on Lützen's bloody field? . . . Swedes! Have you forgotten that the enlightenment of humanity and freedom has always found Swedish people among those zealous guarantors? Norsemen! Have you forgotten truth and that you swore for a free constitution in dear old Norway?"[46]

Like Scandinavians, Irish immigrants felt that they had to compete with the other immigrant groups for recognition as American citizens. Downplaying their Democratic affiliation and openly un-American drinking habits and religious affiliation, Irish leaders pointed to their nationalist devotion and the long tradition of Irish bravery. As allies of loyal Americans, many Irish hoped, they would gain reputation in society after the war. "Irish Americans," an ethnic newspaper appealed to its readers, "we call on you by the sacred memories of the past, by your remembrance of the succour extended to you suffering brethren, by the future hope of your native land here taking root."[47] To make the Irish cause more visible, Thomas Francis Meagher had early conceived the idea of an all-Irish brigade within the northern army. When he rallied support for his project in 1861, Meagher told his audiences that every Irish soldier could "take his stand proudly by the side of the native-born, and will not fear to look him straight and sternly in the face, and tell him that he has been equal to him in his allegiance to the Constitution."[48] Too often, Meagher argued, Irishmen had been abused in the service of the British Empire; now they had the chance to fight for the right cause and for their own pride. Within a week Meagher raised a company of New York Zouaves and joined Corcoran's 69th Militia. Looking ahead to a later fight against England, Meagher was convinced that "if only one in ten of us come back when this war is over, the military experience gained by that one will be of more service in a fight for Ireland's freedom than would that of the entire ten as they are now."[49] Ethnic consciousness ran high. A recruiting poster for the Irish 9th Massachusetts Infantry illustriously combined practically all the promises ethnic leaders could make their fellow immigrants, calling "Irishmen to the Rescue." Apart from a cumulated sum of $138 in bounties, the organizers assured volunteers that their spiritual needs were professionally taken care of by "a chaplain of the old faith." Pointing out Celtic national pride, the poster pledged that "In joining the Ninth, you join your own gallant kith and kin. You will be led to the battlefield by officers of your own ancient race." Finally, Irish recruits should be aware of their tradition of fighting for freedom and join the cause because, "The Union and future glory of this great sanctuary of freedom is in danger."[50]

German ethnic leaders had similar goals as their Irish counterparts when it came to winning society's respect through patriotism. They, too, could name historical references of their ancestors' martial success. Where Swedes recalled the memory of Gustav Adolf and Irish emphasized their fighting tradition, German leaders told the story of Arminius who had beaten back three Roman Legions in the first century. "Whenever and wherever the Germans have participated in the holy war of justice against injustice," the Louisville *Anzeiger* exaggerated, "they have always proven their innate talent to be exceptional warriors, and become covered with glory when the opportunity presented itself."[51] More importantly, the forty-eighters stressed how important it was especially for Germans to defend a united nation, because they had fought against "the provinciality of petty states" before. As Heinrich Börnstein explained, German-Americans "did not want the glorious and powerful Union of the United States to turn from a great and strong nation into an array of independent, small states."[52]

Augmented by the general enthusiasm for the war and the inducement of recruitment bounties, ethnic rivalry spurred immigrant recruitment. German-Americans even experienced such rivalry within their own ethnic group. When excited Germans raised the 9th Ohio Regiment within a mere two days in Cincinnati, the *Illinois Staats Zeitung* immediately demanded that Germans in Chicago were not to stand behind and had to bring out an ethnic regiment, as well. The resulting partly German regiment, the 9th Illinois Infantry, was placed under the command of August Mersey, a former Baden officer turned forty-eighter. Friedrich Hecker, the old soldier from Germany and private in Sigel's 3rd Missouri Volunteers, also aspired to a regimental command in Illinois. Together with Hungarian revolutionary Julian Kuné Hecker organized the ethnic German 24th "First Hecker" Infantry. As a strict disciplinarian and at times despotic commander Hecker soon alienated officers and enlisted men and in December resigned from his first command since the Baden Revolution. After his resignation, the regiment continued to serve under Kuné's compatriot, Geza Mihalotzy.

Hecker received a second chance with the 82nd Illinois Regiment, mustering in from Springfield in October 1862. Among the volunteers in the "Second Hecker" regiment was Friedrich August Bräutigam from Leipzig, who knew Hecker from his Latin Farmer days. Bräutigam had already enlisted in the 24th in July 1861, but fell ill and had to leave the service shortly after. A year later, he took the opportunity to again join Hecker's command and signed up for the 82nd Illinois. By that time, recruitment had already slowed down, and Bräutigam noted that the otherwise German regiment included a company of Scandinavians as well as several Swiss recruits from the town of Highland.[53] Interestingly enough, Bräutigam never mentioned the all-Jewish Company C "Concordia Guards." The German Jews of Chicago had funded and raised this company, led by Edward S. Salomon (no relation to the Wisconsin Salomons) who would later succeed in command when Hecker was wounded in the battle of Chancellorsville. According to Kaufmann, this company "was added to Hecker's regiment in recognition of Hecker's efforts for the emancipation of the Jews."[54]

Illinois eventually sent three German and six predominantly German regiments to war. Several of their members were not actual immigrants, as in the case of the usually considered ethnic 43rd "Körner" Infantry from the Latin Farmer area around Belleville. Its soldiers were mostly second-generation Germans, and the regiment under its Württemberg-born Colonel Julius Raith, a veteran of the Mexican War, included two fully Swedish companies. Among the overwhelmingly German regiments were the so-called Thielemann Dragoons. Rittmeister Christian Thielemann had raised a German cavalry company at the very beginning of the war consisting mainly of veteran soldiers. In August 1861, an excited crowd of German and American citizens greeted Thielemann's stylish dragoons in Chicago, when they paraded through the streets together with the partly German 44th Illinois Infantry led by Colonel Carl von Knobelsdorff. The dragoons would eventually become Company A of the 16th Illinois Cavalry with Thielemann as colonel.

Raising another two regiments, Irish immigrants figured prominently in the Illinois ethnic recruitment effort. Actually, the 23rd "Irish Brigade" under influential Democrat and second generation Irish James A. Mulligan had already mustered in from Chicago almost a month before Hecker's first regiment in June, revealing an equally high enthusiasm to volunteer among Chicago's Irish. August 1862 saw the completion of the second Irish regiment, the 90th Illinois Infantry, under Timothy O'Meara. Mustering in in September, Chicago's "Irish Legion" earned a fine fighting record.

Of the other midwestern states, Ohio had the largest contingent of ethnic regiments. Originally commanded by American Colonel Robert L. McCook, the 9th "Turner" Infantry was the first of eventually six German regiments from that state. "Die Neuner," as the Germans called their regiment, soon became a powerful symbol for the German-American patriotic devotion to the Union as well as for the spirit of the forty-eighters. Like several other ethnic units, McCook's regiment proudly carried individual flags alongside the regimental and national colors. When the regiment was about to muster in, German women of Cincinnati presented the regimental flags to their husbands and sons in Camp Dennison outside the city. The flags carried the inscriptions *Deutsches Regiment von Cincinnati* (German Regiment of Cincinnati) and *Kämpft tapfer für Freiheit und Recht* (Fight bravely for Liberty and Justice).[55] After a moving speech by McCook, his second in command August Willich had the regimental band play the *Marseillaise* in reference to the French Revolution. The following intonation of the *Star-Spangled Banner* concluded the regiment's dedication to the cause of liberty and democracy. The nomination of an American as commanding officer of an ethnic regiment was a clever choice, as McCook would find it easier to rally official support in Columbus and Washington. Under his able leadership the regiment would produce two battle-tested future regimental commanders, forty-eighters Gustav Tafel and August Willich. The regiment soon won admiration for their brave fighting, earning the respectable nickname of "Bloody Dutch" by their enemies. The 28th and 37th Infantries became the official second and third German regiments from Ohio. Gustav Tafel was given command of the 106th "Fourth German" Ohio Regiment. The two regiments immediately following Tafel's, the 107th and 108th Infantries, were also ethnic in makeup, forming the Fifth and Sixth German regiments.[56] In addition, four more regiments of infantry and the 3rd Cavalry from that state included up to half German-born soldiers.

One Irish regiment came from Cincinnati at the beginning of the war. Irish-born Major Joseph W. Burke raised the 10th "Montgomery" Infantry, but surrendered its command to William Haines Lytle from Ohio. Similar to the appointment of American commanders to other immigrant regiments like McCook, this decision ensured higher acceptance of ethnic regiments when it came to state funding and public approval. Like several other Irish units, the "Bloody Tinth," as it came to be called, earned a distinctive reputation for its members' fondness for both fighting and drinking.[57]

Probably as many Irish as Germans volunteered from Indiana. Although ethnic politicians argued for a German Indiana regiment, most of their fellow immigrants joined mixed units and it was not until late August that Governor Morton mustered the 32nd Infantry into federal service from Indianapolis. Its commanding officer, August Willich, had enlisted in the German 9th Ohio as a private and soon rose to lieutenant colonel. Always the plain professional soldier, Willich was disgusted with the ubiquitous pushing for advancement and the political bickering around ethnic recruitment. All the communist forty-eighter wanted was to fight for the righteous cause. Maybe this was why "Papa Willich," as he came to be called by his soldiers, became one of the most admired immigrant officers in the war. Unlike most regiments at the beginning of the war, the 32nd marched out of Indianapolis in a solemn procession, befitting Willich's character as an earnest and serious leader of men. The unit would earn one of the finest reputations as a gallantly fighting regiment of the war. Four months after Willich's Germans, the Irish 35th Infantry left Indianapolis in December under the command of Irish-born Colonel Bernard F. Mullen, an active member of the Fenian Brotherhood. Several other Indiana regiments had good portions of German and Irish soldiers, and at least two infantry regiments each were half German and half Irish, respectively. The soldiers in these regiments seemingly got along well and contrary to other units such as the 5th Pennsylvania Cavalry, records tell of no difficulties between the ethnic groups in these regiments. This regiment counted several Jews among its German members, and Jewish Colonel Max Friedmann had early in the war provoked hostile reactions by appointing Dutch immigrant Rabbi Arnold Fischel as chaplain. Such a decision probably did little to increase sympathies between the Germans and their Irish Catholic comrades.[58]

Although Wisconsin had a high proportion of first- and second-generation Germans among its population, enthusiasm for the war was low. Of course, older German immigrants had already assimilated and probably a good many of them volunteered in mixed regiments. In addition, seven regiments were not purely German but included a high portion of immigrants, such as the 27th Infantry under Colonel Conrad Krez and Colonel Fritz Anneke's 34th Wisconsin. The state produced only two fully German regiments, both from Milwaukee. The 9th "Salomon Guards" Infantry formed in October 1861 under forty-eighter Carl Eberhard Salomon, who had earlier commanded one of the Missouri regiments. Colonel William H. Jacobs organized the 26th Wisconsin. Participating in many battles, this regiment became "one of the finest military organizations in the service." In his discriminating list of the "fightingest" Civil War regiments, Fox called the 26th Wisconsin a "German regiment whose gallantry and soldierly bearing reflected credit upon its nationality."[59]

On the whole, however, enthusiasm for the war was remarkably low among Wisconsin Germans because the whole conflict seemed too remote for many immigrants. Interestingly enough, the home state of Carl Schurz, who had campaigned so passionately for a war against slavery, was also the only state where Germans protested against army service once conscription came into effect in 1862. Immigrants opposed unfair quotas, unequal bounties, and as good Democrats many did not agree with federal interference with state affairs. In Milwaukee, German-American workers attacked recruiting agents trying to gather conscripts and in late November of that year, ethnic opposition to the draft culminated in a bloody riot in Ozaukee County. Recruiters even found it difficult to find men willing to sign up for the famous ethnic 26th Infantry. Considerably less in numbers, Irish immigrants in Wisconsin came forth similarly slowly. Two Madison regiments, the 11th and 17th, had about half their members listed as Irish-born, with a full company of French immigrants blazoning the latter. Scandinavians, in contrast to many Germans and Irish, volunteered readily for the Union. Recruiting among Wisconsin's Norwegians and Swedes, Hans Christian Heg rallied enough recruits to raise the 15th Infantry, soon to be known as the Scandinavian Regiment. Ready to be mustered into service in February 1862, Heg's regiment paraded proudly through Madison and received its regimental colors in front of the capitol by Governor Louis P. Harvey.[60]

Surrounded by antifederal sentiment, little ethnic recruiting occurred in the border states of Maryland, Kansas, and Kentucky. Two partly, if not predominantly, German regiments came from Maryland. Just like the 3rd Maryland Infantry, the 5th included several German companies. A Jewish immigrant and forty-eighter from Brandenburg was instrumental in raising the latter, spending his own money in organizing the regiment. Leopold Blumenberg had served in the Prussian-Danish War as one of only few Jewish officers in the German army. Later Blumenberg fled an increasingly anti-Semitic atmosphere in Prussia and came to Baltimore in 1854. There he became a successful businessman, engaged in ethnic and Republican politics, and founded the German *Unionsverein*. Subject to abuse from his pro-southern neighbors, the German Jew nevertheless remained true to his unionism, and in September 1861, the 5th Infantry mustered into federal service under his command.[61] The German population in Kansas brought forth enough volunteers to man several companies of the 1st and 2nd infantry regiments. Kansas sent probably as many immigrants to war as Kentucky. Some 2,000 Germans from the Bluegrass State joined the Union army, many of them in the 5th and 6th Infantries.[62]

Ethnic recruitment met much greater success in Missouri where immigrants had already volunteered in substantial numbers before the first call for troops. After the reorganization of the three-month regiments, the 12th, 15th, and 17th Regiments remained almost exclusively German units and many other regiments had a considerable admixture of German, Polish, or Hungarian immigrants. Besides Hassendeubel's 17th Turner Infantry, the 12th Missouri has been called the most quintessentially German regiment by William Burton. More than 90 percent of its members were immigrants, the vast majority of them Germans with some French, Danish, and Swiss at their side. A mere sixty-one recruits were American-born, several of them second-generation immigrants. One of the most famous of all forty-eighters, Peter Joseph Osterhaus had organized the regiment among mainly urban and Latin Farmer immigrants from St. Louis and nearby Illinois. Shortly after the regiment had mustered in in August, Osterhaus left to take command of a predominantly ethnic Missouri brigade and passed on regimental command. A fellow forty-eighter, Otto Schadt had already served as captain in Rifle Company A of Börnstein's three-months' regiment.[63] When Schadt saw himself forced to leave the service for health reasons in March 1862, the regiment found its most effective leader. One of the Belleville Latin Farmers and close friend of Osterhaus, Mecklenburg nobleman Hugo von Wangelin had enlisted in the 12th as a private and soon advanced to its major. As regimental leader and subsequent brigade commander, Wangelin stood out in more than fifty battles and engagements. Wounded several times in the war, Wangelin lost an arm in the battle of Ringgold, Georgia, in November 1863. Kaufmann tells the story of Wangelin's surgery, insisting that when the surgeons tried to sedate the officer, "Wangelin refused them, saying that a soldier could stand a little cutting. He whistled 'Yankee Doodle' as the saw went through his bones."[64]

Although known as the "Swiss Rifles" because it formed around two companies from Highland, the 15th Missouri Infantry under Colonel Francis J. Joliat consisted initially of up to two-thirds Swiss immigrants and second-generation Swiss. The rest of the original recruits were almost exclusively Germans from St. Louis. Of course, sharing the same language, the regiment's soldiers all must have seemed German to many Americans. As the war went on, Germans came to dominate the regiment, although it continued to carry a Swiss flag. One of the famed Hungarian forty-eighters, General Alexander Asboth, lauded the 15th Missouri after the Battle of Pea Ridge as "the efficient Swiss regiment . . . whose beautiful flag floated so picturesquely throughout the battlefield."[65] Joliat had to resign in November 1862, due to failing health, and the regiment continued to serve valiantly under its new colonel, Joseph Conrad from Hessian Nassau. A graduate from the Military Academy of Hesse, Conrad was a former major in Sigel's 3rd Missouri and effectively led the regiment in several battles, among others at the terrible slaughter at Chickamauga where it suffered a total of a hundred losses.[66]

Irish Americans also enlisted from Missouri. Most notably, an ethnic cavalry company called "Irish Dragoons" formed in the summer of 1861 under Captain Patrick Naughton, in the heavily secessionist area of Jefferson City. The company subsequently was attached to the Irish 23rd Illinois regiment. The Irish of St. Louis contributed a whole regiment. The members of the 7th Missouri Infantry soon lived up to their reputation as the boisterous part of that city's immigrant population and became known for similar vices as their comrades of the 10th Ohio. As one sergeant-major from Illinois wrote when his regiment encountered the Irish Missourians in August 1861, "the 'Missouri Irish Brigade' arrived here yesterday from Boonville. It is said that there are 800 men, and the first day they came here there were 900 fights."[67] The men of the 7th Missouri soon proved that they could fight in battle as well, however. At Corinth in Mississippi, in October 1862, the regiment's officers earned praise from their brigade commander for relentlessly pushing forward their men "with great promptness and efficiency on all occasions." Especially commending the enlisted men, their commander continued, "All praise is due for their subordination, perseverance, endurance, and soldierly conduct, making an unprecedented advance in the rear of a desperate and determined enemy without rest or supplies." Finally, their proneness for brawling saved two skirmishers when they were captured by the retreating rebels. Undaunted, the Irishmen attacked their guard, "took his arms and came back to the command, capturing a rebel captain on their return."[68]

The state with the longest tradition of German settlement, Pennsylvania, put five German regiments and at least one more half-ethnic German unit in the field. In addition of course, numerous Pennsylvania organizations had high proportions of second-generation Germans and descendants of even earlier "Pennsylvania Dutch" among their members. The first German regiment was the 27th Pennsylvania Infantry or "Washington Brigade." This regiment had already formed in Philadelphia in January 1861, from different German militia companies under the command of Jewish immigrant Max Einstein. Einstein had arrived in America from Württemberg in 1844 and settled in Philadelphia where he achieved considerable status among the city's Germans and Jews. Early in 1861, Einstein invested his personal fortune to consolidate the militias and organize them into the German and partly Jewish 27th Infantry. In April, his command was part of a Union escort that traveled to the defense of the threatened national capital. Unfortunately, the still unarmed and not yet sufficiently drilled regiment had to change trains in Baltimore and on its way between two stations encountered the scorn of local citizens who rose up against northern troops marching through their city. An angry mob attacked the federals, and although the police stood in to protect the regiment several soldiers were wounded and killed. The 27th, like so many other Civil War regiments, later saw a change in commanders. Colonel Einstein resigned under somewhat dubious circumstances following arguments with his superiors. Adolph Buschbeck from Koblenz continued to lead the regiment with distinction through several battles until he took command of a brigade and later a division in the partly ethnic Eleventh Army Corps. Praising Buschbeck's ability, Kaufmann claims him to be "one of the most splendid figures of the Civil War and, alongside Willich and Wangelin, one of our primary German fighting generals. He was always at the front, and his war record shows him participating in many decisive battles."[69] In September 1861, two largely German regiments mustered in in Philadelphia. Colonel Johann A. Koltes from Trier had emigrated in 1844 and was a veteran of the Mexican War when he organized the 73rd Regiment, which included several Irish and English immigrants. Like Max Einstein, Bremen-born immigrant Henry Bohlen used private means to organize and furnish the 75th Pennsylvania Infantry.[70]

Certainly the most famous commander of Pennsylvania Germans was Alexander von Schimmelfennig. Born in Prussian Lithuania, Schimmelfennig had early entered the military profession in his home country after attending a military school. Like many of his fellow officers, Schimmelfennig changed sides during the Revolution of 1848 and fought with Sigel and Schurz in the Palatine. Emigrating in 1853, Schimmelfennig made his home in Pittsburgh and after the fall of Fort Sumter took command of a German regiment, the 35th Pennsylvania Infantry, forming in this city. Petty bickering and jealousy toward the forty-eighter, however, led to the disbanding of the regiment and to its eventual reorganization as the 74th Infantry. Schimmelfennig himself soon won a brigade command, but the professional soldier would throughout the war lament the political influences on the military and the army's inept leadership. As part of the partly ethnic Eleventh Corps, Schimmelfennig's regiment together with the 75th Pennsylvania, Hecker's 82nd Illinois, and several other German and mixed ethnic regiments later suffered from malicious nativist attacks following their defeat at Chancellorsville.[71]

Like their German fellow immigrants, the Irish had already several militia companies in service in Philadelphia, among them the Meagher Guards. Together with other units, they had merged into a militia regiment under the command of Welsh-born Colonel Joshua T. Owen in April. Mustered in as the 24th Pennsylvania Infantry to serve for three months, the men willingly extended their terms of service in August. In reference to Corcoran's already famous 69th New York, the unit leaped ahead of the mustering schedule and took on the designation of 69th Pennsylvania Infantry. Dubbed the "Philadelphia Brigade," the regiment gained a solid fighting reputation and according to Fox "fully sustained the reputation of the Irish soldier for gallantry in battle."[72] Another Irish regiment came from Philadelphia in the summer of 1862. The 116th Infantry under Colonel St. Clair A. Mulholland would see much active service as part of General Meagher's Irish Brigade. Recruited among the miners of Schuylkill County in the fall of 1861, the 48th Pennsylvania Infantry naturally had a great number of Irish among its members, although it was not an exclusive ethnic regiment.

In some Pennsylvania regiments, Germans and Irish served side by side. When the 98th Infantry formed in the early fall of 1861 among Philadelphia Germans, its recruits received exotic reinforcements. The Jackson Rifles, an Irish militia company from nearby Manayunk, joined the regiment as its Company A. Apparently no one in the regiment under the able command of Württemberg-born Colonel John F. Ballier had any problems with serving alongside Irish comrades. The 5th Cavalry under the command of Lieutenant Colonel William Lewis and later led by German Lieutenant Colonel Christian Kleinz, was even half German and half Irish. This regiment, in contrast, suffered from constant quarrels between both ethnicities.

Due to their predominance among the immigrants in the New England States, Irish regiments were the only ethnic units from Connecticut, New Hampshire, Maine, and Massachusetts. Given the prevailing Know-Nothing sentiment in much of New England, however, it is worth noting that these states fielded Irish regiments at all. The 9th Connecticut Infantry under Colonel Thomas W. Cahill of Irish descent, like the other New England regiments, was not a 100 percent immigrant in composition but included Americans and Germans in its ranks. However, its members perceived it as an ethnic organization and were proud of its predominantly Irish character. Members of the 9th got drunk every now and then, and when the regiment participated in the occupation of New Orleans in April 1862, one soldier "left his camp without orders in the night and was found dead the next morning in an obscure street, having probably been engaged in a drunken brawl."[73] From northeastern Maine came the 15th "Old Fifteenth" Infantry, mustering in under its Colonel John McCluskey in December 1861. When the regiment left the state in February, it bore a proud green flag adorned by the Irish harp and shamrock. It was not until September

1862 that New Hampshire sent its 10th Irish Infantry, under Colonel Michael T. Donohoe, to the war. Barely drilled, the regiment participated in the disastrous battle of Fredericksburg in December, although it did not take a prominent part. Nevertheless, Colonel Donohoe lauded his men that "Under the circumstances, I feel that they did well, having never been under fire before, and being witness to many ineffectual attempts of both new and old troops to break the enemy's lines, and seeing the immense destruction of men, which would naturally disconcert new troops."[74]

The first Irish regiment to come from Massachusetts was the 9th Infantry. Organized among members of the disbanded Columbian Artillery by their former captain Thomas Cass, the regiment took to the field from Boston in June 1861. In remarkable contrast to earlier nativist opposition to the Boston Irish, now the whole city saw the splendidly outfitted regiment off and witnessed as Governor John A. Andrew promised that the Union made no difference between native-born citizens "and those born in other countries." Fighting hard throughout the war, it became one of those regiments "whose gallant service on many fields attested the oft-acknowledged valor of the Irish soldier."[75] As in other ethnic units, flags as the most visible signs of identification with their ethnic cause became strong symbols for the Irishmen of the 9th Massachusetts. As the recruiting poster for the 9th promised prospective recruits in bold letters, the regiment always carried an Irish flag together with the Star-Spangled Banner. Their national banner alongside the American flag demonstrated commitment to both their own and the Union cause. After the battle of Kinney's Farm, Virginia, in May 1862, Colonel Cass proudly reported that "The starry banner of the Union, side by side with our green flag throughout the fight, came out of it unscathed, while the latter was pierced by eight buck-and-ball shots and the lower tie torn away."[76] The second Irish regiment from the Bay State, the 28th Massachusetts Infantry, became a part of the famed Irish Brigade. Both Corcoran and Meagher had lobbied for more ethnic Irish regiments since the beginning of the war, and in December 1861, the "Faugh a Ballagh" (*Clear the Road*) Regiment was mustered in. Command of the regiment fell to Irish-born Colonel William Montieth who had to deal with considerable difficulties among his mixture of ethnic and native American soldiers. Together with their comrades from New York and Pennsylvania in the other units of the Irish Brigade, however, the men of the 28th Massachusetts proved excellent fighters until their regiment mustered out after three years and a total loss of 847 killed and wounded.

By far the most ethnic regiments came from New York, the state with the largest city and the most important immigration port during the war. The Empire State raised eleven German and eight purely or predominantly Irish regiments as well as several regiments with high proportions of these two immigrant groups. In addition, New York saw more or less successful ethnic efforts to raise Italian, French, Polish, and Scottish regiments, and it produced a few obscurely mixed ethnic regiments.

When Corcoran's Militia was sworn into federal service as the 69th New York Infantry in November 1861, it received its regimental colors during a festive ceremony. One officer proudly described the regiment's flags:

> The regimental flags were of a deep rich green, heavily fringed, having in the centre a richly embroidered Irish harp, with a sunburst above it and a wreath of shamrock beneath. Underneath, on a crimson scroll, in Irish characters, was the motto, "They shall never retreat from the charge of the lances." . . . The staff-mountings were silver-plated; the top being a pike-head, under which was knotted a long bannerol of saffron-colored silk, fringed with bullion, and marked with the number of the regiment.[77]

The first Irish regiment to join the Union army, the 69th participated in the first battle of Bull Run where Colonel Corcoran was captured. Under the leadership of Robert Nugent, the regiment later formed the core of Meagher's Irish Brigade together with the 63rd New York under Colonel John Burke who was later succeeded by Lieutenant Colonel Patrick D. Kelly and the 88th "Mrs. Meagher's Own" Regiment led by Colonel Henry M. Baker.

Returning from captivity in the summer of 1862 as a national and ethnic hero, Michael Corcoran set out to raise another Irish brigade, called the Corcoran Legion. Recruitment among New York Irish was no longer easy after the first wave of enthusiasm for the war among the immigrants had ebbed away. Therefore, many recruits for these new regiments came from lower and sometimes outright criminal classes such as several soldiers of the 155th Infantry. Its members came partly from New York jails and contributed to the nickname of the "Wild Irish" Regiment. Far from being purely Irish, the 155th included in its ranks Scottish and Swedish as well as Spanish and Swiss men and noncommissioned officers. Germans at some point even outnumbered Irishmen in one company. Organizing the 170th "Fourth Corcoran Legion" in Brooklyn and New York City, Irish-born Colonel James P. McIvor had to struggle with the ubiquitous blight of many Irish units. McIvor even complained about the excessive drinking among his officers and feared that if no measures were taken, "there will not be a Line officer for duty in the Regt."[78] Rounding up the Corcoran Legion were the 164th "Phoenix Regiment" or "Corcoran Guard," 175th, and 182nd New York regiments. Although recruited under less than desirable circumstances, the Legion proved a dependable brigade all the same. As with so many other ethnic regiments, their Irish character faded with the years, and by 1863 two companies of the 175th New York were completely German. Four more New York Regiments were predominantly Irish at the time of their organization, the 11th New York "First Fire Zouaves," the 20th New York Militia "Ulster Guard," Colonel John H. McCunn's 37th "Irish Rifles," and the 105th New York Infantry from Upstate New York.

Without any doubt, the most baffling mixture of ethnic soldiers existed in the 39th New York "Garibaldi Guard." The regiment originated in futile Italian, Hungarian, and Spanish attempts to form ethnic regiments, which only produced ethnic companies in New York City. Regimental flags in the case of the 39th New York must have confused onlookers more than they pointed to the ethnic pride of its members. In addition to the Star-Spangled Banner and the Italian tricolor, the regiment's Hungarian-born Colonel Frederic George d'Utassy, whose real name was Strasser, had the regiment carry a Hungarian flag, although only a few of his fellow countrymen served in the unit. The others, among them Turks, Italians, French, Germans, Swiss, and others, did not seem to care. General George B. McClellan later recalled a highly amusing, although probably exaggerated, episode that tells of the polyglot makeup of the Garibaldi Guard. Returning one night from outside the encampment, McClellan wrote in his memoirs, "I encountered an outpost of the Garibaldians. In reply to their challenge I tried English, French, Spanish, Italian, German, Indian, a little Russian and Turkish; all in vain, for nothing at my disposal made the slightest impression on them, and I inferred that they were perhaps gypsies of Esquimaux or Chinese."[79] It seems likely that the regiment never developed a real identity, while instead its three German and one Swiss company as well as the two Sicilian companies may have formed distinct entities. The regiment was captured at Harper's Ferry in September 1862, and soon after paroled. Colonel d'Utassy was later dismissed from the service after a court-martial involving charges of fraud. The regiment eventually was reorganized under more able commanders like forty-eighter Hugo Hildebrandt, who led it gallantly at Gettysburg. Another motley crew of various ethnicities formed the so-called "Enfants Perdus," a New York independent battalion also mistakenly called the "German Legion." The Enfants Perdus never earned a fighting reputation. On the contrary, they made a rather unfavorable impression in the battle of Olustee in Florida in February 1864, when they retreated to the rear without orders. "My own men behaved well, devotedly, and individually so," a captain of the regular artillery later reported. "My attached 'Enfans Perdus' did not. They clustered and gabbled in all languages; some were punished."[80]

Of two attempts to form French regiments in New York, only one materialized with considerable success. Plagued by the inefficiency of their commander Colonel Lionel Jobert d'Epineuil, the 53rd New York was conceived as an attractive Zouave outfit, but it went under in confusion and dissolved early in 1862. The 55th New York Infantry formed around the Gardes Lafayette and upon its muster-in in August 1861, took on the militia's designation and a French flag. The Gardes Lafayette consisted in good part of French immigrants but Germans, Irish, and Americans also manned the ranks, eradicating the regiment's supposedly French character. Command fell to its organizer, a French nobleman by the name of Count Philippe Régis de Trobriand. A writer and journalist before the war, he had edited the *Courrier des États-Unis*; and with his previous military training and experience from France, he proved to be an able officer and brigade commander. De Trobriand described his six largely French companies as posers who knew exactly when to show off: "At reviews and drills where they attracted attention, they made a fine figure and maneuvered with unity and precision. At those drills where no one was watching them, they did neither better nor worse than their comrades."[81] Still, the 55th fought well and after one year of service had already lost over 400 men. Due to these losses, the regiment was merged with the 38th New York Infantry at the end of 1862.

Wladimir Krzyzanowski would emerge as a charismatic ethnic leader and the highly respected commander of the 58th New York Polish Legion. After his emigration the revolutionary soon made friends with forty-eighters like Carl Schurz, and became an ardent Republican fighting for the abolition of slavery. A civil engineer in the Midwest and in Washington, DC, the immigrant went to New York and joined the Union army at the first call for volunteers. He had already raised a militia company, the "United States Rifles," which together with other units such as the German "Humboldt's Jägers," the "Polish Legion," and the "Gallatin Rifles," consolidated into the 58th Infantry. Mustering in in October, the regiment counted Germans, Poles, Danes, French, Italians, Hungarians, and Russians among its members. As a Polish newspaper reported, the 58th New York was "built around a hard core of freedom fighters—men like its commanding officer, Colonel Krzyzanowski, who had struggled for freedom in Europe and who knew the full value of the deep underlying cause which they instinctively knew lay beneath the simple cause of American union." Nicknamed "Kriz" by his faithful soldiers, the Polish officer earned many laurels in battle and became one of the war's ethnic heroes.[82] Another heavily Polish regiment was the 31st New York under Colonel Calvin E. Pratt, distinct by their traditional Polish square-cornered hats called *schapska*.

Like many other militia companies, the New York City Scottish Highlanders offered their service to the government in the first weeks immediately after Lincoln's call. Commanded by the secretary of war's brother, Colonel James Cameron, the regiment soon was known as "Cameron's Highlanders" and took on the designation of 79th Infantry after a famous Scottish regiment. Scottish immigrants actually constituted the clear majority of men and officers, although several Americans and even Irish joined the unit. When the regiment left New York City for Washington in late May on its way to become a gallant fighting outfit, "it received a flag bearing a thistle, listened to speeches lauding the glories of Scottish soldiers on historic battlefields, and enjoyed a parade down Broadway—a parade complete with pipers playing the pibroch."[83] The Scotsmen's initial dress uniforms of traditional kilts naturally attracted extra attention among New Yorkers already used to exotic ethnic groups. The Highlanders established a gallant fighting reputation in the first major battle at Bull Run where Colonel Cameron was killed. Referring to the fighting tradition of the Scots, Fox praised the regiment, whose members "fully sustained the honor and military reputation of their native land, and fought for the government of their adoption as gallantly as ever Scotchmen fought on native soil or on foreign fields."[84] A second endeavor to raise a Scottish regiment evolved around the Scottish Highland Guards from Chicago. However, there were far too few Scots in the Chicago area to form a whole regiment, and from the beginning its organizers called on all available recruits, promising that the regiment "will be composed chiefly of Scotchmen and the descendants of Scotchmen, although good men of other nationalities will not be excluded from entering its ranks."[85] Finally the 65th Illinois went to the field as a partly ethnic regiment under its Scottish Colonel Daniel Cameron, Jr., in May 1862.

In addition to their presence in many of the mixed ethnic and even in Irish regiments, the impressive number of German and partly German regiments from New York attests to the success of ethnic recruitment efforts in that state, and especially in New York City. Together with others, Carl Schurz had been an active recruiter and to his direct credit go, among others, four German cavalry companies attached to the 1st New York Cavalry. The 4th Cavalry commanded by German Christian F. Dickel also included a good portion of German immigrants in its ranks. Although no forty-eighter himself, Georg von Schack nevertheless was a devoted German nationalist. The Prussian officer had taken leave of absence to join the Union army and took over command of the 7th New York Infantry in January 1862. A German newspaper correspondent later reported that he had observed "the Seventh New York regiment, a purely German unit under Colonel von Schack, with black, red, and golden colors."[86] This tricolor flag had derived from the uniforms of rifle companies during the wars of liberation against Napoleon and later had come to symbolize the German national movement. In the Union, the flag represented the spirit of 1848 and the fight for personal liberty and national unity. Promoted brigadier general during the war for his professional service, von Schack afterward decided not to return to his native Prussia but handed in his resignation and became an American citizen.

Although the Steuben Rifles had recruited among the Germans of New York City, their first commander had been American-born John E. Bendix. Thus, the honor of being called the "First German" New York went to the 8th New York Infantry. This unit was the brainchild of forty-eighter Ludwig Blenker from the Palatine. Blenker's career was a most picturesque one, correlating with his captivating appearance. Born in Worms, Blenker had served in the Bavarian Army and had escorted Prince Otto from Bavaria when he ascended the Greek Throne in 1837. In 1848, Blenker led the Baden revolutionaries as a colonel and later participated in the Palatine campaign where he won fame for his skills and charisma as a military leader. After his emigration in 1850, Blenker settled in Rockland County, New York—involuntarily—as farmer and businessman. A talented and mesmerizing orator like Carl Schurz, Blenker quickly learned how to pull the right strings and lobby in his own favor. Thus, he encountered little difficulty when he set out to raise a German regiment in 1861. In his memoirs, Schurz described the excitement in New York when the First German Infantry finally paraded through the city on May 26, providing entertainment for both ethnic and native onlookers:

> [As] Blenker's Regiment marched off, everybody cheered them on. Every German in New York was out on the streets, joined by thousands of men and women of different nationalities who had heard of the imposing colonel and his men. And their expectations were not disappointed. The regiment in its light grey uniforms . . . was a splendid sight to see both regarding equipment and its military bearing. Colonel Blenker marched at the head of his regiment on foot, amazing the spectators with his goose step.[87]

Similar to Blenker's regiment, many ethnic units at the beginning of the war sported individual costumes, often tailored after the uniforms of their home countries. A bewildering variety of uniforms reflected immigrant regiments' ethnic origins. Blenker's gray was styled after the colors of Prussian uniforms. The regiments of the Irish Brigade had green collars in addition to shoulder straps of the same national color. The Gardes Lafayette wore a distinct light blue modeled after the French army's uniforms, while the 31st New Yorkers sported their *schapskas* in red and white. Most conspicuously, the Highlanders of the 79th New York Infantry tried to retain kilts as part of their uniform, until discarded for practical reasons. Finally, the 39th New York donned red flannel shirts in recognition of Garibaldi's famous "Red Shirts." During the organization of the Union army later in 1861, most of these exotic costumes disappeared and were replaced by the standard Union blue.[88]

The "United Turner Regiment" had already formed in May in New York City under the command of Colonel Max Weber, another former Badenian officer who had joined the revolution in 1848. Mustered in as the 20th New York Infantry, the regiment also carried the German Republican Colors besides the American flag. As with other volunteer regiments, the presentation of the pennants to the United Turners was part the regiment's ceremonious departure from New York City amid cheerful excitement. Large crowds, among them many German societies, lined the streets as the regiment paraded from the Turners' Hall up the Bowery to Union Square. Militia and Turner companies as well as rifle clubs joined in the procession on to City Hall. There the regiment received its flags and one of the most respected German-Americans, Friedrich Kapp, presented a sword of honor to Weber, explaining to his avid audience that "A German soldier has a double fame in this war. He enters for his adopted country, and he has to do honor for the German name."[89]

The 29th "Astor Rifles" organized under Colonel Adolf von Steinwehr in New York City and were mustered in on June 6, 1861. One of the few nonforty-eighters to rise to generalships during the war, Steinwehr had been born into a German officers' family in 1822 and was an educated Prussian officer as well as a teacher at the Potsdam Military Academy. Emigrating to America in 1847, Steinwehr served in the Mexican War and after a brief return to Germany settled down permanently as a

Latin Farmer in Connecticut. The professional soldier combined a Prussian military education with experience and knowledge of the American military and, according to Kaufmann, there "is no doubt that von Steinwehr was the most thoroughly trained of all the German officers in the Union army."[90] Because others were much more active in promoting their own careers than this professional soldier, Steinwehr soon found himself serving under General Ludwig Blenker. In October 1861, Steinwehr received his brigadier general's star and served well throughout the war, emerging as one of the heroes at Gettysburg. Kaufmann relates that it was Steinwehr "who recognized the importance of Cemetery Hill as a point of defense and immediately made use of it."

Historian Ella Lonn has stated that "Few of the German regiments enlisted more attention than the DeKalb Regiment, or the Forty-First New York."[91] Deriving from a German militia company by the same name, the DeKalb Infantry mustered into federal service in Yorkville on the same day as the Astor Rifles. Like its commander, forty-eighter Leopold von Gilsa, two-third of the regiment's officers and men were veterans of the Prussian-Danish War. This composition made the "Second Jäger Regiment," as it was also called, a highly professional unit. So many Germans from New York volunteered during the first months of recruiting that they could actually choose among several ethnic regiments. Four months after Steinwehr's regiment, the "Fifth German Rifles" left New York City under Colonel Georg von Amsberg. This regiment, formed primarily among immigrants from the northern parts of Germany and Prussia, accordingly was also dubbed the "Plattdeutsch" Regiment. Also recruited in New York City, the 46th "Frémont Rifles" led by forty-eighter Colonel Rudolf von Rosa had already mustered in and departed for Washington several weeks earlier, in September.

Named after one of the most famous German forty-eighters, the "Sigel Rifles" had attracted many immigrants before the war. Four companies of that militia together with another six companies of the German Rifle Militia organized into the 52nd New York Infantry from Staten Island and marched off to Washington in November under its Colonel Paul Frank. When Frank later took over a brigade, the regimental command went to Carl Gottfried Freudenberg. The boy forty-eighter proved his valor in many bloody battles and by the fall of 1863, hard fighting had taken its toll on the men. Reporting from Virginia in October, Freudenberg stated that his regiment consisted then of "over 600 being conscripts, with only about 80 veterans." Yet these green troops served very well, the commander added. "They bore the fatigue of the severe marches admirably, and acted under fire better than could have been expected of recruits."[92] Eventually the 52nd became the only German regiment from New York to make it into Fox's list of the Civil War's hardiest regiments. Losing 350 officers and men in the war, Freudenberg's soldiers "fought for the flag of the Union as gallantly as ever Germans fought on the battle fields of their fatherland."[93]

Mustering in from Hudson in October, the 54th New York Infantry under Kossuth's former adjutant Eugen Kozlay from Hungary earned the nickname "Schwarze

Jäger." Recruited mostly among Germans, Poles, and Hungarians from New York City and Brooklyn, the Black Rifles very probably had a good number of Jewish members and included up to three officers of the Jewish faith. This is probably the reason why Kozlay's unit stood out by employing one of the extremely few Jewish regimental chaplains in the Civil War. By law, only ordained Christian ministers could become regimental chaplains, and Fischel's appointment to the 5th Pennsylvania had been revoked by the secretary of war. Thanks to relentless Jewish lobbying, however, the law was changed in 1862, and in April 1863 Rabbi Ferdinand Leopold Sarner from Lissa in Posen became the 54th Infantry's Jewish chaplain. It is certainly worth noting that despite the fact that the majority of Kozlay's officers were no Jews, they nevertheless backed Sarner's election. Sarner made a strong impression both by his thorough education and his willingness to join the regiment in battle. Unfortunately, he was wounded seriously in the battle of Gettysburg and subsequently had to resign.[94]

Baron Fred W. von Egloffstein mustered in a regiment including many former German officers, the 103rd New York. The "Third German Rifles" earned a fine record and subsequently came under the command of forty-eighter Wilhelm Heine, a brevet brigadier general by the end of the war. Less fortunate in the choice of their eventual commander were the men of the 68th "Second German Rifles," a partly ethnic unit under the initial command of Lieutenant Colonel Albert von Steinhausen. When the men's enlistment term expired in early 1864, the unit underwent reorganization and political scheming wrested the command from Steinhausen's hands. Instead, a dubious soldier of fortune became the new colonel, Prussian Prince Felix Salm-Salm who had already led the First German Rifles after the discharge of Blenker in 1863. The prince, later under arrest and a fugitive to Mexico, proved of little military worth and represented the less valuable contributions to the German-American cause in the Civil War.[95] Several other New York regiments were about half German in makeup, among them Krzyzanowski's 58th Polish Legion and the 119th Infantry under its colonel with the Americanized name of John T. Lockman.

The recruitment of ethnic regiments reflected the degree of political activity among the various ethnic groups in the Union at the mid-century. Only those groups with sufficient numbers as well as active lobbyists and their own ethnic cause would eventually succeed in contributing immigrant regiments to the northern army. Even though English immigrants, for example, constituted an important minority in the Union army and served in numbers much higher than their ethnic group's portion in American population, they never organized in ethnic regiments. Despite some efforts early in the war, the absence of an influential ethnic elite and the indifference of most Englishmen toward a unified ethnic cause prevented the formation of English regiments. Contrary to Irish activists, Englishmen never felt that they had to promote political goals through their participation in the Civil War. Welshmen simply never argued for an ethnic regiment. They had a strong ethnic consciousness, but in their devotion to the Union cause they were content serving alongside Americans. Some Welsh and English companies formed within mixed regiments, but they sprang from the local character of recruitment rather than from organized ethnic efforts. As the most invisible immigrants, British volunteers generally blended in with their American comrades who in most cases probably not even recognized them as foreigners.

Swiss, Dutch, and Belgian immigrants, on the other hand, simply did not figure prominently enough in the population to form separate ethnic regiments. They also never felt the urge to compete with the dominant German ethnic group for societal acceptance. Dutch and Belgians as a whole do not seem to have been enthusiastic about the war but instead viewed it as "the necessary defence of a government ordained by God."[96] There were few isolated Dutch companies in Michigan regiments and Belgians sometimes served together with French soldiers. If they did not mingle with Germans or French, Swiss immigrants stood out in several ethnic companies throughout various Midwestern regiments like the 15th Missouri. In addition to the Swiss "Garibaldians," Swiss riflemen served in the famous 1st United States Sharpshooters organized by Hiram Berdan and subsequently led by Colonel Caspar Trepp from Switzerland, "an officer of the highest merit, and one whose military knowledge and achievements have long been the admiration of all who knew him."[97]

Because early in the war it was of utmost importance to raise a strong field army as soon as possible, recruitment had mostly concentrated around the infantry. Therefore, many immigrants who had originally been trained in other branches of the service enlisted in the rapidly forming infantry regiments. It soon became clear, however, that the Union needed more experienced men in the most professionalized arm, the artillery. In July 1861, the Union chief artillery officer remarked that "The German regiments contain a number of artillery officers and soldiers. I suggested the propriety of placing, for the present at least, those regiments in the forts that the guns may be served by drafts from the instructed men. One company, Captain Morozowicz's, of the De Kalb regiment, is composed almost exclusively of old German artillery soldiers, and should there be a lack of field artillery, could readily be made available."[98]

Throughout the war, then, besides their presence in the numerous ethnic and mixed infantry and cavalry regiments, immigrants also figured prominently in the artillery. While most Americans regarded service in the artillery as inferior to the dashing cavalry and the infantry, trained European artillerists could prove their worth in that branch and from the beginning excelled as instructors and battery commanders. In turn, with their need for experienced soldiers the Union artillery benefited particularly from immigrant veterans. Although the Union had no purely ethnic artillery regiments in the field, there were numerous batteries manned and commanded at least partly by immigrants. Up to 140 northern batteries were commanded by Germans or descendants of German immigrants. In addition, countless artillerists came from other countries like Hungary, Poland, and Sweden.

Swedish recruiter and trained artillery officer Axel Silfversparre raised and commanded a battery of the 1st Illinois Light Artillery, consisting of some fifty Swedes and twenty-five members of other nationalities. They manned four field guns, and after five weeks' training went to the field and joined General Grant's army. In the battle of Shiloh in April 1862, Silfversparre's battery stood out through their excellent training and their coolness in battle. Teaching his men the professional artillery service he had learned in his old home country, Silfversparre equipped his battery with spades and axes so they could build earth walls around the guns to protect themselves from enemy fire. Ordering his soldiers to cool the barrels down with water in-between rounds, Silfversparre's cannons fired up to five times as quickly as others. In addition, the Swedish battery was one of the first units to use canister made from wire, inflicting heavy casualties among the enemies. Serving in the 1st New York Light Artillery, Captain Carl Berlin saw many engagements and led his artillery with an equal degree of professionalism. Chief of Artillery Hunt later testified that Berlin "is an educated and accomplished officer, formerly of the Swedish artillery, from which he resigned to continue in our services. His professional and technical knowledge have been especially valuable."[99] The most successful Swedish artillery commander was Charles J. Stohlbrand. Stohlbrand in 1861 organized a battery from Chicago for the 2nd Illinois Light Artillery with seventy recruits, among them several fellow Swedes. Captain Stohlbrand soon showed himself worthy of a higher command and already in December was in charge of the whole regiment with five batteries. One of his batteries, "Adolph Schwartz's Battery," was German except for nine members. In 1862, Stohlbrand commanded the artillery brigade of the Fifteenth Army Corps under General William T. Sherman, who reportedly said about the Swede that "there is no braver man and no better artillery officer in the whole army."[100]

Numerous artillery officers brought with them experience from previous German, Hungarian, and Polish army service. Former artillery officers Franz Backof, Klemens Landgräber, and forty-eighter Johann Albert Neustädter formed the first of German batteries in Missouri at the very beginning of the war. All three would serve credibly throughout the war and earn repeated praise for their effective and accurate handling of the guns under their command. Several other German batteries came from Ohio, among them Hubert Dilger's. A former artillery officer in his native Baden, Dilger certainly was one of the outstanding officers in that branch and there can be no better compliment then Kaufmann's assertion that infantry "always went into battle in a better spirit when it knew that Dilger's Battery was also there."[101] Louis Schirmer's and Michael Wiedrich's New York batteries excelled among others at Cross Keys, Chancellorsville, and Gettysburg.

Historian Ella Lonn has identified some additional batteries consisting of different ethnicities. The 5th New York Independent Battery, for example, united in its ranks British, German, Irish, French, Swiss, and Swedish immigrants together with soldiers born in Canada, Cape Colony, and the West Indies. Another independent battery, the 34th New York Light Artillery, was almost half-American, but included several Germans, Irish, Englishmen, French, Danes, Swiss, as well as one Scot and Hungarian each. Irish immigrants manned a few New England batteries, such as the 3rd Rhode Island Heavy Artillery and the 3rd Connecticut Light Artillery, which were both heavily Irish.[102]

It is impossible to round up a definitive number of all ethnic regiments and batteries in the Union army for several reasons. First of all, in several cases the designation of an "ethnic" regiment was misleading and based more on imagination than on facts. As historian William Burton in his study on the war's immigrant regiments has shown, the number of ethnic units "depends upon the ethnic pride of the counter, the month and year of the count."[103] Consciously or not, immigrants would often exaggerate the number of ethnic members in their regiments. Serving in the 116th New York Infantry, for example, German Albert Krause perceived his regiment to be half German, but the muster rolls show that only one of the companies consisted of 50 percent Germans. Obviously, the immigrant confined his social contacts to the fellow immigrants of his company, implying that their number in the rest of the regiment was equally high. On the other hand, Burton admits that in addition to the identified ethnic regiments there may have been "a small number of regiments whose membership was largely made up of a single ethnic group, but where there is no evidence that either the men themselves of the larger society identified the unit as ethnic."[104] This is an important restriction, because the existence of such regiments would prove the high degree of assimilation among the members of such nominally ethnic units.

Organizational changes in the army and the inevitable losses on the battlefields also prevented the number of ethnic regiments from remaining stable and controllable. At the beginning, most volunteer regiments were recruited for three months, like the ethnic St. Louis regiments. When their terms of enlistment were up in summer, several of these regiments disbanded and their members went home to their families and farms. When it became apparent that the war was no three months' affair, enlistment terms changed to two or three years, or the duration of the war. As casualties mounted, those ethnic regiments remaining in service often received nonethnic recruits to replenish their depleted ranks and gradually lost their ethnic character. Johann Buegel made similar observations as many of his comrades in other originally ethnic regiments when he noted in his diary after the Battle of Pea Ridge: "Our 3rd M[issouri] Regiment received reinforcements of 4 companys Irish and a certain Colonel Sheppert (called Sheephead) became our commander. Thus our regiment was at full strength again, 6 German and 4 Irish [companies]."[105] Likewise, the Gardes Lafayette was even less a French unit than before after they had merged with the 38th New York. On the other hand, it was exactly this replenishment that steadily increased ethnic membership in mixed or predominantly American regiments. As the war went on, the original intention of many ethnic and American recruiters to raise Irish, German, French, or purely American regiments became obsolete.

Although ethnic units made immigrants highly visible in the Union army, however, only a small percentage of foreign-born soldiers served in these units. Instead, the vast majority of immigrants from the start enlisted in nonethnic regiments and seems to have integrated into the army without much commotion. Of the estimated 200,000 German soldiers in the war, for example, not more than 36,000 served in ethnic regiments. Even adding the German companies in mixed regiments, the number of immigrants from Germany and Prussia in ethnic units would never reach 100,000. It is clear then that more than half of all German soldiers fought in nonethnic environments. Percentages for most other ethnic groups, including the Irish, may even be higher. Thus, Prussian and German immigrants disappeared in the Union army just as surely as Poles and Italians. Belgian, Italian, and French immigrants integrated as thoroughly as Bohemians, Czechs, Austrians, and Hungarians.[106]

Undoubtedly, many immigrants would have preferred to join ethnic regiments but never had the opportunity to do so, as was the case with the failed Italian efforts. On the other hand, the vast numbers of immigrants volunteering for American regiments testify to their willingness to assimilate as readily as English or Welsh soldiers. Even though ethnic spokesmen often emphasized their respective groups' extraordinary role in the Civil War, immigrant soldiers more often than not identified at least as much with the American cause.

THE FORTY-EIGHTERS: LEADERSHIP IN TIMES OF CRISIS

After Frémont's defeat in the election of 1856, Carl Schurz had confided to his friend Kinkel in Germany that "I don't know whether this struggle can be decided without powder, but I doubt it."[107] Schurz was right; and when his prophecy became reality, he and his fellow forty-eighters were among the first to reactivate their military careers and assist the federal cause. The efforts of the forty-eighters and active Turners showed in every city and town where ethnic companies and regiments formed. In Wisconsin, Governor Friedrich Salomon encouraged immigrant recruiting, while Carl Schurz used his powers to raise immigrant troops in New York and Washington. In St. Louis, forty-eighters organized and commanded four of the first five Union regiments, and several veterans of the German and Hungarian revolutions enlisted in these regiments as privates to demonstrate democratic egalitarianism. Some of these volunteers eventually made their way to larger commands, like Friedrich Hecker. The turmoil following the Camp Jackson affair had also provided immigrants with their first martyr of the Union cause. A former Prussian officer and veteran of the Polish and Hungarian revolutions, Konstantin Blandowski had been an active Turner and instructor of the first St. Louis volunteers whom he now led as captain in Börnstein's regiment. As the victorious regiments marched their captives back to the city, an infuriated mob attacked the immigrant soldiers. Wounded by a gunshot, Captain Blandowski died of complications on May 25, the first immigrant officer to die for the North. Although Blandowski had been born in Jarnowitz in Upper Silesia, Germans immediately claimed him as one of their own, demonstrating their devotion to the Union.[108]

Eventually, forty-eighters would figure prominently, if not always successfully, among immigrant Civil War general officers. Of the twelve German-born generals, eight were veterans of the revolutions. Unfortunately, their appointments were not always grounded purely on professional ability. Instead, some of them became political generals whom many of their own fellow immigrants so disliked. Forced to acknowledge his political support, for example, Lincoln in 1862 rewarded Carl Schurz with the generalship he had longed for. The president originally had summoned the ethnic leader as minister to Spain, but Schurz talked the president into giving him a field command. From the beginning Schurz's promotion provoked heated discussions in the German-American press. In fact, disapproval of Schurz's appointment was one of the few topics on which Democratic and Republican papers could agree. This criticism was certainly justified to a certain point, because the forty-eighter had no adequate military experience in leading large bodies of troops. His active participation in the revolutionary campaigns in Baden had been largely confined to his bold liberation of Kinkel, and as a general Schurz never scored a victory.

In stark contrast to Schurz, Peter Joseph Osterhaus rose to fame and glory and has been praised as one of the true German military geniuses in the Civil War. Born in Koblenz, Osterhaus was a Prussian officer of the reserve when he joined the revolutionary forces in 1848. Following his emigration, Osterhaus had first settled in the Latin Farmer district around Belleville, but later moved to St. Louis. When the ethnic regiments formed in April, the veteran enlisted in Börnstein's 2nd Infantry. Immediately elected captain, Osterhaus soon became major and commander of the regiment's sharpshooter battalion. Through his credible service in several battles Osterhaus quickly advanced to brigade and division commander, and even led the Fifteenth Army Corps for some time. Advancing from private to brigadier general, the forty-eighter served throughout the whole war and stood in thirty-four battles. His extraordinary career bears testimony for the merits capable immigrant officers could earn in the American volunteer army. Highly lauded by everybody who knew him, Osterhaus probably received the finest praise from an American officer in the black regiments who attested the immigrant to have "given me aid when others refused it. He speaks word of encouragement when others discourage & denounce us. He fights the battles of his Country and asks for no one to applaud him. May he always be as successful & brave & good as he has been."[109]

Franz Sigel eventually became the great tragic figure of the German-American story in the Civil War. After organizing and commanding the 3rd Missouri, Sigel went all the way to major general, largely due to political pressure by the German community. The choice seemed logical at first because Sigel possessed a thorough military education and was one of the most experienced forty-eighter veterans. Unfortunately, his whole military career in the Union army was marred by personal disputes with superiors that led to his repeated resignations out of hurt pride. Despite his indisputable personal bravery, Sigel never excelled on the battlefield because he lacked both instinctive subordination and the ability to independently lead large bodies of troops. A master of organization and perfect in the art of strategic retreat, however, Sigel commanded the unwavering devotion of his troops until he was relieved in July 1864 following the defeat at New Market.[110] In May, a Confederate force including several hundred cadets of the Virginia Military Institute had beaten the forty-eighter in the Shenandoah Valley, and Sigel had once more retreated, exhibiting a lack of aggressiveness in his superiors' eyes. Because of his popularity with the German-Americans and the publicity of his alleged nativist derision by the authorities Sigel's fate has always overshadowed the splendid careers of other forty-eighter commanders such as August Willich or Friedrich Salomon.

Two Hungarian forty-eighters also received generalships. Szeged-born Julius Stahel had been a bookseller in Pest before the revolution. Acquainted with leading nationalists like Petöfi, Stahel joined the Honved army and won a decoration for bravery. Emigrating in 1856, Stahel settled in New York City where he engaged in journalism and made friends with many German-Americans. At the outbreak of the war he helped to recruit for Blenker's 8th New York and initially served as the regiment's lieutenant colonel. After a short spell as commander of the First German Regiment following Blenker's appointment as brigadier general, Stahel himself was named general in November 1861. A reliable officer and outstanding cavalryman who fought in several battles, the forty-eighter left the army in 1865 holding the rank of major general. His fellow immigrant, Alexander Asboth, was one of the defective Austrian officers who had joined the Hungarian revolution and later shared Kossuth's exile in Turkey. In 1851 the Hungarian lawyer came to the United States and worked as an engineer for famous New York architect, Frederick Law Olmstead. In July 1861 Frémont called him to St. Louis as chief of staff where Asboth put to use his military experience in organizing Union regiments. A brigadier general by March 1862, Asboth commanded a division under Sigel and later headed the Department of Western Florida. Kaufmann, in his twisted effort to include as many immigrants as possible in his array of German Civil War officers, called both these distinguished generals "German-Hungarian."[111] Anselm Albert, a native of Pest and forty-eighter who succeeded Sigel in command of the 3rd Missouri Volunteers, shared their fate when Kaufmann made him the "German Colonel Albert."[112]

Many other forty-eighters were able to reactivate their military careers and obtain officers' commissions at the outbreak of the war. Probably only few were happier to leave behind an unrewarding civil life full of hardship than Leopold von Gilsa. The

Prussian nobleman had made a living by singing and playing piano in the shabby bars of New York City's Bowery district when the outbreak of the Civil War offered him a second chance as military officer. A true professional soldier, Colonel von Gilsa distinguished himself at the head of his DeKalb Infantry and later as brigade commander, but like many other immigrant officers was never appointed to a higher rank that would have befitted his ability. Von Gilsa serves as an example for the several hundred forty-eighter officers who contributed their experience to the Union cause in ethnic and nonethnic volunteer regiments. Because no ethnic Hungarian regiment had formed, several veterans of the Honved army took commands of mixed regiments during the war. The most impressive example certainly is Frederick Knefler who enlisted in the 11th Indiana Infantry under Lew Wallace of later *Ben Hur* fame. Knefler eventually rose to lead the 79th Indiana Infantry and stood out through his bravery in such bloody engagements as Shiloh, Stones River, Chickamauga, and Missionary Ridge.

For a small group of forty-eighters, finally, the Civil War offered yet another career opportunity in the military. Julius Reichhelm, the Catholic who had turned against the institutionalized Church in Germany, voted Democratic in 1860, but soon after staunchly supported the Union and Lincoln. After his son had run away to fight with Sigel in Missouri, Reichhelm followed the call of his friend Friedrich Hecker and became the regimental chaplain in his 82nd Illinois Infantry. Reichhelm turned out as a most extraordinary chaplain. True, he would preach to his men, but his "sermons, while more patriotic than strictly religious, promoted the spiritual welfare of the regiment, its devotion to the Union, and a cordial comradeship among its members." Reichhelm would never remain behind in a battle. He assisted the surgeons in tending to the wounded and he buried fallen soldiers in solemn ceremonies on the battlefields. Sometimes, his biographer adds, "the fighting blood of the family asserted itself, so that he was also known as the 'Fighting Chaplain of the German Division,' who thought it his duty to be in the thickest of the fight, where the need of a chaplain seemed to him to be the greatest."[113] Other revolutionary veterans turned regimental chaplains had even less spiritual ambitions. August Becker, the chaplain of the 8th New York was a journalist and socialist whom his comrades called "Red Becker." Because according to regulations a regimental chaplain had to be an ordained minister, the soldiers in Osterhaus' 12th Missouri Infantry founded their own free congregation and made freethinker Albert Kraus its reverend. Like Reichhelm, Kaufmann tells, in battle Kraus "always stood in the firing line and assisted the wounded."[114]

Whether they recruited ethnic regiments, commanded troops in battle, or served as role models for other immigrants, most forty-eighters—including Irish leaders Meagher and Corcoran—promoted ethnic consciousness among Civil War soldiers. Even if only a fraction of foreign-born soldiers served in ethnic regiments, German, Hungarian, and Polish revolutionary veterans contributed greatly to the Union cause by rallying their fellow immigrants around the banners of republicanism and freedom.

Even soldiers in nonethnic regiments were proud to call Sigel or other forty-eighters their compatriots and "I fights mit Sigel" became a common motto among German soldiers. Carl Hermanns probably would have found most of his fellow immigrants in accord when he boasted in a letter to his family that in this war it was the Germans "who are fighting best, the bravest of all being the German Major General Sigel."[115]

FOUR

SERVING THEIR
ADOPTED COUNTRY

Ernst Hoffmann from Koblenz had lived in the United States several years when he graduated from St. Louis Medical College in 1861. Married to a local woman, Hoffmann, like many other immigrants in the border region, soon found himself immersed not only in a national conflict, but also in a question of loyalty to his own family. In a letter to Missouri Senator B. Gratz Brown, he explained his personal situation in drastic words. Both his wife and her parents, he wrote, were southern sympathizers and "to the utmost opposed to me as a Republican." Refusing to surrender his political convictions, Hoffmann's conscience nevertheless forbade him "to talk disrespectful to aged parents & wife, which are ever & allways introducing & advocating what I must call treason at home." Therefore, leaving his home and enlisting in the federal army remained the only way to "prove it to the lettre that I mean & carry out what I advocate as a Republican & in order that I might be spared to listen to treasonable language which I despise from the bottom of my heart, much more so if spoken by them who are connected to me by family ties."[1]

Johann Buegel had experienced similar conflicts in St. Louis. Following the Camp Jackson affair, Buegel observed that friends and even family and kin distrusted each other. Not only were "opinions and views highly diverging," Buegel wrote in his diary, "yes, in one and the same family one was Unionist and the other Confederate (also called secesh or rebel). Every one feared each other."[2] Peter Smith, another German immigrant, also found strong words condemning secession and the southerners he would be fighting in the nonethnic 8th Missouri Infantry. He had taken up the "weapon of death," Smith wrote, "for the purpose of doing my part in defending and upholding the integrity, laws, and the preservation of my adopted country from a band of contemptible traitors who would if they can accomplish their hellish designs, destroy the best and noblest government on earth."[3] It probably would not have needed much propaganda to convince men like Hoffmann, Buegel, and Smith that joining the military was the best way to protect their homes and lives. Out of necessity, immigrants along the border had been ready for the war for some time before Lincoln's call for volunteers forced everybody else to take sides.

The motivation to join the army out of an immediate and real danger was unknown to immigrants and Americans living to the north and east of Missouri. Because the coming war did not touch them as immediately, they needed an additional impetus to enlist. Such a motivation could be patriotism, the fight against slavery, prospects of bounty money and regular pay, lust for adventure, ethnic pride, or personal honor—or any mixture of these. Usually patriotism played a role. Many immigrants had come to the United States as a country guaranteeing personal and political freedom. For them, the feeling of duty to their new home country was a major motivation to join the fight against what they saw as an unjustified rebellion of the southern states. Krzyzanowski wrote in his memoirs that "I, too, was seized with the fever and left the quiet of my home to enlist as a volunteer. . . . I enlisted partially out of my gratitude to this country, and partially out of memories of my boyhood in Poland."[4] A sergeant in the nonethnic 116th New York Infantry, Prussian Albert Krause told his family in 1862, "I am marching into battle with courage and desire. The [United] States have adopted me, I have been able to earn a living, and now, when the country is in peril, I should not defend it with flesh and blood?"[5] It was fortunate for the immigrants that slave holders had started the war, Peter Klein wrote from California, because now the Germans could prove that they were the "most ardent defenders of the Constitution" and earn their due respect among the Americans. "Now the Americans do not make fun of us any more because they know that we are the main pillar on which rests their country and their freedom."[6]

Irish immigrants fighting for the Union often had hard times explaining why they did so. Defiantly, an Irish private in the 28th Massachusetts wrote to his family in Ireland that he defended the United States as his new home: "This is my country as much as the man who was born on the soil."[7] As a member of the celebrated Irish Brigade, the immigrant certainly had many likeminded Irish among his comrades, even if his family obviously needed additional information on why he had joined the war against the South. Born in Canada, Peter Welsh was of Irish descent and strongly identified with the Irish-American cause. Writing to his father-in-law to explain why he had enlisted, Welsh made it clear that "when we are fighting for America we are fighting in the interest of Irland [sic] striking a double blow cutting with a two edged sword For while we strike in defence of the rights of Irishmen here we are striking a blow at Irlands enemy and oppressor."[8] While many Irishmen made a

clear distinction between their national cause and the American war, Joseph Tully of
Corcoran's 69th New York openly cheered the opportunity Irish-Americans were given
to demonstrate "their devotion to the Union" as well as the "pride in the character of
their race and fatherland."[9] Enlisting in the Irish 116th Pennsylvania, soon to become
a part of the famed Irish Brigade in August 1862, William McCarter gave a most
vociferous reason for answering the call to arms. He had volunteered, McCarter wrote
in his distinguished style that made his memoirs an extraordinary piece of literature,
"because of my love for my whole adopted country, not the North, or the South, but
the Union, one and inseparable, its form of government, its institutions, its Stars and
Stripes, its noble, generous, brave and intelligent people ever ready to welcome, and
to extend the hand of friendship to the downtrodden and oppressed of every clime
and people."[10] Already in May of the previous year, McCarter's fellow Irishman James
Patrick Sullivan had left his job as a hired farm hand in Wisconsin to become on of
the first volunteers for the 6th Wisconsin Infantry, a mixed American and immigrant
outfit that would eventually form part of the celebrated Iron Brigade of the Army of
the Potomac. Sullivan put it simply: "I wanted to do what I could for my country,"
he explained his motivation to join the federal ranks.[11]

Corresponding with immigrants' various ethnic and national backgrounds, asser-
tions of patriotism had different underlying causes. Germans and Irishmen wanted to
prove their loyalty and diminish possible suspicions of seclusion, while British immigrants often felt a strong urge to demonstrate their patriotism because they were aware
of the still strained relations between their old and new home countries. In his letters,
Titus Crawshaw never demonstrated any ethnic pride. Rather, he felt an individual
obligation to the Union that caused him to join a native American regiment. After
enlisting in the 3rd New Jersey Volunteers, Crawshaw wrote home in November 1861
that "in my opinion I have done just right. I hope the Secessionists will be wipt till
they will behave themselves for at least 100 years. If the Unionists let the South secede
now the West might want to seperate next Presedential Election."[12] Crawshaw and
other Englishmen demonstrated their willingness to fight the Confederacy, fearing
that England might enter the war on the southern side.

Naturally, immigrants would profess loyalty to their adopted country and their
unwavering patriotism in any kind of official communication, especially when they
applied for officers' commissions. Philipp Weinmann, who later led a highly successful
unit of African-American sharpshooters, also expressed his willingness to serve the
Union: "Sir! I am a Foreigner by birth, but my only Intention is, to do all I can for
the Benefit of my adopted country."[13] Similarly, at the "breaking out of this base &
unjustifiable rebellion" Hungarian forty-eighter Ladislas Zsulavszky above all wanted
"to offer my feeble services to my adopted country."[14]

Everywhere, immigrants were willing to leave their homes and fight the rebellion.
Peter Karberg from Schleswig had taken up teaching in Lansing, Iowa, where he
had become an ardent unionist. Like so many other immigrants, Karberg and his

brother traveled to Missouri in April to join the ethnic regiments forming in St. Louis. Upon their arrival they learned that a third brother had just come over from Germany and entered the army as well. In New York City, combative forty-eighter Joseph Weydemeyer volunteered for the federal army in April and, although in his midforties, specifically requested an assignment in Missouri where he could participate in active fighting. At age seventeen, Julius Reichhelm's son Eduard decided to defend the Union in 1861, but met his father's objection when he wanted to enlist in Weber's 20th New York Turners. Eduard would not stay home, however, but ran away and joined Sigel's Volunteers in St. Louis. Franz Wilhelmi did not feel restrained by his parents, but by state authorities whom he accused of not battling the rebellion determinedly enough: "I hope the Southern forces will soon surrender. I want to return to civil life, but only with honor. The motive of patriotism, together with disgust because of the indifference and indecisiveness of our government caused me to leave civil life and enlist in this time of emergency."[15]

How earnest the dedication to the Union as their new home country may have been for immigrants, patriotism often went hand in hand with more profane motivations. The lust for adventure and excitement without doubt motivated many young immigrants as well as juvenile Americans longing to participate in the fight. As the German-language *Staats Zeitung* reported from Minnesota in late April, the same enthusiasm that had earlier seized other cities to the south and east had finally reached remote St. Paul as well: "A wonderful enthusiasm has gripped our population which had initially reacted with caution to the call for volunteers. Now, men long past the military age have contracted the war fever, and boys under age eager to take up arms had to be sent back by the mustering officers."[16] Furthermore, as soldiers the young men were sure to travel a lot and go to parts of the country they would never see otherwise. A newly arrived Norwegian immigrant had been lucky enough to find employment at a sawmill in the summer of 1861, when a fellow immigrant recruited him for Heg's Scandinavian regiment. Bersven Nelson agreed, because "I would have an opportunity to travel and to see a great deal."[17] Like Nelson and many other immigrants, Louis A. Gratz from Posen enlisted not only out of devotion to the Union, but also for the thrill of soldiering. "Carried away by the general enthusiasm," Gratz confessed to his diary, "I became a soldier . . . And should it be my destiny to lose my life, well, I will have sacrificed it for a cause to which I am attached with all my heart, that is: the liberation of the United States."[18] Gratz had emigrated from Posen without monetary means and like many other Polish Jews started out as a peddler in America. At the outbreak of the war enlistment in the 9th Pennsylvania "Lochiel" Cavalry at least promised steady pay in addition to the seemingly exciting life in the army. Gratz soon discovered his love for soldiering. Putting every effort in studying the English language, the immigrant quickly made his way up the ranks and eventually was made a major in the 6th Kentucky Cavalry.

Gratz's case was typical for innumerable immigrants who were stranded penniless and saw volunteering as a way out of their misery. Joining the army promised financial security for unemployed Irishmen, newly arrived impoverished Jews from Poland, farmers unable to pay rising rents, or German craftsmen who had lost their jobs to industrialization or wartime depression. Wilhelmine Schlüter from Baltimore wrote to her daughter in Germany in December 1861, "We have a great famine here. People have no work. All business is down. The men leave their wives and children and become soldiers because there is no other work."[19] Friedrich Schmalzried from Württemberg earned meager wages as a farmhand and lamented that although he labored hard, "I have often been treated unjust and mean from which I suffered badly." Schmalzried saw his chance to escape this unsatisfactory situation and improve financially when the war broke out. With no ethnic bonds whatsoever, Schmalzried thought "that I could try that as well." He enlisted in a completely nonethnic company of the 1st Michigan Cavalry and wrote to his friends in Germany that "it is not bad here, we are treated alright and have enough to eat, and the pay is as well as anywhere else."[20] When Congress appropriated means for enlistment bounties to fill the quotas, this immediate cash-in-hand provided additional enticements to enlist. "Yes, and then there was a bounty of a hundred dollars," Bersven Nelson later remembered, "and thirteen dollars a month, free clothes, and free food. This seemed good enough to me."[21] Throughout the war recruiting agents lured immigrants right off the boats as soon as they reached the harbors, promising bounties, pay, and regular rations. This is one reason why so many Irish and German recruits joined New York regiments during the war. Wilhelm Albrecht from Schwerin enlisted in the 59th New York Infantry only three days after he had arrived in Castle Garden on August 27, 1861. Joining the army was easy, because "as soon as one set a foot on dry land, the recruiters came swarming from all sides." In a letter back home Albrecht described the unscrupulous methods of recruiters. Because he had "not the slightest idea of the American recruitment swindle, the same happened to me as to many others, I made a mistake. I enlisted in a regiment which, as I unfortunately only found out later, did not suit me at all." The German recruit soon found a particular fault with the 59th Infantry: "This regiment consisted mostly of Americans and Irishmen; therefore I did not like it."[22] After three months Albrecht left his regiment without permission. When he met a fellow immigrant from Mecklenburg who served in the 30th New York Light Artillery, the deserter decided to join that predominantly German outfit and served throughout his enlistment term.

Decidedly more idealistic in their views about the American conflict were the forty-eighters and other abolitionist immigrants. Having campaigned to elect Lincoln and the Republicans, they had hoped for an all-out war against slavery already in 1860. Several of them, like Carl Schurz and Heinrich Börnstein, had early believed in the inevitability of an armed conflict over slavery. Likewise, many Hungarian revolutionary veterans were enemies of slavery and from the beginning welcomed every opportunity to fight that institution actively. Commanding the 24th Illinois Infantry after Hecker's resignation, Colonel Mihalotzy with his regiment made an early stand against that inhuman institution when he refused to enforce the Fugitive Slave Law and return fugitive slaves who had escaped to the regiment's camp. Several Hungarian and German officers in the army formally offered their resignations when army orders forced them to hand over runaway slaves.

In August 1861, August Horstmann from Oldenburg enlisted in the 45th Fifth German or "Platt Deutsch" New York Infantry composed mainly of his fellow northern Germans under the command of forty-eighter Colonel Georg von Amsberg. Born in 1835, Horstmann was too young to have participated in the revolutions, but he ardently embraced the cause of freedom and the abolition of slavery. A captain by September 1863, Horstmann told his parents in Germany why he had joined the army: "Because the freedom of the oppressed and the equality of human rights must be won first! For us, this war is a holy fight for principles that will deliver a deadly blow to slavery and triumph over the southern aristocracy."[23] Also an ardent abolitionist, Wladimir Krzyzanowski called the Civil War "the noblest deed in a hundred years, the war to liberate the slaves." The Polish immigrant was convinced that "No civil war was ever fought for so noble a cause."[24] Friedrich Martens, the declared enemy of slavery, volunteered upon the first call for troops in April 1861. He enlisted in a German company of the 6th Illinois Infantry, and proudly told his family in Holstein that he had joined the war "to suppress and root out" slavery "in all of its horror." Confident that his family would agree with his step, he challenged his father, "Now, father, I would like to know how you would think about a son who safely staid home while the enemy was at the door to suppress and wage war on freedom, our dearly conquered freedom; would I still have the right to live in this land, to savor its freedom if I were not willing to fight and need be to die for this freedom."[25]

Among immigrants, the calls for a war against slavery seem to have been louder than among Americans in general. Polish revolutionaries like Krzyzanowski as well as forty-eighters who had rebelled against inhuman oppression in their homelands together with many English, Scottish, and Welsh immigrants accepted service in the army as a welcome chance to strike a blow against slavery. Two Welsh immigrants wrote to their relatives from Ohio in June 1861 that "rivers of blood will flow through the fruitful and once glorious fields of America before peace returns because of the anger and hatred of the two parties for each other. The cause of the trouble is the self-seeking and fiendish lust of the slave dealers to spread slavery throughout the land and to govern and oppress black and white under foot."[26] Humphrey Roberts may have joined the army afterward, but if he did, the fight against human bondage would have been his main motivation, as it was for his Welsh friends who had already enlisted in the 18th and 22nd Ohio regiments. Another Welshman from Wisconsin promised a friend back home that slavery must be destroyed, because "While such a monster lives here justice can never be on the throne. Every man has the same right to freedom, whether he is white or black."[27] Largely workers and small subsistence farmers, these immigrants embraced a notion of universal freedom for all races, just as Scandinavian immigrants did from their Protestant egalitarianism. Repeatedly, these immigrants voiced their conviction that the very existence of slavery desecrated the ideals of liberty and equality that had drawn them to the United States. Swedish 1st Lieutenant J. B. Rudberg from the 43rd Illinois "Körner" Infantry described how closely many Protestant immigrants connected slavery to aristocracy when he wrote that "we are only wishing that the war might soon come to an end. But only a good end, a complete victory, the extermination of slavery and the suppression of the pride of the Southern aristocracy."[28]

Opposition to slavery also motivated many German immigrants in the midwestern and border states to join the army. Less abolitionist in sentiment, these volunteers feared the extension of slavery primarily for economic reasons and often expressed racist sentiment. As Dietrich Gerstein told his brother back in Germany from his farm in Michigan, "while we have to struggle terribly hard to bring in one harvest, the south garners twice as much easily, thanks to their laborers with the woolen heads."[29] It is clear that Gerstein, opposed to the institution of slavery as he was, fought against economic competition more than for the slaves' freedom. Gerstein hesitated long before he finally enlisted in the 29th Michigan Infantry as one of only four Germans in his company. Magnus Brucker from Baden had studied medicine and very probably participated in the 1848 Revolution before he emigrated the following year and settled in southern Indiana, where even parts of the immigrant population sympathized with their slaveholding neighbors across the Ohio. Against considerable opposition, the physician became an active Republican and joined the overwhelmingly Anglo-American 23rd Indiana Infantry early in 1862. He fought against slavery, he wrote to his wife, because it was "the ruin of the free white laborer." Before the war, Brucker had not agreed with what he termed the "agitation of the northern fanatics," but as the war dragged on, he reached the conclusion that the Union had to destroy slavery, and "open the whole country to free labor, and to keep it free for our children and grandchildren." As Brucker indicated, a good number of immigrants were openly opposed to the liberation of the slaves and would not participate in a war against slavery. He cared not, Brucker told his wife, what the population of Troy thought of him, "whether they call me Black Republican, Abolitionist, Lincolnite, or Yankee Vandal as the rebels call us, black or white."[30] Numerous German and Irish Catholic immigrants and orthodox Lutherans had remained true to their Democratic creed, and many of them made it clear that under no circumstances were they supporting a "nigger war." Friedrich Schmalzried, a devout Lutheran and Democrat, detested the notion of abolition. Writing from the battlefields in Virginia in 1862, Schmalzried vented all his detestation for Republicans and abolitionists when he grumbled that "it is about time to elect righteous men to leaders and not traitors; it would be best for this country to have fed all those Abolitionists to the cannons at Richmond." Even amidst a bloody war against the South, Schmalzried identified others than the Confederates as the real enemies, promising that "as soon as we are done here we will be marching north, well armed, and send the Blackley Abolitionists to hell together with all their niggers; they must not think that we are all Republicans here in the army, no not at all."[31] Valentin Bechler from Karlsruhe voiced a similar opinion when he told his wife in November 1862 from his camp with the 8th New Jersey Infantry that "I wish all abolitionists were in hell."[32]

Daily confronted with the institution of slavery, immigrants in the South often had a simple motivation to side with the North and join the federal army, if that was at all possible. Whether it was their refusal to assist in a war against the legitimate government or their abolitionist convictions, the urge to enlist in Union regiments was strong enough for several thousand foreign-born southerners to cross the lines and sometimes even desert the Confederate army. During the secession crisis, immigrants in the Deep South had often found themselves in the uncomfortable situation that southerners would only accept their presence if they stood loyally behind the Confederacy. As soon as foreigners expressed doubts about the legitimacy of southern secession or question the rightfulness of slavery, they had to face repression and outright violence in many cases. "I do not like to leave Texas, that beautiful country that has offered me happiness and contentment for so long," a Latin Farmer from the German colony of Milheim in Austin County wrote in April 1861, "but I have to go, because I can never accept system that allows slavery to be the fundament of the nation state."[33]

When the war came the Confederates obviously saw service in the army as an appropriate way of demonstrating loyalty. While recruitment went considerably well among Irish southerners and enough Germans to raise several ethnic companies and even regiments, local authorities often simply pressed immigrants into the army. Another southern forty-eighter, Oswald Dietz, was forced into Confederate service in Texas. Serving as captain of engineers at Galveston, Dietz was able to desert in March 1864, and joined the Union army to fight "under the flag he loved."[34] Likewise, many Swedish settlers left the South to avoid conscription and hostile reactions. The *Hemlandet* newspaper covered many stories of these war refugees. Wisconsin immigrant farmer Heinrich Hütter knew several fellow immigrants who had settled in the South. Writing to his siblings back in Germany in August 1862, Hütter pondered their fate and feared the worst: "All foreigners, like Jentges, who were in the South when the war began with North America, were forced to join the army. He is either off to war or has been killed. In my opinion he is dead."[35]

When the Union army conquered New Orleans in April 1862, many loyal citizens there took the oath of allegiance and enlisted in the army. Yet by far the largest number of foreign-born southern Union soldiers came from Texas, where Germans, Swedes, and Poles had always constituted the most visible group of nonslaveholding settlers. After the Lone Star State had left the Union and officially joined the Confederacy, a large part of its immigrant population refused to join the southern cause. When Confederate conscription threatened to affect more and more unionists and harassment became increasingly violent, many immigrants and loyal Americans tried to make their getaway. In March 1862, the commander of San Antonio, Colonel Henry E. McCulloch, complained that many Germans "are leaving here to avoid a participation in our struggle."[36] In July of that year a refugee party consisting of sixty-three Germans, five Americans, and one Mexican, set out from Austin to make their way to Mexico and from there to Union territory. Confederate troops pursued the unionists and attacked their camp at the Nueces River. Determined to die rather than be captured and pressed into the Confederate army, the unionists under the leadership of German Fritz Tegner "offered the most determined resistance," according to Lieutenant C. D. McRae. In his report McRae further stated that the Germans "fought with desperation, asking no quarter whatever; hence I have no prisoners to report."[37] Kaufmann reports that nineteen immigrants fell in the battle and that the Texans killed nine wounded after they had taken the camp. The rest escaped capture, but several died afterward in the barren wilderness along the Mexican border, while six more were eventually caught and shot to death. Only five lived to join a loyal Texas Union regiment.[38]

Other loyal immigrants tried to get around Confederate conscription by enlisting in frontier guards and volunteer militias that did not have to participate in the war. A schoolteacher by profession, Ferdinand Ohlenburger had settled near the German town of Fredericksburg and in 1862 joined a German frontier militia company to evade the draft. In a postwar letter Ohlenburger described the situation that had led him and many others to make such a decision. "We did not have many secessionist[s] here at that time," the German claimed,

> but what few there were, everybody was afraid of; because they were types of the lowest character & bragged upon, that they produced some Dutch fruit on the life oaks, which never had grown here before. I was conscripted & to try to save myself (& by the begging of my wife) [from getting] hung, as I was notified by a mob to join the army or run the consequences, I joined a company of Texas Rangers, all of whom were Union men out of Gillespie County, Tex. This was no volunteerly act on my part under the circumstances. I was forced.[39]

Like other militias, however, his unit was soon integrated into the southern army against the terms of their enlistment. In late 1863, Ohlenburger managed to desert and join the federal army. Several other immigrant Texans shared Ohlenburger's fate, among them three of Stanislas Kiolbassa's sons and other Poles from Panna Maria. Pressed into Texas regiments, these immigrants deserted to the northern lines the first chance they got. At the battle of Arkansas Post in January 1863, the

Kiolbassas together with more than 1,500 largely German and Polish-born Texas soldiers surrendered willingly to the federal troops. The prisoners were confined in Camp Butler in Illinois, whose commander attested that "nearly one-half the prisoners confined here were pressed into the Confederate service and are anxious to take the oath of allegiance and then join loyal regiments."[40] Contacting fellow immigrants across the lines, Peter Kiolbassa and several others eventually enlisted in Colonel Thielemann's ethnic 16th Illinois Cavalry. A similar case occurred later in the same year when Colonel Mullen and his chaplain, Father Peter Paul Cooney, asked permission to receive several hundred captured Irish Catholics from the rebel army into the 35th Indiana Infantry to replenish its ranks. The Union army gladly received these defected southerners in its ranks. After all, by enlisting ex-Confederates the North proved its cause was right and even attractive to its enemies.[41]

Other Europeans had only come to the United States to participate in the war. Many of them had been educated officers in their home countries and hoped to enhance their experience by participating in actual combat. A Hessian nobleman, Wilhelm von Bechtold told the secretary of war in 1864 that he had come to America "with the sole intention of seeing real warfare in the ranks of the Federal Army." Although von Bechtold had abandoned a military career to fight for "the noble cause of the United States," he had no intention to emigrate, and returned to Germany after the war.[42]

Although the Union government never actually endorsed recruitment in foreign countries, many Europeans came to America during the war with the explicit intention to participate in the war. A good number of them were mercenaries, who offered their military training and experience to the government and hoped for quick advancement in the army. These immigrants would not fight for the Union out of patriotic motivations, and some of these mercenaries also fought on the Confederate side. Welsh-born adventurer Henry Morton Stanley, who would win fame tracking down missing explorer David Livingstone in Africa in 1871, for example, readily volunteered for the southern army in New Orleans. Captured at the battle of Shiloh, the ex-Confederate easily changed sides and enlisted in the Union Army. Recruiting for the Union, Carl Schurz made several obscure acquaintances with immigrants who desperately tried to get commissions in the Union army. One of them, he recalled, was "A young man, calling himself the Count of Schweinitz, and carrying the uniform of the Austrian Ulane lancers." Schurz tells that the count "introduced himself with clever eloquence and produced papers which seemed to be authentic and proved his statements. However, in his conversation there surfaced a certain slyness that aroused my suspicion."[43] Later Schurz would find out that this imposter had been a former orderly who had stolen his superior's uniform.

Still, most Europeans sailing to the United States to participate in the war probably pursued professional goals earnestly. Former professional soldiers like Bechtold came form various countries to test their education in active service. A similar interest brought members of the medical profession to wartime America. Carl Uterhard was a successful physician who owned a medical practice in Warnemünde in Mecklenburg. In 1862 he wrote to his mother that he gave up his practice and went to the United States "for the main reason that I will be able to work with the sick and wounded while at the same time learning a lot."[44] Like Uterhard, many other physicians and medical students viewed service in the Civil War armies as a venue to enhance their professional knowledge and gain experience. In a strict sense, all these foreigners do not count as immigrants, as the greater part of them returned to their home countries after the war—as did Bechtold and many Swedish officers. Still, these highly trained professionals were often of considerably higher benefit to the Union than show-offs and soldiers of fortune like Prince Salm-Salm or Frederic d'Utassy.

Whether immigrants felt patriotic devotion to the Union, whether they abhorred slavery or got carried away by the excitement—most of them acted out of a combination of motivations that often involved a certain degree of ethnic consciousness. Civil War volunteer regiments formed and mustered into service under state authority, and their basic organizational units were companies. Often originating in preexisting local institutions like militia companies or other social organizations, volunteer companies gathered from towns and villages, urban neighborhoods, or around persons of influence. Naturally, ethnic environments would produce ethnic companies, even if in the end they did not accumulate into ethnic regiments. The immigrant colony of Bishop Hill, for example, raised a Swedish company in early 1861 under the name of *Svenska Unionsgardet* ("Swedish Union Guard"). No Scandinavian regiment came into existence in Illinois, so the Swedes joined the partly German 57th Illinois Infantry as Company D under their captain and future regimental commander, Eric Forsse.[45]

Active recruiters like Forsse usually were elected captains by the men of their companies and thus received officer's commissions. In addition to militia commanders who led their companies into regimental organizations, many immigrants who had gained local authority before the war now vied for commissions by recruiting ethnic volunteers. Dietrich Tiedemann from Hannover had already before the war organized the Illinois St. Clair County Volunteer Militia among fellow Germans. Immediately after Lincoln's call for troops Tiedemann wrote to Governor Richard Yates that "I hereby tender a full Company of Volunteers, to serve at the Call of the Governor."[46] His unit became one of several German companies in August Mersey's 9th Illinois Infantry. Captain Friedrich Krumme from Kalbe in Saxony had raised the 46th Illinois Infantry's Company C among the Germans of Freeport, which remained an ethnic company. Hungarian veteran Geza Mihalotzy had raised Hungarian and Bohemian immigrants as the Chicago Lincoln Riflemen. With his unit incorporated into Hecker's 24th Illinois Infantry, Mihalotzy was elected lieutenant Colonel. As the *Illinois Staats Zeitung* stated with considerable pride, fifty-four ethnic companies, mostly derived from militias, had formed in the state and been accepted into service by the end of April 1861.[47]

Like the Bishop Hill Company, other Scandinavian units recruited under the leadership of former Swedish and Norwegian soldiers in midwestern cities, such as Charles Stohlbrand's battery from Chicago. Following Hans Mattson's call for volunteers in the *Hemlandet*, seventy Swedish and thirty Norwegian recruits enlisted in his Scandinavian Guards. Mattson's unit became Company D of the 3rd Minnesota Infantry, a regiment composed to a good extent of Scandinavians and Germans. The St. Paul, Minnesota, *Press* congratulated Mattson "for the splendid company of Swedes and Norwegians of which he is in charge. A better company of soldiers has never before been recruited for service."[48] Captain Mattson would later become the regiment's commander after its initially popular Colonel Henry Lester had disgraced the regiment by surrendering against the men's will. Other prominent recruiters who would eventually lead regiments were ethnic heroes Thomas Francis Meagher and Wladimir Krzyzanowski. Latin Farmer Adolf Dengler, one of the idols of the Baden Revolution and close friend of Franz Sigel, organized a company from Belleville and enlisted them in Sigel's regiment. Captain Dengler later became colonel of the Körner Infantry.[49]

In addition to militias and *Turnvereins*, members of ethnic social clubs such as singing societies, rifle clubs, and even theater circles would volunteer as entire companies. As was the case in many American volunteer companies, members of such locally recruited ethnic units often had known each other and established close personal ties before the war. Thus, early volunteering ensured that relatives and neighbors remained together and formed a large number of ethnic companies and artillery batteries. The comfort of a common language, often enough one other than English, could be an important factor of identification. Friends and members of an ethnic club or organization speaking the same mother tongue would gather, discuss the issues over a couple of beers, and then volunteer. After his initial service in Sigel's three-month regiment was over in September, Johann Buegel received his discharge and returned to St. Louis. Meeting his friends at a local wine hall, Buegel remembered that "I found already three companies of my old comrades who had enlisted for another three years in the 3rd Missouri Regiment." After short consideration Buegel also joined the regiment. Besides the motivation to join his old comrades, Buegel gave another convincing argument, when he added that he preferred to "go now voluntarily rather than be forced to later on."[50] Especially when it came to reenlisting after the initial three months, many immigrants—as well as native Americans—signed up together with their old companies.

For many immigrants, language served yet another purpose. Young men, often not long in the country, usually did not speak English well enough to feel comfortable among Americans. Therefore, enlistment in an ethnic company not only strengthened ethnic consciousness and togetherness, but also ensured the functioning of military drills. On the other hand, immigrants in mixed and predominantly American regiments often met linguistic barriers. Paul Petasch had left his native

Dresden in the summer of 1861 and shortly after his arrival in Chicago enlisted in the ethnically mixed 55th Illinois Infantry for the thrill of soldiering and the promise of steady pay. Although fairly educated, Petasch did not master the English language very well. The resulting lack in communication brought him trouble at least once when he did not feel well while on guard duty and his sergeant ordered him to see the regimental surgeon. Petasch refused, "because the doctor himself told me that he could not understand much German."[51] The Saxon private without doubt would have preferred to have more German-speaking comrades in his regiment consisting of Swedish, Irish, American, English, and few German soldiers and officers. Language was also an obstacle for wartime newcomers who entered the ranks shortly after their arrival, most often because enlistment bounties promised quick money. Especially ports like New York City and Boston received large numbers of these volunteers. As Governor John A. Andrew complained in 1864, over 1,200 newcomers from Germany and Switzerland speaking "hardly a word of English" had arrived in Boston within weeks, ready to enlist in Massachusetts regiments. Linguistic tensions could pose serious problems in combat situations, as was the case in the 20th Massachusetts Infantry. Shortly before the battle of Reams' Station in August 1864, the regiment received 200 German raw recruits who neither spoke nor understood English. During the closing campaigns against Richmond in 1865, Lieutenant Colonel Cannon of the 40th New York Infantry encountered the same problematic situation. "In consideration of the large number of recruits in the ranks, many of them being ignorant of the English language," the commanding officer reported, nevertheless "the conduct of the regiment was very satisfactory."[52]

A common denomination or religious belief could also be instrumental for immigrants to enlist together, especially for minorities like Irish and German Catholics who together constituted a little over 10 percent of all Union soldiers. It was only natural that Catholics, often victims of prejudicial antipathy, would prefer to serve alongside their brothers in faith rather than with Protestants or nonbelievers. In some cases, as in the recruiting efforts for the 9th Massachusetts Regiment, religion would even be instrumentalized to bring forward ethnic volunteers. Additionally, chances were that in a Catholic unit a Catholic priest would serve as regimental chaplain and tend to the men's spiritual needs. Father Peter Paul Cooney of the Irish 35th Indiana Infantry serves as a case in point. Admired by his men, the priest not only held services and prayers, but also looked after the wounded in the heaviest of battles. Deeply moved by his chaplain's gallant bearing during the battle of Stone's River in Tennessee in January 1863, Colonel Mullen in his official report asserted that to "Father Cooney, our chaplain, too much praise cannot be given. Indifferent as to himself, he was deeply solicitous for the temporal comfort and spiritual welfare of us all. On the field he was cool and indifferent to danger, and in the name of the regiment I thank him for his kindness and laborious attention to the dead and dying."[53] For many Catholics, religious ties were even stronger than ethnic boundaries. Thus, French or even German Catholic priests served in Irish regiments. Other immigrants did not feel a strong need for professional spiritual guidance. In the 3rd Minnesota Infantry, Hans Mattson's Swedish company would gather every evening for informal masses and sing psalms, a custom that eventually spread to all of the predominantly Lutheran Protestant regiment. In several other regiments Swedish soldiers were known to combine military discipline with religious services. Swedes and Norwegians rarely figured prominently enough in a single regiment to elect chaplains of their own. Hans Heg's Scandinavian Regiment, the 15th Wisconsin, was the only Civil War regiment with a Scandinavian chaplain, Danish Reverend Claus Lauritz Clausen.[54] Flocking together in companies such as in Hecker's 2nd Regiment or in Einstein's 27th Pennsylvania was especially important for immigrant Jews who often felt segregated from society as much as from their fellow immigrants.

Wherever immigrant regiments formed, these units seemed the natural choice for volunteers who consciously followed the calls for ethnic pride. A considerable degree of social pressure in heavily ethnic areas and especially in urban neighborhoods certainly led many immigrants to enlist in these regiments. Aggressive recruitment campaigns served to increase ethnic consciousness among foreign-born volunteers. When Sigel's 3rd Missouri formed to strike against Jackson's militia, Buegel described the ethnic fervor that had gripped the German soldiers: "After several toasts 'long live the Union' and 'down with the traitors' had been made and several glasses had been emptied, we marched off. . . . The majority [of the soldiers] possessed some education and civility, and most importantly everyone was eager to teach the German-haters an unforgettable lesson."[55] Similar emotions prevailed in most other ethnic regiments. When in the summer a company of the German 37th Ohio Infantry left Cincinnati, "the unconquerable . . . Haberbusch did his rounds with a yodeling yell and a full bottle, lifting everybody's spirits with the following words: 'Boys, as soon as we join the regiment, let's show the rebels how we'll lick them, we'll have the war over with in no time.'"[56] Combining patriotic devotion to the Union with ethnic pride, August Horstmann probably acted from motivations similar to many of his comrades in immigrant units. Even if he fell "fighting for the freedom and the preservation of the Union of this my adopted home country," the sergeant-major soon to be lieutenant of the 45th New York Infantry wrote to his family in Germany, "you must not worry about me, because many brave sons of our German country have already died on the field of glory and many more will yet fall at my side!"[57]

Sometimes, immigrants traveled considerable distances to join ethnic regiments and help increase their visibility. Members of *Turnvereins* had an especially strong desire to serve in German units. When Pennsylvania Turners could not be accommodated in a German Pennsylvania regiment, they joined Steinwehr's 29th Infantry in New York. Likewise, Turners from Philadelphia, Cincinnati, Detroit, Milwaukee, Davenport, and other midwestern cities sent detachments to fill the 17th Missouri Turner Regiment forming around a core of St. Louis Turners in July 1861.

Immigrants not only crossed state lines to join regiments of their choice; often, whole companies traversed national boundaries to help fill regiments of other nationalities. Several German regiments included Scandinavian companies, such as the "Galesburg Company" C of the 43rd Illinois Infantry under its German Captain H. M. Starkloff. In most cases, however, ethnic companies would simply join any regiments forming in their city or state without regard to their composition. As long as immigrants could serve alongside fellow ethnic soldiers in their immediate surroundings, many of them seem to have cared little about the makeup of the regiment they were part of. Thus, German, Scandinavian, Polish, or other immigrant companies were common in mixed and largely American regiments throughout the northern armies. These companies would often take pride in their distinctiveness, such as the Welsh Company C of the 56th Ohio Infantry, or the 7th Minnesota Infantry's "Scandinavian Guards."[58]

Whatever their motivations to join the army, the majority of foreign-born volunteers did not enlist in companies or regiments in which their own ethnicity dominated. Certainly, in many cases immigrants would have preferred to join such units if they had had the opportunity. Evidence suggests, however, that for the majority ethnic pride and group consciousness did not play the most important role when it came to volunteering. When the Germans of Indianapolis offered their services to Governor Oliver Morton, they explicitly declined to raise separate regiments. "Because now it was time," a chronicler of the Indianapolis German community later held, "to bury all national differences and instead be indivisibly American."[59] For most immigrants, the decision to join the army seems to have been an individual one. Some German immigrants even served in Irish regiments. Württembergian Eugen Reistle from Ludwigsburg had joined the 10th New Hampshire Infantry in September 1862, and soon advanced to the rank of sergeant. Reistle seemingly got along well with his comrades and obviously did not encounter the ethnic tensions so common between German and Irish immigrants. Carl Bonath, on the other hand, asked the commander of the 7th Minnesota Infantry for a transfer to another company after his Irish captain had twice reduced him in rank for incompetence. Offended by such allegations, the former professional artillerist from Germany wanted to "get out of Capt. Gilfillan's reach."[60]

Deliberately or not, most immigrant volunteers made their decisions in favor of mixed or predominantly American units. They encountered strange environments and shared life in camp and on the battlefield with their American comrades, even if many of them might have preferred the comforts of their familiar traditions and language. Sergeant Albert Krause felt as much at home in his regiment as possible, but after three years' campaigning, he had a forlorn feeling, serving "All alone in a foreign country amidst foreign people speaking a foreign language." Krause obviously had little contact with his German regimental comrades, because "The Germans here all speak English, even among themselves."[61] Gustav Keppler had left his native

Württemberg in 1862 at age nineteen and settled in New York City among the German-speaking population. Soon Keppler found himself in economic distress and enlisted in the 14th New York Cavalry, a largely nonethnic unit except for several Irish members. As Keppler told his family in Ludwigsburg, "I am all on my own; I have little contacts with the others, who for the most part are Irishmen of the lowest class." The only two friends speaking his language he had lost. A German comrade had died of fever, Keppler wrote, and a former merchant from Switzerland had "received a gunshot in his backside and because they could not remove the bullet, he was discharged."[62]

Ludwig Kühner from Baden had settled together with his brother in northern Ohio, where a small emigrant settlement had totally integrated into its American, Republican environment. By the time both joined the army, Ludwig had already anglicized his name to Louis Keener. Although several of his friends and three brothers-in-law enlisted around the same time in the fall of 1861, they entered different native American units and obviously showed no intention of serving together. For Keener, who had left his wife and children behind and gave up a thriving farm, the decision to join the war was not an easy one, all the more so as "our vicinity has not yet suffered from the war as the battlefields are far away in the slave states." However, it was the duty of every loyal citizen to stand up for his country in times of need. Writing to another brother in Germany, "the majority of young and single men have volunteered to defend our freedom. . . . We have not been drafted, neither have money or lust for adventure driven us; it is hard to leave behind wife and children and to go into battle, but we have no other choice if we want to retain our and our children's freedom."[63] Serving in the 15th Independent Battery of Ohio Light Artillery, Louis survived the campaigns in the west and returned safely to his farm and family after his three-year term had ended.

For a small group of immigrants, retaining their spiritual freedom and independence was more important than going to war and joining the military. Pacifist enclaves like the Shaker villages in Kentucky and New York or the German communal settlement of Amana in Iowa refused to take up arms and tried to stay clear of the surrounding conflict. This was not always possible, of course, as guerrillas and irregular marauders cared little for pacifism or religious isolationists. Kentucky Shakers in South Union and Pleasant Hill who included American as well as German, English, Catholic French, and Swedish members, suffered severely from the war. In addition to the ongoing guerrilla fighting around their settlements that often resulted in burned and plundered buildings, army foraging deprived them of their horses and carriages. Usually, however, at least the regular army officers respected their attitudes and Confederate General John Hunt Morgan even protected them from guerrilla attacks. In return, the impartial Shakers fed both armies and during the war gave out more than 50,000 meals to Union and Confederate soldiers. A few young members from Pleasant Hill even broke their pacifist vows and volunteered for the Union. As journalist and chronicler Charles Nordhoff noted, these prodigal sons "returned after the war ended, and were reinstated in the society after examination and confession of their sins."[64] Federal authorities accepted the conscientious objection of religious groups and orders and exempted them from general conscription. In November 1862, the State of New York declared that the Shakers and Quakers could not be called to armed service. When four members of the Benedictine Order were drafted from Pennsylvania in late 1862, the Irish Archbishop of Baltimore together with the German abbot of the Benedictine monastery in Latrobe, Pennsylvania, united in their protest. President Lincoln intervened personally, and in November the War Department ordered "that the members of the Benedictine order are relieved from military duty."[65]

Except for the miniscule number of conscientious objectors to the war and several other immigrants who opposed what they perceived as an unjust attack on the South, hundreds of thousands of foreign-born Union soldiers augmented the northern armies. Whether they joined ethnic units or not, most immigrants acted from motives very similar to those of their native American comrades. Indeed, Americans would have found that they had much more in common with most immigrants than they thought. Immigrants joined the army to defend their home and the Union, they volunteered because of the thrill of making war, and they hoped for advancement in the ranks and social reputation. Many foreign-born Union soldiers, like many Americans, fought to destroy slavery or at least put a stop to its further expansion. Ethnic Americans, however, often acted out of an additional set of motivations that drove many of them to join the army. They were united in the desire for acceptance in American society through war service. Faithful service in the military, many immigrants hoped, would earn them respect and prove their worth as full citizens as well as reduce antiforeign sentiment. Finally, ethnic rivalry was the single unique motivation for immigrants to join the army. While Americans would brag about their home states or towns, their affiliation to political parties or denominations, they never had to compete with ethnic groups for societal recognition. Immigrants who organized and volunteered for distinct regiments, on the other hand, often had the clear-cut goal to protect their own interests.

Still, from what the volunteers told their friends and families it seems safe to assume that patriotism and loyalty to the new homeland were the main and major motivations for Americans and immigrants alike to join the army. Historian Ella Lonn was certainly right when she claimed that "Relatively seldom was wholly undiluted devotion to the ideal of liberty the motive, though comparatively seldom, at least during the early years of the war, was that motive entirely absent."[66] Immigrants, especially political fugitives and idealistic forty-eighters, knew the debt they owed the country that had welcomed them. Of course, not all immigrants had felt the urge to participate in that country's conflict right away. Physician August Achenbach had emigrated from Westfalia in 1857 and taken up medical practice in Allegheny

City near Pittsburgh. At the outbreak of the war Achenbach continued with his civil profession, until "The battle of Shilo[h] was fought, and as I heard of so much suffering of our gallant boys there, I couldn't stay longer at home, I went down to Shiloh on my own risk and expenses with the purpose to help as a private physician for a short time as good as in my power."[67] Achenbach again assisted privately during the Seven Days' Battles around Richmond, when finally he discovered that he had the patriotic duty to enlist as a soldier. After a thorough examination the physician became a regimental surgeon in the 7th New York Steuben Rifles.

A sense of duty to a free country combined with the desire to gain recognition in society might well have been the principal motivations for a majority of immigrants, outspoken or not. In an affectionate letter to his wife, Hans Mattson revealed complex reasons for his decision to fight for the Union. Speaking for many, if not most, immigrants in the northern army, Mattson realized that Americans rightfully expected immigrants to join their cause if they wanted to be accepted as citizens. "A little hatred had previously existed between our people and the Americans," the Swede admitted. "Now there was more reason for it. People began to ask, 'Why don't you do anything for the defense of your country and yourselves?' . . . I meditated long; I prayed for God's guidance, I partly realized the sacrifice I should be making for myself and for you. . . . The difference between us and the Americans will disappear so much the faster."[68]

The Battle of Bull's Run. This cartoon from 1861 ridicules the Union army's flight back to Washington, DC, after the battle of Bull Run. Blenker's Brigade (no. 16) is covering the retreat in the right middle of the picture. The brigade's rearguard action at the first major battle in Virginia laid the foundation for Blenker's fame (Lithograph by A. Pfott. Library of Congress, Prints and Photographs Division).

Headquarters of Blenker's Brigade. Taken around October 1861, this photograph shows the inflated staff of the German Brigade. Blenker is standing in the front row (middle) with his right hand on the belt, with Julius Stahel to his right (Library of Congress, Prints and Photographs Division).

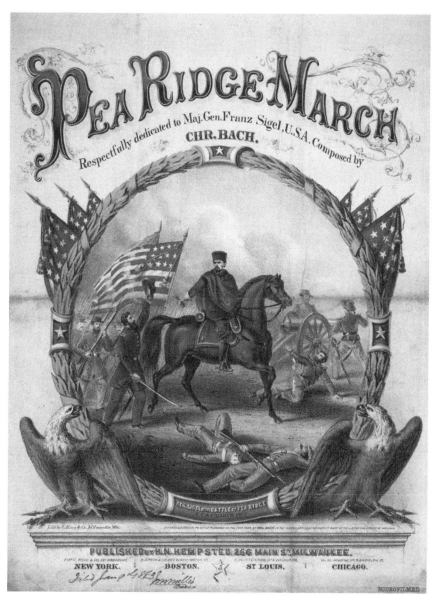

Pea Ridge March. Respectfully Dedicated to Maj. Gen. Franz Sigel, U.S.A. Cover of sheet music composed by Chr. Bach from Milwaukee in dedication to Sigel's contribution to the Union victory at Pea Ridge, which greatly enhanced the forty-eighter's popularity (Library of Congress, Prints and Photographs Division).

Carl Schurz. The most influential German-American in the nineteenth century, Schurz had become a hero of the German Revolution when he freed his fellow forty-eighter, Gottfried Kinkel, from Rastatt prison. As major general, Schurz received bitter criticism for the largely ethnic Eleventh Corps's alleged cowardice at the battle of Chancellorsville. After the war Schurz served as U.S. senator and secretary of the interior (Library of Congress, Prints and Photographs Division).

Hubert Anton Casimir Dilger. Captain Dilger was a former artillery officer from Baden who commanded Battery I of the First Ohio Light Artillery. One of the outstanding European professional soldiers who helped establish the federal artillery's superiority during the war, Dilger would definitely have deserved a higher rank in the army (Library of Congress, Prints and Photographs Division).

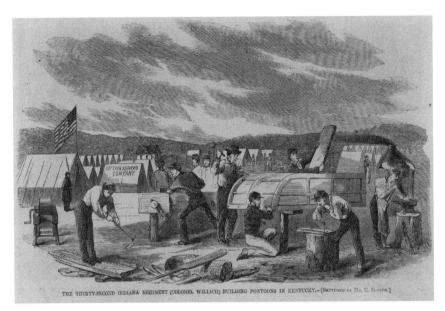

THE THIRTY-SECOND INDIANA REGIMENT (COLONEL WILLICH) BUILDING PONTOONS IN KENTUCKY.—[SKETCHED BY MR. H. MOSLER.]

The Thirty-Second Indiana Regiment Building Pontoons in Kentucky. Under the command of their beloved Colonel August "Papa" Willich, the 32nd Indiana would eventually become one of the finest and hardest fighting Union regiments in the western theater of the war (Wood engraving published in *Harper's Weekly,* December 14, 1861. Library of Congress, Prints and Photographs Division).

Major General Peter Joseph Osterhaus. A Latin Farmer who at the outbreak of the war enlisted as a private under Sigel in St. Louis, Osterhaus quickly rose to colonel of the 12th Missouri Infantry and eventually division and corps commander. Serving with distinction in several theaters of the war, this exceptional officer had stood in thirty-four battles when he left the army in 1866 (Library of Congress, Prints and Photographs Division).

GENₗ MEAGHER AT THE BATTLE OF FAIR OAKS Vᴬ, JUNE 1ˢᵀ 1862.

The bayonet charge of the Irish Brigade at this battle, was the most stubborn, sanguinary and bloody of modern times. Again and again they advanced with the cold steel, and were as vigorously met by the the enemy. In one place on the field of carnage, three men were found on each side, that had fallen by mutual thrusts. But at last the battle terminated in favor of the Union arms, the Rebels gave way in flight, and the victorious 'Army of the Potomac' continued their advance on Richmond.

General Thomas Francis Meagher at the Head of His Irish Brigade at the Battle of Fair Oaks. The caption reads, "The bayonet charge of the Irish Brigade at this battle, was the most stubborn, sanguinary and bloody of modern times. Again and again they advanced with the cold steel, and were as vigorously met by the enemy. In one place of the field of carnage, three men were found on each side, that had fallen by mutual thrusts. But at last the battle terminated in favor of the Union arms, the Rebels gave way in flight, and the victorious 'Army of the Potomac' continued their advance on Richmond." Note the distinct Irish flag carried by Meagher's troops (Library of Congress, Prints and Photographs Division).

Jumping the Ditch–St. Patrick's Day at the Army of the Potomac–Sports of the Irish Brigade   . This drawing depicts the enthusiastic and often raucous style of celebrating Meagher's brigade was famous for throughout the Army of the Potomac (Library of Congress, Prints and Photographs Division).

Brigadier General Michael Corcoran, famed Irish nationalist and one of the first commanders of Irish troops in the Union army. Captured early in the war, Corcoran returned in triumph and raised the Corcoran Legion in New York (Library of Congress, Prints and Photographs Division).

Father Thomas Scully, regimental chaplain of the Irish 9th Massachusetts Infantry, wearing the liturgical vestment used for service in the field. Largely Catholic, Irish-American soldiers stood out by their religious rites. Like language, religion was an important aspect of identification for many immigrants in the Union army (Library of Congress, Prints and Photographs Division).

Officers of the 69th New York Infantry proudly pose with their colors. Originally raised by Michael Corcoran around members of his 69th New York Militia, this regiment formed the core of the Irish Brigade and became a synonym for Irish bravery (Library of Congress, Prints and Photographs Division).

Brigadier General Robert Nugent, the last commander of the Irish Brigade. The emblem on Nugent's cap is that of his regiment, the 69th New York Infantry, richly embroidered with Irish shamrock (Library of Congress, Prints and Photographs Division).

The Fight in the Corn Field; The Irish Brigade Driving the Rebels Out, on the Right Wing. Already decimated after continuous and costly fighting, the Irish Brigade made one more memorable stand on the second day of the battle of Gettysburg (Drawing by Arthur Lumley. Library of Congress, Prints and Photographs Division).

Lieutenant Colonel Alexander Repetti, 39th New York Infantry. The Italian veteran wears the colorful dress uniform of the *Garibaldi Guard* sporting a hussar jacket and the fancy broad-brimmed felt hat of Garibaldi's *Bersaglieri*. Repetti proudly poses with the Italian flag the regiment carried alongside the Stars and Stripes and the Hungarian tricolor, inscribed "*Dio e Popolo*" [For God and the People] (Library of Congress, Prints and Photographs Division).

Captain Charles Schwarz, 39th New York Infantry. The captain of the *Garibaldi Guard's* German Company C posed for this photograph in the characteristic flabby flannel shirt styled after the famous "red shirts" worn by Garibaldi's troops (Library of Congress, Prints and Photographs Division).

Colonel Ernest M. P. von Vegesack, 20th New York Infantry. Vegesack had been a captain in the Swedish army before coming to the United States at the outbreak of the war. After short service on McClellan's staff the professional soldier became a captain in the 59th Ohio and finally took command of the German *United Turner Regiment*, which he reportedly called "certainly the best in the whole army." The highly lauded officer distinguished himself at Antietam and left the army as brigadier general. He later returned to Sweden (Library of Congress, Prints and Photographs Division).

Colonel Géza Milahótzy, 24th Illinois Infantry. Early in the war, the Hungarian had organized the Chicago Lincoln Riflemen, composed of Hungarians and Bohemians. Milahótzy took command of the 1st Hecker Regiment after the forty-eighter's resignation. He was killed near Chattanooga in 1864 (Library of Congress, Prints and Photographs Division).

General Julius Stahel, the highest ranking Hungarian in the Union army, helped to recruit for Blenker's 8th New York "First German Rifles." Stahel initially served as lieutenant colonel until he took over command of the regiment (Library of Congress, Prints and Photographs Division).

Baron Philippe Régis Denis de Keredern de Trobriand. A novelist and editor of the French-speaking New York *Courrier des Etats Unis* before the war, Trobriand became colonel of the 55th New York Infantry, "Gardes Lafayette." The Frenchman was a major general by brevet at the end of the war and continued to serve in the military. Trobriand is shown in this photograph in his uniform as a brevet brigadier general, the rank he held when retiring from the regular army in 1879 (Library of Congress, Prints and Photographs Division).

FIVE

ETHNIC VISIBILITY
IN THE EARLY WAR

The first months of the war did much to forge American public perception of ethnic visibility in the Union army. Because immigrants had reacted so promptly to Lincoln's call for volunteers, and because ethnic newspapers and agitators had so fervently pushed for ethnic recruitment, a disproportionately high number of immigrants served in the three-months' regiments from the start. Obviously, regiments like the 8th New York Infantry that paraded through New York City led by officers in foreign dress uniforms shouting German commands, and Irish outfits proudly sporting bright green flags increased the impression that a good portion of the young volunteer army consisted of immigrants.

Ethnic companies and regiments had readily rushed to arms upon Lincoln's first call for troops in April, and consequently they figured prominently in some of the opening campaigns of the war. Indeed, immigrants participated in most engagements of the first year and in several cases their conduct and their commanders' conduct determined how Americans would judge ethnic soldiers throughout the entire conflict. Even more visibly to many, European and American notions of discipline and professionalism often collided, leading to prejudice on both sides. Finally, some foreign-born officers exhibited strange behavior unknown to Americans. Their love of pomp and decorative outfits turned public attention toward the military's immigrant element especially during the critical time of army organization and identity building among the Union troops. Two ethnic commanders, forty-eighter Ludwig Blenker and Thomas Francis Meagher, became particularly known for their outlandish and

eccentric bearing. Both made their first appearance at the very beginning of the war in
the first Battle of Bull Run, Blenker at the head of an ethnic brigade and Meagher as a
captain in Corcoran's 69th New York Regiment. After his regiment had left New York
cheered on by excited crowds, Blenker received command of the Union's first ethnic
brigade. Colonel Steinwehr's 29th New York Astor Rifles joined Blenker's own 8th
New York, now under the command of Lieutenant Colonel Ludwig Stahel together
with D'Utassy's Garibaldi Guard and the 27th Pennsylvania that had recovered from
the humiliating treatment in Baltimore. Blenker's brigade and Meagher's regiment
were part of General Irwin McDowell's 30,000 men massing outside Washington.
Although he could count on several regiments and former militia units trained and
ready to fight, McDowell's force was a motley mixture of largely untrained recruits.
Pressed by public demands for a quick and decisive victory over the equally green
southern troops and by Lincoln's order to take offensive action, the commanding
general moved south although he would have preferred to drill his army into fighting
shape first.

In northern Virginia, Confederate General Pierre G. T. Beauregard had taken
positions south of Bull Run, while a smaller force under General Thomas J. Jackson
was out to defend the Shenandoah Valley. McDowell also divided his troops, marching
one army against Beauregard, and sending another under General Patterson to hold
Jackson at bay. Jackson, however, with his 9,000 "foot cavalry" speeded past Patterson
to join Beauregard and set the stage for the battle that would bring him immortal
fame. With the intention to outflank the Confederates, McDowell crossed Bull Run,
but his inexperienced troops mistook the campaign for a Sunday walk under the
hot Virginia sun. Without adequate discipline and control by their overburdened
officers, the Union army ran into the southerners in the morning of July 21. Because
Beauregard was not yet prepared for battle, the attacking Union regiments threw
the enemy back and quickly gained substantial ground. Just when Union victory
seemed certain, however, General Thomas Jackson prevented a Confederate rout
by steadfastly defending a chain of hills "like a stone wall" against the advancing
federals.[1]

One of the regiments rushing against Jackson's Virginians was the 79th New York
Highlanders, the Scottish regiment in which some kilts still were to be seen even in
battle. Cameron's Highlanders valiantly attacked the Confederates several times but
finally had to give in to Jackson's stubborn resistance, suffering some of the heaviest
losses that day. When Colonel Cameron was killed in one of the attacks and all their
efforts ended in frustration, the Scots finally broke. In disorderly retreat from the
field the men of the 79th passed their Irish comrades who had been held in reserve as
part of General William T. Sherman's brigade. Corcoran's regiment immediately took
the place of the fleeing Highlanders and attacked the Confederates at Henry House
Hill. After several charges against enemy lines, Captain James Kelly later reported, the
Irishmen had to fall back under southern artillery fire, "owing principally to the panic

of the regiment which preceded us, and then, under a desperate fire, retired to the line from which we had advanced on the battery, and then endeavored to reform." Kelly argued that his regiment tried to hold a defensive position, but when fresh southern troops arrived and turned the federal defeat into a totally uncontrollable rout, the panic became general "and the Sixty-ninth had to retreat with the great mass of the Federals."[2] At that time, Meagher had been wounded and had his horse shot under him. Trying to rally his men, Corcoran was also wounded and captured by the Confederates. Now all hell broke loose for the beaten northerners. In wild chaos the whole army pressed over a single stone bridge to the other side of Bull Run and ran back to safety in Washington. Only a few commanders were able to keep discipline and order among their men.

This was Ludwig Blenker's hour. As part of Colonel D. S. Miles' reserve division, Blenker had positioned his brigade strategically on the heights east of Centreville, with Einstein's Pennsylvania regiment detached to the village for the protection of the headquarters and hospital. When Union defeat became apparent, Miles ordered Blenker to retreat with the rest of the Union army. Probably disobeying Miles's order on purpose, Blenker later stated in his official report that he had instead received orders to advance. Thus, the brigade marched down the road leading from Centreville to Bull Run that "was nearly choked up by the retreating baggage wagons of several divisions, and by the vast numbers of flying soldiers belonging to various regiments." With Stahel's First German Rifles in the first line, the brigade entrenched in a strong defensive position along the road. While the uncontrollable Union flight continued until late in the evening, Blenker proudly stated, his brigade stood its ground and repulsed several half-hearted attacks "from various sides by the enemy's cavalry."[3] As amazed by their victory as the federal troops were by their defeat, the Confederates never managed to deliver a massive counterattack and eventually withdrew. Blenker's men remained in their positions until ordered to fall back to Washington around midnight. On their march back Stahel's regiment salvaged six abandoned cannons as well two stands of colors left behind by Union soldiers. Although Blenker's men did not get the chance to prove their valor that day, they nevertheless proved that they could retain discipline and stand their ground even amidst the surrounding chaos and the otherwise poorly led actions of the army. After nineteen hours the German Brigade reached Washington the following evening. Together with the 69th New York Infantry, Blenker's men were among the few Union regiments marching into the capital intact and in good order. Cheered on by citizens in the streets, this achievement naturally served to increase ethnic visibility and strengthen the immigrants' self-consciousness. Casualties in the first major battle exceeded the wildest expectations on both sides. The Scottish Highlanders had lost over 200 men and officers and the Irish Regiment only slightly less. General Sherman, who had not held the Irish in high esteem before, now reversed his opinion and praised their good conduct. Acknowledging their enemy's bravery in battle, a southern report admitted that "No

Southerner but feels that the Sixty-Ninth maintained the old reputation of Irish valor—on the wrong side."[4]

War was on in earnest now and everyone realized that it would not be over in a matter of weeks. Consequently, President Lincoln signed the necessary bills to enlist an additional 1,000,000 volunteers. The growing army needed more commanding officers, and among those who profited from this development were Blenker and Meagher. Because Corcoran was still in captivity, Meagher was offered command of the reorganized 69th New York Infantry. Aspiring to higher goals, Meagher declined and instead went on to organize his personal dream, an all-Irish Brigade. During a successful recruiting campaign, the charismatic speaker convinced his listeners of the righteousness of the Union cause and won over many undecided Irishmen in New York and Boston. By the end of 1861, his Irish Brigade consisting of the 63rd, 69th, and 88th New York Regiments together with the 2nd New York Artillery Battalion officially had become the Second Brigade, First Division of the Second Army Corps in the newly created federal army gathering in northern Virginia. Taking command of the brigade in October, Meagher received his appointment to brigadier general in the following February. The Irish revolutionary had a clear vision; he wanted his brigade to become an aggressive and effective fighting unit that would do honor to the Irish cause and ensure its members and their fellow immigrants a respectable position in postwar American society. Therefore, he explicitly ordered his regiments equipped with large-caliber smoothbore rifles that caused the greatest possible damage at close-range encounters with the enemy. Telling his soldiers what he expected of them, the general called upon the Irish to always thrust themselves "into the thickest of the most desperate fight."[5] Meagher certainly knew how to inspire his devoted men. His usual appearance in dashing full-dress uniform perfectly complimented his inflaming rhetoric. "He possessed high-toned sentiments and manners, and the bearing of a prince," Chaplain William Corby of the 88th New York Infantry related of Meagher in his memoirs. "He had a superior intellect, a liberal education, was a fine classical writer, and a born orator. . . . Wherever he went he made himself known as a 'Catholic and an Irishman.' "[6] Although heavily criticized for his habitual drinking that tended to intensify stereotypes about Irish addiction to alcohol, Meagher nevertheless proved an able and daring commander who would lead his brigade to undying fame.

At that time in Virginia, Meagher's flamboyant bearing and charismatic character stood out from the rest of the Union generals, with one exception. A similarly captivating speaker and equally keen on impressive public appearances, Ludwig Blenker through his persistent lobbying had also secured a considerable enlargement of his command after Bull Run. In addition to his original brigade, now under the command of Brigadier General Stahel, his newly created division embraced two more brigades. Colonel Adolf von Steinwehr led the Second Brigade consisting of his old 29th New York, the half-German 68th New York, the 73rd Pennsylvania, and the 54th New York Black Rifles. Colonel Heinrich Bohlen's Third Brigade comprised Colonel

Krzyzanowski's 58th New York Polish Legion and the 74th and 75th Pennsylvania Infantry regiments. Completing the largely ethnic force, Leopold von Gilsa's 41st New York DeKalb Infantry and Dickel's 4th New York Cavalry served as unattached regiments together with two German batteries under Captains Michael Wiedrich and Julius Dieckmann. In his description of Blenker's Division Kaufmann in his usually ethnocentric way pockets all the various immigrant groups in the division as German and even claimed that all the officers "were Germans." This was not true, of course. Besides Hungarian, Polish, Italian, and Austrian officers in the Garibaldi Guard and the Polish Legion, several Americans served under Blenker's command as well. Kaufmann was, however, right in pointing to the explicitly ethnic characteristic of the division, adding that "the language of command was German, and even the uniforms recalled the fatherland."[7] Blenker himself saw to it that the ethnic composition of his division received the necessary attention. In a general order, he even decreed that "the designation of the *division* under my command is not *15th Division*, but . . . Blenker's Division."[8] All official correspondence was to use this name exclusively, and eventually even most American officers and generals complied.

Blenker's and Meagher's ethnic organizations were part of the newly created Army of the Potomac under its commanding general, thirty-five-year-old West Pointer, George B. McClellan. Hailed as the "Young Napoleon," McClellan would soon excel as a brilliant organizer but an overtly cautious general who repeatedly hesitated to take the offensive. For the time being, however, his first and most important task was to whip into shape the largest army the continent had yet seen. As a professional officer "Little Mac" recognized the already existing discipline among the veteran European units, and as a vain and self-important careerist he probably marveled at Blenker's ability to show off. McClellan later recalled the visibility of Blenker and the ethnic troops in his army in an amusing and much-quoted depiction. "The most entertaining of my duties were those which sometimes led me to Blenker's camp," the general wrote in his memoirs, to see the "circus" or "opera," as his adjutant called it.

> As soon as we were sighted Blenker would have the 'officer's call' blown to assemble his polyglot collection, with their uniforms as varied and brilliant as the colors of the rainbow. Wrapped in his scarlet-lined cloak, his group of officers ranged around him, he would receive us with the most formal and polished courtesy. Being a very handsome and soldierly looking man himself, and there being many equally so among his surroundings, the tableau was always very effective, and presented a striking contrast to the matter-of-fact way in which things were managed in the other divisions. In a few minutes, he would shout, "Ordinanz numero eins!" whereupon champagne would be brought in great profusion, the bands would play, sometimes songs be sung.[9]

McClellan certainly was sympathetic toward Blenker's ethnic soldiers who brought luster to the Union army. "His division was very peculiar," he wrote. "So far as the 'pride, pomp, and circumstance of glorious war' were concerned, it certainly outshone all the others."[10] According to Chaplain Corby, the brassy appearance of Meagher's staff in every respect matched that of the Blenker Division. It was "composed of gallant young officers, who were decked out not only with the regulation gold straps, stripes, and cords on their coats, trousers and hats, but they had also great Austrian knots of gold on the shoulders, besides numerous other ornamentation in gold, which glittered in the Virginia sun enough to dazzle one."[11] When in 1862 the 116th Pennsylvania Infantry joined the Irish Brigade, its commander Lieutenant Colonel St. Clair Mulholland was also impressed by Meagher and his entourage. With dry humor, the Irish colonel remembered that the Irish Brigade's officers "seemed to wear a great deal more gold lace than the regulations called for."[12]

Apart from its splendor, as a professional officer McClellan appreciated the discipline in his German division. "Their drill and bearing were also excellent," the general acknowledged, giving as a reason that "all the officers, and probably all the men, had served in Europe."[13] Indeed, it was probably the most important overall contribution of experienced European officers to contribute their military knowledge to the organization of the Union army during its first year. While immigrants with military experience understood the importance of thorough training as a crucial requirement for success on the battlefield, in the early days of the war many American volunteer officers did not. To most American volunteer soldiers, strict military discipline was a novel and awkward constraint on their traditional individualism. Soldiers were quick to challenge the superiority of their officers, whether immigrant or American, and often enough simply did not see the need for exact drill and exhausting military exercise. As a result, many immigrants in turn looked down upon the American volunteers. A German observer remarked of a regiment marching off from New York, "their negligent bearing could not impress me, still having in mind the parade step of the Prussian battalions."[14] Critical immigrant observers even attributed the defeat at Bull Run to lack of serious training and discipline, and some were quick to point out the exceptional role played by the German Brigade. A German mining agent in Tennessee told his family back in Prussia that "In the battle of Manassas a few German regiments have parried and covered the wild rout and flight of the northern Yankee boys as well as they could."[15] A former noncommissioned officer in his native Brunswick, Emile Dupré found equally little praise for the green American army and their conduct in the war thus far. The "cowardly Americans will soon be glad to have German officers in leading positions. Right now I am Captain in the Pioneer-Corps in Washington, but I don't know how much longer I want to keep this rank, because this here is probably the lousiest military leadership in world history." Referring to the recent Union disaster, Dupré added, "just think that a week ago on Sunday a battle was fought in the vicinity of Washington at Bull's Run where whole regiments threw away their rifles, sabers and revolvers, even though no one was wounded, and ran back here as fast as they could."[16]

Like Dupré, former soldiers from Europe found that their idea of professionalism did not coincide with the American way of soldiering. Usually, volunteer companies elected their officers and more often than not social status and wealth secured an officer's commission rather than military experience. Even worse, regimental commands and even generals' appointments went to civilians and influential political lobbyists. August Valentin Kautz had emigrated with his parents from Baden in 1828 when still an infant, and after his service in the Mexican War had been admitted to West Point. Like other professionals, immigrant and American, Kautz saw considerable danger in appointing commanding officers from civilian life. Serving in the regular cavalry at the outbreak of the war, the veteran soldier detested the ubiquitous rush for promotion in the volunteer army. "Officers, who had failed to do themselves credit as Commanders of Companies," Kautz complained, "were Colonels of Regiments and demanding to be made Brigadier Generals. They did not seem to reflect upon the responsibility they were seeking, as though the war was going to be a holiday affair and the care of thousands of human lives was a task of easy execution; as though nothing was required to make a man a General except the shoulder strap that indicated rank."[17] A rare Welsh critical voice, James Griffiths from Cincinnati, told his family: "Unprejudiced opinion has it that the war would have been over long ago if all our generals had been able men but it is sad to think that many of them have turned out otherwise."[18] Of course, there were able political generals as well. One of the best examples was Thomas Meagher, who proved to be a capable and valiant leader in battle and possessed the full confidence of even veteran officers.

Like all commanders of significant ethnic military organizations, Blenker and Meagher naturally attracted more or less qualified aspirants for commissions and personal importance. However, it was Blenker who outdid all others in collecting an entourage of dubious immigrants convinced of their superior qualifications. As Carl Schurz has noted, "Our war had attracted many German officers hoping for advancement in the army, among them noblemen with high honorary ranks. Some of these gentlemen were attached to General Blenker's staff as adjutants. Thus he was able to surround himself with a kind of royal suite that distinguished itself by many lofty titles."[19] Schurz politely kept silent about the talents of many of Blenker's officers like the Prince of Salm-Salm. Others did not; the staff of the German division at some point consisted of more than eighty officers, and many critics agreed that it only served as a way station for questionable characters wasting public money. Blenker never kept strict control over his staff. Instead, he let his officers require special favors for the troops such as generous beer rations and their own bakery. Allegedly, Blenker's division spent several thousand dollars on beer every month. Even worse, Blenker's tendency to show off and the ostentatious luxury prevailing in his camp contrasted strikingly with American republican plainness. This pompous style and unusual conduct soon caused heavy criticism, in no minor degree from Germans who feared the negative effect on their public status. As Otto Heusinger, a noncommissioned officer in the 41st New York Infantry would later recall in his memoirs, "Blenker's love of luxury simply had to become the matter of unfavorable attention by dissatisfied Germans, usually gathering in large numbers in New York beer halls. Fierce articles appeared in German newspapers abusing Blenker, completely denying him any talent as general, and insinuating that he had a disreputable background."[20] One of the most prominent and outspoken critics of Blenker was his former forty-eighter comrade from Baden, Max Weber, who in 1861 refused to incorporate his New York Turner Regiment in the German Brigade. Fellow exile Gustav Struve, now a captain in the 8th New York, resigned under protest when Prince Salm-Salm became commander of the regiment. Carrying the class struggle of the forty-eighters into the American army, Struve refused to serve under a showy nobleman who only pretended to fight for democracy. Eventually, the kind of ethnic visibility Blenker and his staff officers embodied did nothing to make Americans in the Army of the Potomac sympathetic to the alien element in their midst.[21]

It is no wonder that the appointment of political officers alienated immigrant professionals who, despite their ability and knowledge, found themselves serving under ineffectual superiors. Untrained in the art of pulling the right strings and often too proud to boldly ask for promotion, foreign-born officers fell victim to a system preferring influence over skill. All the more amazed was a correspondent of the German-language *Morgenblatt für gebildete Leser* when he received his commission. "A German officer without monetary means or connections in an American native regiment," the immigrant wrote "that is very unusual."[22] Another immigrant who had already served one year in the military of his native Brunswick, told his parents in 1862 about the amateurish system of electing officers: "Advancement is fast here, but when the war is over school is out, and these gentlemen who have a grandiose living now, will again be laborers, waiters, and barbers."[23] On the other hand, the war provided a career leap for many an immigrant who had not made it in Europe. An anonymous writer complained to the *New York Times* that "an educated Artillerist or Engineer would be so, we do not doubt. But certainly it is unwise to accept foreign birth and inability to speak the English tongue as prima facie evidence of military education and experience. There are many German officers now on their way to America, or forming their plans for coming, because they have not the ability necessary to do well at home."[24]

In addition to the absence of thoroughly trained professionals, many European officers detected yet another reason for the lack of discipline in American volunteer regiments. In their opinion, the missing social distance between officers and men undermined the necessary strict authority. Traditionally, officers in European armies had come from the upper and noble classes. Thus, many immigrants in prewar America still saw social caste barriers as an indispensable prerequisite of a disciplined and effective army. Certainly it was unfamiliar for many former European officers to deal with citizen-soldiers and some, like August Kautz, reacted accordingly. Even though he had practically spent his entire life in America, Kautz held on to typical European notions. As a captain in the volunteer army he expressed his disgust "with the messing arrangements, Soldiers & Officers all sit at the same table."[25] Immigrant soldiers serving in the ranks, on the other hand, often preferred this American egalitarianism because it made them feel respected. A German noncommissioned officer wrote that "I never hesitate to speak just as freely and frankly to our colonel as I might to one of our sergeants."[26] Albert Krause also enjoyed the remarkably relaxed atmosphere in his regiment. "There is strict authority in the military," he told his family, "but only while on duty, afterwards the general is not worth more than the private."[27] Mecklenburg physician Carl Uterhard also favored the lack of class distinctions in the American army. Recalling a train ride from New York to the national capital, Uterhard was fascinated that "all the people on my train were commissioned officers and soldiers on their way to join the army. Generals, colonels, captains, and privates traveled together in the one common class that is unique to American trains. There is no such difference between officers and soldiers like in our country. Soldiers are as much gentlemen as generals."[28]

Social equality across the ranks led many immigrants to identify with the democratic ideals of the Union. A veteran from the 136th Indiana after the war fondly remembered what he called the "Republican plainness" of the federal uniform signaling democratic unity, and stated that many German volunteers "very much liked being called 'the boys in blue.' "[29] Maybe this was a reason why so many immigrants, used to impenetrable class obstacles in European armies, preferred serving in mixed and nonethnic regiments. Although ethnic soldiers frequently scoffed at incompetent American officers, there were also those who disliked the haughty attitudes of ethnic superiors. Wilhelm Albrecht, who had been a sergeant in Mecklenburg, shunned a responsible position and pledged to remain a "free" man in the ranks, "because the self-importance of the officers in the German regiments is tremendous." With his experience, Wilhelm could have become an officer "as well as any other," but he did not want to join the scores of unworthy officers. His goal was to remain an enlisted man because "As such I am just as worthy as an officer in the eyes of an American."[30] Enlisting in the 9th Wisconsin Salomon Guards, Georg Michael Zimmer from the Palatine witnessed the same bickering for commissions in this ethnic regiment that immigrants disliked in American regiments. Zimmer noted in his diary that during the organization of the regiment in September a certain Conrad Brunke, who had recruited several fellow immigrants, demanded that he be given an officer's commission, "because otherwise he would have taken his recruits into another regiment." Consequently, Brunke was made first lieutenant. "No one said anything about military knowledge," Zimmer added sarcastically, "and we could see that he did not have a clue." Zimmer, soon a first sergeant, found the behavior of most of his regimental officers little inspiring. When he finally received his discharge in December 1864, Zimmer did not part in sorrow. Instead, he rejoiced, "Oh, for the first time since

September the 7th, 1861, I felt how wonderful it is to be a free man. It is no small matter to serve under aristocratic officers for three years and nearly three months." With great satisfaction Zimmer related in his diary that "their time has ended as well and from now on they hopefully have to content themselves with a glass of beer instead of champagne." Yet the diary also speaks of Zimmer's affection for Colonel Carl Eberhard Salomon and his brother. When in November General "Fritz" bade farewell to his division, he "gave a wonderful speech and told us that he was very sorry to say goodbye to his old regiment, which he held in high regard above all others."[31]

While German and other immigrant officers were quick to single out missing class barriers as a reason for inferior discipline, Americans certainly had no monopoly on unruly behavior. The men of the 9th Wisconsin repeatedly misbehaved on purpose, just to rebel against being "tyrannized by the aristocratic gentlemen officers." Zimmer took special pleasure in recalling an episode where several companies refused to follow orders at battalion drill. "We will see who has the harder head, you or me," the major threatened the men. However, "instead of better it became worse, and suddenly our Major turned his horse and galloped away as if lightning had struck him. We gave him a cheerful hooray to take with him. . . ."[32] Like Zimmer, Johann Buegel frequently took the liberty of criticizing his German officers. The Lieutenant Colonel, according to Buegel, was "a small man little over 4 feet tall. As small as he was, the larger loomed his ambition, and in his pocket he had a commission as Lieutenant Colonel of our 3'd Mo Regiment. How he had come to the honor of this rank I have never found out. But he had never smelled powder before but he always remained in the background during the time he was with us, and every time we went into action he was sick and stayed behind." Called the "little fool" or "big fool" by the men alternately, Lieutenant Colonel Bischoff had a hard time trying to exert authority, and the regiment repeatedly let him know that his efforts were in vain. On a hot July morning in 1862, Bischoff once more called out the soldiers to reprimand them officially:

> When we arrived on the parade ground, he ordered the regiment to form a hollow square around him and high upon his horse the big fool held a preachment in such broken English that the Irish officers asked, "What that fellow says?" After this ceremony had ended, he called out his orders again, but we all just ran around like sheep. He screamed and howled like a madman; but he could not make us obey. Finally he declared the whole regiment to be mutineers and rebels, and ordered every officer under arrest. The regiment, however, just went away, everyone as he liked.[33]

In addition to such rather harmless incidents, there were instances of violent misconduct in ethnic regiments. The most serious mutiny occurred among the members of the Highlanders after the battle of Bull Run. Angry and disappointed over the whipping they had received, the Scottish soldiers in addition felt that they had been lied to concerning the term of their service. The three months they had signed up for were over and the regiment, like several others, had not yet received any pay. As a consequence, morale was down and smuggled whiskey made the rounds in the camp. When the regiment was ordered to march into Virginia, the men finally abandoned all self-restraint and rebelled against their new commander Colonel Isaac Stevens. Quickly the provost marshal called in regular troops to restore order and arrested the instigators of the mutiny, while those sober enough marched off in formation. As historian William Burton has noted, this incident caused unusually high attention because it involved an ethnic regiment. Pointing to the peculiar situation of immigrant units in the volunteer army, Burton holds that "when things went well, the ethnic group relished the limelight. When unpleasantness occurred, the same public spotlight illuminated the group," and the ethnic soldiers "endured the embarrassment."[34]

While ethnic officers squabbled for appointments in the East, Franz Sigel rose to become the most famous and popular German military leader of the Civil War in Missouri. In June of 1861, General Nathaniel Lyon had officially taken command of the forces around St. Louis, consisting of the five partly ethnic regiments together with several batteries of artillery plus some regular infantry. While Lyon drove a Confederate army under General Sterling Price from their positions at Boonville and the capital of Jefferson City, Sigel penetrated into the secessionist southwest of Missouri to cut off Price's retreat and prevent enemy forces from gathering there. Colonel Sigel commanded the 3rd and 5th Infantry regiments together with Major Frank Backof's artillery on this expedition. Marching through hostile country, the immigrant troops had no choice but to requisition supplies from rural Missourians. In contrast to Meagher and Blenker's troops in the Army of the Potomac, ethnic soldiers in the West soon earned a reputation as savage plunderers among the xenophobic southern population.

On July 5, Sigel's regiments met the rebels at Carthage near the Kansas border. Fending of the enemy in a series of skirmishes, Sigel finally engaged Claiborne Jackson, whose 4,000 men outnumbered his force roughly four to one. Realizing the impossibility of a military victory against the much larger enemy army, Sigel aborted the battle after a few hours and retreated to Springfield. In his report Sigel attested that both officers and men of the two regiments "fought with the greatest skill and bravery. Although more than once menaced in flank and rear by large forces of cavalry, and attacked in front by an overwhelming force, they stood like veterans, and defended one position after the other without one man leaving the ranks."[35] During the battle and the following withdrawal, Major Backof and his battery had effectively protected the infantry movements and prevented Jackson from bringing to bear his numerical superiority. Equally joyous, Lyon in his official report praised Sigel's generalship and "the high soldierly qualities exhibited by his officers and men."[36] Interestingly enough, Lyon's adjutant general would later give a highly contradictory account of what happened at Carthage that day. The two Union regiments, Major John M. Schofield claimed, had been well armed and equipped, with "most of the men old German soldiers." Together with their artillery they should have had no problems in whipping Price's "miserable rabble" of undisciplined and badly organized soldiers. Instead, Schofield charged, Sigel merely repelled a few irregular attacks "which he did with perfect ease whenever they ventured to make them."[37] Even if Schofield underrated the fighting abilities and determination of the Confederates, it seems clear that Sigel could have done better at Carthage. Nevertheless, sympathizers eager for ethnic military success turned that day into a splendid strategic victory and proclaimed Sigel their hero. Notwithstanding Sigel's underperformance, some immigrant officers exhibited great skills at Carthage, like Captain Adolf Dengler, whose Company G of the 3rd Missouri Infantry together with others stood valiantly against several enemy attacks. Likewise, the experienced German artillery constantly demonstrated their superior effectiveness and, according to Johann Buegel, taught the southerners "great respect for our guns."[38]

Soon after these first battles in the West, the enlistment terms of the three-month volunteers ended and Sigel had to persuade many of the soldiers not to leave and return home in the midst of the campaign against Price. However, several hundred men departed and the federal regiments contained a good number of raw and untrained recruits when the two armies met again in August. In the first significant battle in the western theater of the war at Wilson's Creek, Lyon attacked McCulloch and Price in an unfortunate split of forces, which led to Union defeat and the general's death. Although heavily outnumbered again, Lyon's reckless plan of battle called for a two-pronged simultaneous assault from north and south. On August 9, Sigel and Lyon attacked. Sigel commanded the 3rd and 5th Missouri Infantry regiments under Lieutenant Colonel Anselm Albert and Colonel Salomon together with six pieces of artillery and two companies of regular cavalry. After initial federal success on both fronts the tables turned, partly due to a mistake by Sigel who mistook advancing Confederates for Lyon's troops and allowed them to counterattack at close range. Already exhausted by the preceding march, Sigel's recruits were not able to stem the assault and broke in confusion.

Meanwhile, Lyon had begun his part of the battle. The partly German 1st Kansas Infantry together with the 1st Missouri attacked McCulloch's much stronger force and stood their ground "steadfastly under an uninterrupted and murderous fire of artillery and infantry," according to the Kansans' commander. To reinforce these regiments, Lyon personally led the 2nd Kansas into battle when he was shot and killed by snipers. Finally, the Union troops had to give in to the enemy's strength and "retired from the field in good order, preceded by the ambulances containing our wounded." Always in the center of action, the First Kansas lost almost 300 men and officers, many of them from a company of German Turners. Still, as their commander lauded, the regiment "maintained every ground assigned it, without once turning its back upon the foe, for the five long hours during which the battle raged."[39]

Three weeks after their first victorious battle in Virginia, the Confederates could celebrate another success in Missouri. Adding to his criticism of Sigel's action at Carthage, Schofield censured the German for the "mixture of glory, disgrace, and disaster" at Wilson's Creek because he had not come to Lyon's assistance. The battle of Wilson's Creek established well-founded criticism of Sigel's abilities as a field commander. Although highly biased and at times resentful toward Sigel, whom he blamed indirectly for having caused Lyon's death, Schofield was quite accurate in his judgment of Sigel's qualifications as well as his faults. Acknowledging the forty-eighter's talents as a military scholar, Schofield later testified that he had witnessed several instances where Sigel had failed to exert strict authority and instill the necessary discipline among his men. "General Sigel," he wrote, "in point of theoretical education, is far above the average of commanders in this country. He has studied with great care the science of strategy, and seems thoroughly conversant with the campaigns of all the great captains, so far as covers their main strategic features, and also seems familiar with the duties of the staff, but in tactics, great and small logistics, and discipline he is greatly deficient." These defects in practical leadership abilities, Schofield argued, not only caused lack of discipline among his ethnic soldiers, but also made "it absolutely impossible for him to gain the confidence of American officers and men, and entirely unfit him for a high command in our Army."[40] Sigel would see even worse criticism, even though German-Americans firmly backed their hero and rejected such charges as unfounded nativist prejudice.

Hotly contested and still strongly secessionist in sentiment, Missouri remained a center of political and military unrest within the Union. Creating the Western Department in July, President Lincoln named Senator John Charles Frémont commander in St. Louis. The appointment of a political general provoked considerable jealousy among regular army officers and politicians who disliked the radical Republican. Forced to strengthen the Union's grip on the border region, however, the Pathfinder could safely rely on a dedicated part of the population in St. Louis and Missouri. Since his entry on the national political scene as the first Republican presidential candidate, Frémont had been extremely popular with German, Hungarian, and Polish immigrants who admired his steadfast opposition to slavery and his ethnic sympathies. This was their chance to prove their loyalty. "General Fremont is now the general in charge of the Western army," Jette Bruns exultantly told her brother, "and since he is here things are going differently. He is a man full of energy and without prejudice against the Germans."[41]

Personally acquainted with many immigrants, Frémont could count on experienced officers when it came to organizing an army and fortifying strategic posts. Predictably, the appointment of several Hungarians to his staff earned Frémont further defamation for purportedly fancying worthless foreigners over Americans. Among the critics was Thomas Francis Meagher, who had been offered a post on Frémont's staff. Yet Meagher refused, allegedly proclaiming that "I have no ambition to increase the catalog of blunderers and imposters."[42] Meagher's blunt repudiation shows clearly that Frémont was not equally popular with all immigrants. Still, the Pathfinder was the idol of his ethnic soldiers. "Without a doubt," Buegel told his diary, "this army could force the Confederacy west of the Mississippi to law and order within short time."[43] At any rate, Frémont was a shrewd politician who understood the power of the ethnic unionist element in Missouri and knew how to use it. It is worth noting that most of his staff members subsequently served well and disproved accusations of their worthlessness.

Frémont further split public opinion when he shocked the South—and many northerners as well—with a proclamation declaring the property of Missourians in rebellion confiscated and their slaves free. This first proclamation of emancipation in the Union made Frémont an even greater hero to forty-eighters and other immigrants opposed to slavery. The proclamation, the Indianapolis *Freie Presse* wrote, "Is to a patriotic heart what rain is to a dry garden. . . . Three cheers for Fremont!"[44] Similar reactions came from other abolitionist and Republican newspapers that celebrated Frémont's bold step and chided Lincoln for not approving it. Carl Schurz backed the decision unconditionally and saw it as an important means to swing the war in favor of the Union after Bull Run. "There is only one way to decisively turn around the whole affair," Schurz told a friend in Germany, "and that is to proclaim the freedom of all slaves. Of course this is an operation that may cause terrible consequences; it is a veritable Caesarean section—yet I do not see any other way." Hinting at Lincoln's hesitation, Schurz added, "Such a measure demands more courage and determination than the government possesses."[45] Convinced of the evil of slavery himself, Lincoln still refrained from immediate emancipation to keep the Border States from seceding. When Frémont refused to revoke the proclamation, the president annulled it personally.

Ethnic hopes were bitterly shattered when Lincoln finally gave in to mounting criticism, and the Missouri soldiers were notified "that our dear Gen Fremont was relieved of his command." Embittered, Buegel wrote that the "charge was (as rumor had it) that Gen Fremont had organized too fine an army etc. These evil tidings upset the army in such a way that many wanted to throw away their weapons and go home. So big was their bitterness."[46] Soon, radical abolitionists and immigrants all over the Union gathered to protest against Frémont's dismissal and demanded his reinstatement. Gustav Körner personally wrote a letter to Lincoln asking his friend not to abandon the general. Mass meetings that expressed ethnic sympathy with Frémont took place in St. Louis, Chicago, and other northern cities but were to no avail.[47] Major General Henry W. Halleck succeeded Frémont in St. Louis and instantly became unpopular with the immigrant communities there. When Sigel left on sick leave in December, Halleck planned to replace him because his absence caused conditions and discipline among his troops to deteriorate. No friend of foreign-born soldiers in general, Halleck considered the majority of German troops in his department "little better than armed barbarians."[48] An indignant Sigel resigned and once again German-Americans all over the Union rose in protest against this seemingly nativist discrimination, although Halleck had immediately offered to reinstate the general. Sharing the ethnic outrage, the Davenport *Demokrat* placed Sigel's qualities high above those of most American generals when it commented that "if Sigel were made head of the army, he would bring the war to a speedy end."[49] The unhappy episode of Sigel's resignation together with Halleck's strict enforcement of the Fugitive Slave Law of 1850 and his order to summarily eject fugitive slaves from Union territory soon worsened relations with immigrant Missourians. When the *Westliche Post* and Börnstein's *Anzeiger des Westens* still favored Frémont's emancipation plans, Halleck even tried to shut down these ethnic papers. With an unpopular general commanding in St. Louis and public criticism of Sigel's military abilities rising, German support for the Union suffered a severe blow in the West. An officer in the German 17th Missouri Infantry was positive that "If men like Fremont and Sigel had been put into places of important field commands, patriotism would not have degenerated into rheumatism, and the war would have ended before this."[50] Forty-eighter Franz Wilhelmi was one of many immigrants who thought that the Union government and the army deliberately discriminated against immigrants and purposely barred them from advancement, even though the popular general soon returned to command.

Accusations of discrimination in the army became commonplace during the Civil War. In Sigel's case—he resigned again in October 1862—personal animosities between the touchy forty-eighter and a paranoid Halleck (afraid of ubiquitous conspiracy) played probably an even bigger role than the justified doubts about Sigel's qualifications. Certainly his promotion to major general in March 1862 was a result of German-American pressure on the government more than the general's merit. But there were well-founded suspicions of discrimination against foreigners as well. A typical case was that of the 9th Illinois Infantry's commander, Lieutenant Colonel August Mersey. An excellent soldier, the former Baden officer had ably led a division in the German Revolution. In Illinois, however, the immigrant became the target of nativist politicians and officers who envied his position. Ridiculed as the "Fat Little Dutchmen" by some, Mersey was denied the rank of colonel until 1862. Eventually, he commanded a brigade and was able to prove his worth.[51] Physician Carl Uterhard put it bluntly when he wrote to his mother in 1863 that "Americans have an aversion against all Germans and neglect them everywhere." Competing with several others for the post of division surgeon, Uterhard was convinced that an American or Englishman would be appointed whereas "I, a German, will remain behind."[52] Even if Uterhard in his bitterness exaggerated the general situation of advancement in the army, educated immigrant officers indeed were often passed by when it came to promotion. In their disappointment, German-Americans sometimes received encouragement from other Europeans. Swedish immigrant Hans Mattson in a letter to his wife praised German military leadership qualities. Mattson wondered "how many victories the union troops could have counted in this war if it had not been for those much despised Dutchmen.... The great American political officers are a perfect Humbug—if the President would leave the job to some of these Dutch . . . they would have cleaned out secession long ago—but no—political favorites must have a chance to get big salaries, and stealings."[53]

The Irish also had their tragic heroes. One of them was James Shields. A veteran of the Mexican War and brigadier general of volunteers in 1861, the immigrant had seemed the first logical choice as commander of the Irish Brigade. Shields, however, declined the offer and instead vied for a major generalship, which he did not get. Irish-Americans were furious when the war department denied promotion to their meritorious fellow immigrant. Predicting a serious decline in support of the war, the New York *Irish-American* expressed severe dissatisfaction over this alleged case of discrimination in July 1862. "We believed he had attained his merited rank some months ago," the newspaper wrote on behalf of Shields, "but the announcement of this base ingratitude has almost paralyzed our confidence and enthusiasm, and suffused every Irish cheek of Iowa and the nation with a flush of indignant disgust. None have contributed more toward the number and efficiency of the Union army than the country-men and admirers of General James Shields."[54] Used to the long tradition of nativist prejudice and Know-Nothing attacks, the Irish were especially quick to suspect discrimination based on ethnicity in the army. When Meagher campaigned for the Irish Brigade in Boston, he reminded his listeners of the disbanding of the Columbian Artillery in 1855. In joining the Irish regiments, Meagher assured his countrymen, they could contribute toward overcoming nativism. The "Irish soldier will henceforth take his stand proudly by the side of the native born," Meagher called, "and tell him that he has been equal to him in his allegiance to the Constitution."[55]

Much more commonplace than the broken hopes of immigrant officers for promotion was everyday discrimination against foreign-born soldiers in mixed and predominantly native American regiments. Even if the majority of immigrants seemingly got along well with their comrades and officers, there were frequent accusations of discrimination. In August Mersey's partly German regiment, for example, immigrants complained about unfair treatment by their American officers. Although German immigrants constituted a substantial minority in the 5th and 6th Kentucky Infantry, Gottfried Rentschler noted a tendency among their officers to favor Americans in various ways. Writing to his family in March 1864, Rentschler reported that "the treatment or rather mistreatment of the Germans in the army has recently demanded the attention of the German press more than usual." Although his brigade numbered about 600 German soldiers, ethnic companies were treated differently from American ones. "If a full company is needed for some easy service, e.g., Provost-Guard," Rentschler complained, "a German company is never taken. If an entire company is required for rough service, e.g., several days or several weeks as Train-Guard, a German company will be ordered whenever possible." According to Rentschler, Germans in mixed companies had to endure the same abuse: "As a rule, the German has to wade through the mud, while the American walks on the dry road. The German is a 'Dutch soldier' and as a 'Dutchman' he is, if not despised, disrespected, and not regarded or treated as an equal." Rentschler's view was confirmed by an American in his regiment who wrote to his mother that both immigrants and native-born soldiers preferred to serve in segregated companies. Because they could not understand each other, Private Alfred Sampson argued, Germans and Americans "seem suspicious of each other. I am afraid it will be the case all through the army. I think it would be better to have them separate."[56] In accord with Sampson, immigrants in ethnic regiments or companies stressed their foreign identities by keeping up their own language and traditions. Thomas Francis Meagher explicitly set apart his Irish Brigade from the rest of the army as a model command embodying Irish glory. Similarly, Ludwig Blenker clearly defined his command as a separate German force serving alongside American regiments. He did not want anybody to mistake his "Division Blenker" for merely another American division consisting of German soldiers. Other regiments stood out visibly simply by keeping up ethnic customs. Scandinavians, for example, gathered for collective prayer meetings and cooked their traditional food just as Blenker's division baked their own German bread. Historian Ella Lonn has noted that visitors praised the French cooking in the camps of the Gardes Lafayette.[57]

Most visibly, immigrant officers in numerous cases resisted the army's customary prohibition of alcohol and openly allowed the consumption of beer and liquor in their units. Blenker officially obtained the right to allow beer in his division, while others did not even ask for such permission. General "Papa" Willich, in open defiance of temperance requirements, permitted the soldiers of his 32nd Indiana Regiment to drink beer in such quantities as to boost morale. If Willich was strictly against the abuse of alcohol and punished "habitual intoxication," other officers served as bad examples for their men.[58] Carl Uterhard noted with disgust that in his partly German regiment "everybody drinks liquor to celebrate cheerful occasions or suppress gloomy memories. It is consumed not from glasses but from bottles and a saddening drunkenness is the consequence. Dozens of officers are dismissed from the service dishonorably every day in our army because they got drunk madly." The immigrant went on to relate that "an otherwise able and worthy officer" had been recently dismissed, "a Bavarian named Brunner who, after insulting our Brigadier General [Krzyzanowski], went to our Division General Schurz and told him the classical words: 'Lick my. . . .'"[59] In his memoirs David Conyngham recalled frequent and well-attended parties in General Meagher's tent, which became known throughout the Army of the Potomac. Liquor flowed freely at these occasions and their officers' drinking did not go unnoticed with the men of the Irish Brigade. Private McCarter, while sincerely devoted to Meagher as a "whole-souled and perfect gentleman," in his memoirs nevertheless included an incident revealing the general's "most unfortunate, intemperate habits." While on guard duty one night, McCarter discovered Meagher standing in front of his tent in dangerously close proximity to a blazing campfire. "He was very drunk, looked strangely wild and only prevented himself from falling down by his grasp of the center pole," McCarter wrote. The other officers in his tent, presumably drunk as well, did not make any effort to rescue Meagher from his hazardous situation. Suddenly the general let go of the pole and stumbled into the fire, saved only by the guard's quick reaction. McCarter darted toward Meagher and "with the bayonet on my musket, I stopped his progress and threw him back on the ground." General Meagher showed his gratitude by rewarding McCarter with a brand new musket the next day. McCarter added that the problem of frequent intoxication, especially among officers, "was alarmingly prevalent."[60] To his knowledge, however, it was not confined to ethnic officers. Alcohol was the curse of the Union army, and both in times of boring idleness or under extreme mental stress during battles, many an officer during the war would resort to the bottle.

Generally, many immigrants were used to drinking beer and other alcohol in larger quantities than most northerners, especially Puritan New Englanders and reformers advocating temperance. For Europeans, alcoholic beverages in reasonable quantities were part of a regular diet, according to Uterhard's professional opinion. For a nutritious diet the surgeon prescribed due variety of food including "pickles, Sourkraut, Whiskey," as well as lemons and "beer of good quality."[61] While Swedes and Norwegians were used to drinking liquor more frequently than most Americans, as invisible and largely assimilated immigrants they only rarely suffered from nativism and prejudice. It was Irish and Germans who became universally known for their drinking habits. In the camps of German, Austrian, and Swiss soldiers, festivities involving their cherished "Gemütlichkeit" necessarily included drinking alcohol. Schwerin-born Robert Rossi was content with the frequency of such celebrations in his regiment, the German 8th New York. Writing home from Blenker's camp at Hunter's Chapel in northern Virginia in February 1862, Rossi told his sister that "we had punch on Christmas and New Year's Eve and spent the evenings chatting and singing sociably." After a round through all the tents toasting the New Year, "we only went to bed around 3 A.M., every one being dutifully drunk."[62] A year later the situation was a totally different one for the members of the German New York regiments, now part of the Eleventh Army Corps. Camping in the snow on the frozen Stafford Hills north of Fredericksburg, August Horstmann described the depressing way he and his comrades had spent the holidays. Munching salted bacon and crackers, the soldiers had "no punch, no beer nor wine" to cheer up their spirits. The lack of alcoholic beverages was particularly hard for the Germans, so that even "the mutual season's greetings were suspended and most of us were rather in the mood to curse each other."[63] Another German soldier complained to the Milwaukee *Seebote* about the lack of alcoholic beverages that prevented the soldiers in his regiment from celebrating

George Washington's birthday in style. Freely combining the German way of having fun with an American occasion, the immigrant wrote sadly that: "We must celebrate Washington's birthday dry and quietly; no beer or wine [and] be satisfied with cold, wet weather."[64] Thus, immigrant soldiers continued to conduct themselves in a way that even before the war clashed with the expectations of their surrounding society. In the army such deviant behavior was highly visible and naturally contributed to the stereotypical opinions of many Americans. Of course, not every ethnic soldier drank alcohol beyond moderation as many Americans suspected. Private McCarter's memoirs indicated that he abhorred the excessive drinking of some of his comrades and officers. A sergeant in the German 26th Wisconsin, Wilhelm Francksen had already come to America with an alcohol problem, as he admitted himself. Confronted with the almost daily chance of being killed, however, the immigrant soldier realized the danger of intoxication and told his father that "I don't even drink my usual ration of whisky, and I earnestly believe that I will have gotten over my old addiction to liquor once I am out of the military."[65] However, notable examples like Meagher, Blenker, and others outshone such exceptions.

Irish soldiers did their best to corroborate another stereotype, frequently exhibiting a fondness for brawls. Fistfights were common among the members of the "Wild Irish" 7th Missouri just as well as the "Bloody Tinth" and other regiments. Often, these clashes occurred after battles or following exhausting marches and fatigue duties when the men had to vent their frustration. McCarter recalled an episode that was typical for such heated situations. In November 1862, the 116th Pennsylvania suffered from cold, rainy weather and bad roads on the way toward Fredericksburg. One night when the fatigued men halted to set up camp, "Some few of our boys managed somehow or another by 'hook or by crook' to get away with much more than the allowed ration of whiskey this night." The consequence, McCarter explained, "was a free fight, black eyes and bloody noses."[66] In July 1863 in the trenches around Vicksburg, an American soldier witnessed a similar turbulent scene. The Irish 90th Illinois Infantry, Theodore Upson wrote, "came into camp just back of us this morning. And such a time as those fellows did have. They had got into a row about putting up their tents and had a free for all fight and were knocking each other over the head with pick handles, tent poles, or any thing they got hold of." In both cases, the officers broke up the brawls, the colonel of the Illinoisans personally dispersing the ruckus "with a great wide bladed broadsword." However, incidents like these reinforced the general picture of the Irish as unruly rowdies willing to start a fight out of nothing. The well-known facts that Irish immigrants as a whole had voted against Lincoln in 1860, and that numerous Irishmen had enlisted in the Confederate army, further worked to belittle their worth as equal citizen-soldiers in the eyes of Americans. After the Ohio Gubernatorial elections in October 1863, the commanding officer of the 67th Ohio Infantry expressed his low opinion of the Irish soldiers in his regiment. "The Irish as railroad hands are well enough," Colonel Alvin C. Voris lamented, "but as citizens they are sure to be on 'the rebellion side, by Jeazes.' The intelligent colored man is much more respectable and safe as a voter than the Irish. If I had taken a big jug of whiskey, I think I could have controlled the votes of the Irish company."[67] Confirming old stereotypes about racial inferiority, Voris would not even acknowledge the unquestionable positive label of Irish courage in battle.

When Americans stamped them with real or imagined prejudicial tags, immigrants often reacted with their own defensive stereotyping. Resorting to stubborn ethnic pride, foreign-born soldiers frequently pointed to their presumably superior qualities. Observing the daily disputes between German and American soldiers in his Kentucky regiment, Gottfried Rentschler was convinced that "the German soldier is generally far more faithful, conscientious and zealous than the native-born American. This is part of the German nature, which is our reason to be proud of our nation." Besides this patriotic devotion, Rentschler found a big difference in motivations. "The German soldier is obedient and loyal to duty without regard to reward or punishment," he declared, whereas "The American generally considers, only reward, or—The Guard-House. This is caused by the national education on either side, in the broadest sense of the word. Because of the situation as mentioned, you may possibly draw the conclusion that the mixing of Germans and Americans in the Army may be beneficial to both parties, but such conclusion is in error."[68] Referring to the reckless bravery of his ethnic comrades, an Irish soldier challenged the government to "Take the Irish for instance from the army of this union and this war perhaps will last for fifty years to come."[69]

Of course not every American scoffed at immigrants in the army, and there were particularly positive judgments about Germans and Irishmen as well. Superiors and comrades often praised Irish bravery just as they lauded German artillerists and engineers. Something everybody seems to have agreed on was the unsurpassed quality of many German regimental bands. Often recruited from singing clubs and brass bands, these orchestras lifted depressed spirits after terrible battles and lent pleasantness to many a dull evening in camp. General Joshua Chamberlain fondly remembered an occasion at his brigade headquarters: "Here at about four o'clock the fine German band of my First Brigade came over to reciprocate the smiles of heaven by choice music, ministering also to our spiritual upgoings."[70] When General Benjamin Butler inspected the 20th New York Infantry in July 1861, the Turners performed physical exercises for the general and his family before delighting them with fine musical pieces. As Butler recalled, "The melting tones of the zither rang through the air, and in the course of the evening a concert of German music entertained the guests."[71] Always ready to criticize or praise his comrades and superiors regardless of their nationality, James Sullivan recalled that along the 6th Wisconsin's march to Gettysburg the German soldiers lightened the hearts of the regiments with their singing. "We had a German Company F," the Irish sergeant wrote, "the turners, of Milwaukee, and amongst them were some very good singers, and that day they struck up a soul stirring song in German, such as only Germans can sing. I remember we all took step to the time and when they had concluded, we gave them three rousing cheers." Sullivan's Irish compatriots of Company K followed suit and in stark contrast to the Germans sang a few songs "with about as much melody as a government mule."[72]

Ethnic German pride received a major boost when Sigel finally won a celebrated victory over Price and General Earl Van Dorn in early March 1862. Following his reinstatement the forty-eighter led two divisions under Osterhaus and Asboth in Major General Sam Curtis's Army of the Southwest. As in many other western regiments Germans and Scandinavians (as well as Irish and other immigrants) made up a large portion of Curtis's army, while Sigel's divisions were predominantly German in makeup. Osterhaus's and Asboth's divisions included the reorganized 2nd, 3rd, 12th, 15th, and 17th Missouri Infantry as well as the heavily immigrant 36th, and 44th Illinois regiments.[73]

In late February, a sundry Confederate mixture of Missouri state guards, three Indian regiments, Louisiana infantry, Texas cavalry, and several other units under General Van Dorn marched against Curtis's army. Curtis positioned his force near Pea Ridge in northwestern Arkansas and waited for the Confederate attack. Gathering his forces under adverse winter conditions, Van Dorn planned to attack the federal rear at Elkhorn Tavern and at the same time McCulloch's Texans and General Albert Pike's Indians would bind Union reserves near Leetown to the northwest. Curtis ordered some of his troops including Osterhaus's division against McCulloch and Pike. Pitted against American Indians used to guerrilla tactics, Osterhaus and his troops in this battle encountered a kind of warfare entirely different from the European battlefields they had been used to. "The Indians swept forward brandishing rifles, knives, and tomahawks, while barking shrill, unearthly signals," historian Jay Monaghan has written of the savage engagement. As a result, "Osterhaus's trained infantry battalion broke and fled, some scampering this way, some that. Soon Choctaw, German, and Texan were milling in a confused and bewildering rabble, shouting, shooting, and running."[74] Trying to press forward and wipe out the enemy McCulloch was killed and his assault came to a halt. In turn, Osterhaus managed to masterfully rally his troops and succeeded in beating back the attackers. On the main front, Asboth formed his regiments along a reinforcing second line against the Confederate right wing after the first attack at Elkhorn Tavern had been fended off. Then during the night, Curtis called up Sigel's divisions to form for a counterattack on the federal right. Starting the battle in the morning, German artillerists again exhibited what they had been trained for. With an exceedingly well directed barrage the guns of Backof and another German battery from Ohio under Louis Hoffmann pounded the enemy lines and prepared a splendid charge that drove the Confederates from the field. Remaining in reserve as part of Asboth's division, the Swiss Rifles had not even received the opportunity "they so ardently longed for of following their energetic commander, Colonel Joliat, to the heart of the conflict, and of attesting by their blood their devotion to the cause."[75]

The Battle of Pea Ridge finally forced the Confederates out of Missouri and established Union dominance in the Southwest. Of course, the "German victory" won by Sigel and his ethnic soldiers became the principal issue for ethnic and Confederate attention alike. Certainly, southern dislike for the much-berated foreign hirelings did not dwindle after this decisive reverse. Following his defeat, General Van Dorn hurled bitter charges against the German soldiers. As his adjutant general wrote to General Curtis, "Many of our men who surrendered themselves as prisoners of war were reported to him as having been murdered in cold blood by their captors, who were alleged to be Germans."[76] Curtis frankly rejected these accusations, replying that "the Germans charge the same against your soldiers. . . . The Germans in the army have taken and turned over many prisoners and the general has not before heard of any murder charged against them; on the contrary they have seemed peculiarly anxious to exhibit the number of their captives as evidence of their valor."[77] This communication shows the extent to which irreconcilable hatred had mounted between immigrants and Confederates along the border. Corroborating Curtis's statement, a member of the Swiss Rifles later testified that "many of our comrades who fell dead and wounded upon the field were found to have been scalped by the Indians under command of the rebel General Pike." Maurice Marcoot, a son of Swiss immigrants from Highland, Illinois, claimed that "This discovery aroused the most bitter feelings in the ranks and loud and determined were the expressions for retaliation."[78]

Extreme brutality in words and deeds would characterize many following encounters. When a superior force of rebels attacked a foraging party of the 17th Missouri Turners and the Frémont Hussars at Searcy Landing in May, the outnumbered Germans soon had to give in and subsequently fell victim to savage treatment. As Second Lieutenant August Fischer stated in his official report, "My men continued to defend themselves until at last I saw none standing except Sergeant Schaub and myself, upon which I called to him to surrender, which I also did. My sword and revolver were then taken from me, and after having been a prisoner some five minutes I was shot in the shoulder by one of the enemy." Fischer testified that "I have seen the enemy barbarously hacking and shooting our brave wounded soldiers after all resistance on their part was impossible."[79] Finally, reinforcements came to the few survivors' rescue. Among the advancing detachment was Second Lieutenant Friedrich Martens, who later told his family about the affair. Arriving at the scene, Martens wrote, "We saw our comrades butchered, and with the battle cry 'to hell with them rascals' we assailed them." Martens hints at the atrocious retaliation they inflicted upon the Confederates when he continues, "I do not want to tell more now, you don't know how sweet revenge is, and thus you would not understand how I can excuse a retaliation as terrible as it was."[80] This totally unnecessary slaughter remained the engagement with the highest losses for the 17th Missouri during the whole war, with fifteen dead and twenty-six wounded.

While Germans still rejoiced over Sigel's triumph at Pea Ridge, Lincoln gave them even more reason for jubilation. In late March 1862, the president finally gave in to severe criticism by ethnic and radical Republican elements and reinstated John C. Frémont as commander of the newly created Mountain Department encompassing Western Virginia, Eastern Kentucky, and parts of Tennessee. Again, Frémont relied on ethnic officers and appointed several of his old Hungarian friends from Missouri as staff officers—Chief of Staff Anselm Albert, Chief of Topographical Engineers John T. Fiala, and Chief of Cavalry Charles Zagonyi. Their assistants were also Hungarians. Major Adolf C. Warberg and Captain Nordendorf came from Sweden and Chief of Artillery John Pilsen was a former officer from Austria. Former French officer Gustave Paul Cluseret was appointed aide-de-camp by Frémont.[81] Bolstering ethnic presence in the West even more, President Lincoln agreed with Frémont's request for ethnic troops and transferred Blenker's Division to the Mountain Department—against McClellan's protest.

In early March it seemed that the German Division would finally be able to show their worth when Blenker received orders to check the Confederate grip on the Shenandoah Valley under Stonewall Jackson.[82] The campaign, however, soon turned into a tragedy. Leaving their winter camp at Hunter's Chapel in Virginia on March 10, Blenker's troops hurried through hostile country on forced marches along roads soaked from terrible spring rain. Poorly supplied and fed, the regiments left numerous stragglers behind and were forced to live off the land, earning them the hatred of the Virginians. Sympathizing with the victims, a Union general stationed in Western Virginia charged Blenker's men with outrageous behavior: "The Dutch brigades are composed of the most infernal robbers, plunderers and thieves, I have ever seen," General Robert H. Milroy reported in disgust, adding that "our army is disgraced by them." Even though Milroy admitted that this plundering was caused by an extreme scarcity of provisions, he reprimanded the Germans for "leaving women and children crying behind them—but no tears or entreaties stop or affect them, the only answer they make is 'Nix forstay.' "[83] Defending the soldiers' conduct, Milroy's superior, General William S. Rosecrans, offered insight into the deplorable situation of the division on their onerous march. According to Rosecrans the soldiers were "wandering without tents, shelter, or knapsacks, with but four wagons per regiment at first. Their clothing is worn, shoes gone, no pay since December. Not much wonder they stole and robbed."[84] Rosecrans's description was realistic. Constantly harassed by bushwhackers, the soldiers had been battling their way through enemy country for over two months. "In the name of humanity" even the Mountain Department's medical director turned to the adjutant general's office for help. Brigade Surgeon George Suckley explained the catastrophic sanitary condition of the troops and reported that several hundred of Blenker's men had been left behind sick and badly exhausted. In dire need of ambulances to carry the wounded and worn out, the division had not even enough draft animals, "and of those they have and call 'horses' several are little better than living skeletons."[85] In a tragic climax to that disastrous episode, fifty-eight soldiers of the 75th Pennsylvania had drowned and died when their raft fell apart while crossing the Shenandoah River in April. Of its original strength of over 10,000, only 6,000 men were left when the division united with Frémont's army near Harrisonburg after their three months' ordeal.

Meanwhile, General Stonewall Jackson had tied down three Union armies in the Shenandoah Valley and prevented them from reinforcing McClellan in the east. Evading the federal forces several times, Jackson suddenly wheeled around at Port Republic on June 7. Having burned the bridges across the South Fork River, the Confederates left the two advancing Union armies under Frémont from the west and Shields from the east without proper communication. Forming Frémont's left wing, the German Division received its baptism of fire in the battle of Cross Keys the next day. General Stahel's First Brigade encountered General Richard S. Ewell's division around 11 A.M., well covered in a thick forest. Colonel Cluseret's leading Garibaldi Guard "drove the enemy from the woods before them and advanced against their main position," as Captain Horstmann later described the beginning of the battle. Buschbeck's 27th Pennsylvania "skirmished to the left, the De Kalb Regt NY in the center, then our 45 Regt N.Y. & on the left wing the 8 Regt N.Y. Blenker's Rifles." After this aggressive and promising start, the artillery was supposed to take up position and support the attack by pounding the enemy. However, the advancing lines soon witnessed a most bizarre scene that totally confused the situation. Without waiting for the reserve to catch up or giving the batteries time to aim their guns Colonel Franz Wutschel, who most probably was hopelessly drunk that day, prematurely ordered the Blenker Rifles to attack. The regiment sped past the skirmishers, drove in the enemy pickets, and sang folk songs while it charged into the forest. Horstmann could not believe his eyes witnessing how the 8th exposed itself in such a foolish way, until "covered behind in the woods 7 regiments of infantry welcomed them cordially in such a way that 4 regiments fired on this single one while three stood in line with fixed bayonets." The fight was brief and predictable; met by a hail of bullets Wutschel's regiment lost 220 men within a matter of minutes.

Colonel Amsberg, whose 45th New York should have led the attack according to the plan of battle, at once sent the regiment to the rescue, but "the fate of the 8 Regt was already sealed," as Horstmann noted.[86] What was left of the regiment hurried back together with the 45th, chased by the enemy's counterattack. Now General Bohlen sent his brigade, consisting of Kozlay's 54th New York together with the 74th and 75th Pennsylvania, to the field. Their advance blocked by rail fences and other obstacles, however, the regiments had to retreat before the enemy's relentless firing. Fortunately, by that time the German batteries under Schirmer and

Wiedrich had begun to sweep the battlefield and with their accurate fire succeeded in halting the Confederate offensive for some time. Meanwhile Krzyzanowski had brought up his 58th New York from the rear. The Polish commander ordered his men to keep up "a constant fire, which told greatly among the enemy's lines." When the Confederates had approached within close range, Krzyzanowski "gave the command to charge bayonets, and succeeded in driving him back about a hundred yards." This gallant charge may well have saved Frémont's army that day. Unfortunately, this federal success did not turn the battle around. Instead, Krzyzanowski reported: "To my greatest dismay I noticed at this instant two regiments coming out of the woods on the right of the enemy's battery, and having no reserve to fall back on I thought it imprudent to remain any longer, and consequently gave the command orders to retire while a heavy musketry fire was poured upon my men. I retired behind the battery of Captain Wiedrich, who now opened a heavy fire upon the enemy."[87] Coming to the rescue, von Gilsa's De Kalb Regiment and the 27th Pennsylvania under Adolph Buschbeck could not turn the battle around, either. Under the protection of the German gunners the division fell back and left the field to Ewell's southerners who crossed the South Fork and defeated Shields in the battle of Port Republic the next day.

Major Adolf Warberg was not very impressed with Frémont whom he blamed for letting Jackson's smaller army escape. On the other hand, the Swedish officer could not find enough praise for Jackson's superior skills as a general. "What a difference it was to see Jackson's troops in battle," he noted. Led by their famous commander, Warberg witnessed the southern troops "advancing with zealous enthusiasm, the most intrepid calm, completely trusting the commander who understood how to lead them."[88] In stark contrast to the federal commanders and their influence on their troops, Jackson knew exactly how to frequently change positions to keep his soldiers from overexposure to enemy fire. Warberg was amazed by Jackson's constant and irritating troop movements between the left and right wings. In contrast to Jackson's brilliant maneuvers, lack of necessary coordination was partly responsible for the Union defeat at Cross Keys. In his battle report, Captain Wiedrich gave testimony to the badly organized communication between commanders in Blenker's Division. When it had become clear that the batteries could not hold the Confederates at bay, Captain Schirmer had ordered all guns to retire. However, when Wiedrich's battery "was limbering to retire General Bohlen came up and ordered me to stay and keep up the fire, but Captain Schirmer insisted on retiring, and as I had received orders from General Blenker a few days before that all orders from Captain Schirmer should be obeyed the same as before, I withdrew with my battery, against the protest of General Bohlen."[89] General Blenker himself may have been responsible for some of the confusion on the field, as Eugen Kozlay later hinted. In his official report the Hungarian stated that "through the engagement I received a great many conflicting orders, coming from staff officers unknown to me, which I disobeyed."[90] However, most detrimental to the success of the German division was Wutschel's misconduct as commander of the 8th New York. Generally called "schnapps head" by the regiment, the Austrian forty-eighter was known to get drunk frequently. Intoxicated and worn out after the previous grueling march, Wutschel disgraced his rank and uniform in the battle by dismounting and running about behind his regiment. Lacking both dignity and leadership qualities, Wutschel even threw himself to the ground pretending to be wounded. To restore the honor of the regiment, his officers brought up formal charges against Wutschel who was dismissed dishonorably a few weeks later.

With all efforts to hunt down and destroy Stonewall Jackson's army futile, the Union forces withdrew. On June 26, President Lincoln dissolved the Mountain Department and incorporated its troops into the new Army of Virginia. This order also signaled the end of Blenker's Division, which was merged into the First Corps. His command broken up, Blenker received orders to report to Washington. He never again saw active command and was discharged in March 1863. Mentally and physically broken, the formerly dashing officer died half a year later. With all its exemplary discipline and its esprit de corps, the Blenker Division never had the chance to display its ability in battle. Blenker had never led a division before the Civil War, and he did not live up to expectations. However, all possible experience probably would not have enabled him to succeed against an adversary like Jackson. It had simply been the German's bad luck to run into the unconquerable southern general in his first and only major battle. Soon to leave western Virginia after their defeat, the soldiers in Colonel von Amsberg's 45th New York Infantry still burst with self-esteem. August Horstmann believed that "the enemy has great respect for the German soldiers, and even the farmers show up from all around to see the flying Dutchmen as they call our German division."[91] When several months later the regiment again suffered defeat by Jackson's troops, this sobriquet would take on an entirely different meaning.

SIX

TO FREDERICKSBURG:
SLAUGHTER AND GLORY

By spring of 1862, George McClellan had succeeded in forming a powerful, well-organized army full of confidence in its leader. As historian Paul Jones has put it, "McClellan convinced the Army of the Potomac that he was their man; and they were his."[1] Especially the men of Meagher's Irish Brigade, the only remaining ethnic organization left in the Army of the Potomac after the transfer of Blenker's Division, repeatedly expressed their devotion to the commander-in-chief. "Little Mac" had instilled in them and their immigrant comrades scattered by the thousands throughout the army self-confidence and the important feeling that they were making a valuable contribution to saving the country.

Still, the general had rejected repeated urges by Lincoln and others to set his force in motion and conquer Richmond. Finally, in March some 130,000 Union troops embarked down the Chesapeake Bay to the mouth of the James River from where they marched against the Confederate capital. Slowed by bad spring weather and muddy roads, the federal army approached its objective after two months, when General Joseph Johnston's Confederates attacked the leading Fourth Corps under General Erasmus D. Keyes at Fair Oaks and Seven Pines, several miles east of Richmond. Starting around 1 P.M., on May 31, the battle lasted for about five hours and forced the hard-pressed federals into a vulnerable defensive position. The roaring sound of the battle had alarmed the troops lined up to the north of the Chickahominy, and Major General Edwin V. Sumner told the brigade commanders of Richardson's Division to get ready to cross the river in the evening. This was exactly what Meagher and his Irishmen had been waiting for. Leaving behind all excess baggage the Irish Brigade moved out immediately "with unremitting celerity, ardor, and eager readiness for action." As Meagher later reported, "On the line of march we met several soldiers and other parties returning from the field of action, who informed us that the Federal arms had met with a severe reverse, and that as some New York troops were implicated it was specially incumbent on us to redeem the honor of our State and the fortunes of the day." Shortly after 9 P.M., the brigade entered the battlefield and the men were instantly shocked "by the appearance of numbers of surgeons and chaplains with lanterns in hand searching over the ground to the right and left of our advance in column for the dead and wounded, who they said were scattered in every direction around." While Meagher's surgeons and chaplains assisted in caring for the wounded, the officers and men stacked their arms and settled down for a short night, anticipating a Confederate attack the next morning. At 4 A.M., on June 1, scouts discovered two Confederate brigades approaching through the woods surrounding Meagher's troops on the federal left flank. The 69th and 88th New York Regiments were "under arms and ready for action the same hour" and after a hasty breakfast of hardtack and water lined up for battle. Shortly after, General Sumner rode up and addressed the men with few encouraging words. Speaking from Meagher's heart, the corps commander told the Irish soldiers "that they had been held back ever since they joined the service, but now their time had come."[2]

The advancing troops were those of General James Longstreet who expected to attack the seemingly exposed vulnerable flank of Keyes's corps, but instead hit Sumner's fresh division. After some skirmishing the battle started in earnest. For one and a half hours the opposing forces exchanged musket volleys at close range, inflicting heavy casualties on both sides. Colonel Paul Frank's German 52nd New York Infantry stood in the first line and bore the first impact of the Confederate assault. His report gives evidence of the fierce fighting his regiment had to stand on that morning. "About 7 o'clock A.M., the Third Georgia Regiment came up in line of battle, in four ranks, as near as from 15 to 20 paces (the woods being too thick to allow a proper aim at a farther distance), when I gave the command 'Fire by file,' the fire from both sides continuing about fifteen minutes." Immediately after the Georgians had retired, a North Carolina regiment came up and took their position. The murderous fire at close distance continued for another thirty minutes until the enemy fell back. There was no time for rest, though. Soon after an Alabama regiment formed in front of the Germans, when suddenly enemy fire hit them from behind. The rebels had broken through the federal line to their left and threatened to envelop Frank's regiment. To save the line, Major Carl Freudenberg fell back with a part of the regiment and succeeded in driving back the attackers. As Frank recalled, the engagement "with the Third Alabama lasted about one hour. Seeing that my left was exposed and entirely unprotected for the moment I advanced in line of battle within about 30 paces from the end of the woods, this movement enabling me to see all the movements of the enemy before they entered the woods, at the same time keeping my men under cover."[3] Frank's Germans managed to fend off yet another attack, while Meagher's two regiments formed in line of battle to relieve the exhausted troops. After four relentless hours in action, the soldiers of the 52nd New York had only a few rounds left when Colonel Frank finally gave orders to withdraw.

At the head of the 69th New York Infantry Meagher now took over. The regiment maintained its ground against further enemy assaults without faltering and Meagher later commended the "incomparably cool" conduct of his soldiers. "The officers and men," he wrote in his report "stood and received the fire of the enemy whilst they delivered their own with an intelligent steadiness and composure" that would have done credit to more seasoned veterans. Standing prominently by the regimental colors, Colonel Nugent bravely led his regiment and inspired his men as he "over and over again repeated the order to fire on the enemy."[4] Finally, the Confederates ceased their attacks and fell back. The Irish had saved the day with their gallant resistance and had laid the foundation for their future fame. However, victory had come at terribly high cost. Over 5,000 Union soldiers and officers had been killed, wounded, or captured, while Confederate casualties amounted to over 1,000 more, by far surpassing those of Bull Run on both sides. Overwhelmed by these numbers, Colonel Frank found it necessary to mention the services of Assistant Surgeon Rappold, "the only regimental surgeon present, who distinguished himself highly, attending to his duties under the heaviest fire and caring for the great number of wounded transferred to the hospital." Likewise, Meagher would not close his report without mentioning the unremitting efforts of his surgeons "even in the very heat of the conflict, and whilst it was dangerous for them to discharge their duties." Always the refined gentleman, Meagher added that "It is a source to me of the greatest satisfaction that the brigade which I have the honor to command can reckon with confidence on the services of such skillful, daring, and intrepid surgeons."[5]

Although victorious, a hesitant McClellan failed to keep up the pressure with his superior army and instead allowed the Confederates to withdraw and reorganize. As a consequence, the Union commander soon experienced the daring aggressiveness of his new adversary. After Johnston had been wounded in battle, General Robert E. Lee took command of the Confederate forces around Richmond, now called the Army of Northern Virginia. Although outnumbered, Lee decided to throw the northerners out of his home state and in a series of battles forced McClellan to fall back south to his new base of operations at Harrison's Landing on the James River. Lee found a congenial partner in General Stonewall Jackson, who had hurried his army east to Richmond after his dazzling successes in the Shenandoah. During the following Seven Days' Battles, General Jackson relentlessly harassed the retreating Union army's flank, several times threatening to break and rout the enemy. It was in these battles that the men of the Irish Brigade and their comrades in the Irish 9th Massachusetts finally established their enduring fame for reckless bravery and unflinching persistence even in the hottest of actions.

After two defensive battles at Oak Grove and Mechanicsville, Lee struck McClellan's army again on June 27 at Gaines's Mill. The 9th Massachusetts under its able Colonel Thomas Cass, together with two other Union regiments, took the full blow of Confederate General A. P. Hill's attack on their corps in the rear of the army. After preventing the enemy from crossing the Chickahominy in a fierce exchange of musket fire, the 9th fell back when the Confederates crossed at another ford. With Jackson's Virginians arriving on the scene, the Confederates attacked again along the whole front and seriously threatened the Union's right flank under General Fitz-John Porter. Reinforced by the nonethnic 29th Massachusetts Infantry, Meagher's brigade was encamped at Fair Oaks Station and had not yet participated in the battle. Now the Irish were ordered to aid their hard-pressed comrades together with another brigade under General French. Crossing the Chickahominy, they encountered Union soldiers who had deserted their ranks and fled in panic from Jackson's assault. Recognizing that this collapse might endanger the whole army, French ordered Meagher to deploy a company "and with fixed bayonets to drive back the runaways." While Captain Felix Duffy stemmed the wave of fleeing soldiers, the rest of the Irish Brigade steadily advanced against the enemy. Again the 69th and 88th New York formed the first line, with the 63rd New York and 29th Massachusetts following close behind. Hindered by the disorderly retreat of federal soldiers and constantly fired upon by Confederate artillery, the Irishmen nevertheless "preserved an unwavering and undaunted front" that eventually thwarted the Confederate attack.[6] Meagher's brigade and the 9th under Cass had contributed more than their fair share in saving the Army of the Potomac from a severe thrashing, but again at appalling costs. Listed in Fox's register of the bloodiest battles, Gaines's Mill cost the 9th Massachusetts 231 men and officers, among them six line officers killed.

Lee continued to push his enemy southward, although McClellan could score defensive victories at Savage Station and White Oak Swamp on June 29 and 30. The final battle of the Peninsula Campaign took place at Malvern Hill where the Confederates made a last attempt to strike at the retreating federal army. However, the Army of the Potomac occupied a strong defensive position on high ground surrounded by swampy marshland and buttressed it lining up some 250 cannons. When the Confederate vanguard came into range on July 1, this artillery phalanx opened up a momentous bombardment that entirely prevented Lee from bringing to bear his field guns. In the unfolding battle several desperate Confederate attacks failed, thanks in part to the gallant fighting of Irish and German soldiers. Part of General Samuel Heintzelman's Third Corps, the 7th New York Infantry had not seen much service during the preceding battles. Leaving their camp at Savage Station late on June 30, the Steuben Rifles marched through the muddy White Oak Swamp and arrived at Malvern Hill the next morning. Near Nelson's Farm at the federal right flank, Colonel Georg von Schack formed his regiment in line of battle to cover the Union batteries stationed there. Around 5 P.M., then, the Germans and two other regiments of their brigade received orders to march to the front, where they engaged the Confederates heavily for two hours. Impressed by his troops' steadfastness on that day, brigade commander General John C. Caldwell later testified that "these regiments fought till every round of ammunition was exhausted, and then stood without flinching the fire of the enemy when unable to return it." Caldwell did not forget to mention Colonel von Schack and his Major Friedrich Gaebel who "behaved with great coolness and gallantry."[7]

The men of the Irish Brigade, like their German comrades, had endured an equally strenuous night march and were glad to get some rest behind the guns lined up at Malvern Hill. Thrown into battle at the center of the Union front in the late afternoon, Meagher's regiments marched forward in the usual order with the 69th and 88th New York Infantries in the van. "The advance of the regiments," Meagher reported, went on "with a rapid step, displaying their colors," and their movement "was marked by an alacrity and enthusiasm which found their expression in vehement cheers, which had the effect of rallying several fragments of regiments that had, after bravely sustaining themselves under an overpowering fire, been forced to retire from the front."[8] Reportedly, one Confederate officer groaned upon discovering the advancing Irish Brigade, "Here comes that damned green flag again."[9] Soon after, the 69th hit the enemy and immediately began to pour "an oblique fire upon them with a rapid precision and an incessant vigor which had the effect of almost instantly staggering and silencing for some moments a fire which seemed to be almost overwhelming." While the supporting two regiments protected nearby artillery, Colonel Nugent and Major James Quinlan's Irishmen exchanged unrelenting fire with the Confederates until after nightfall. Then, lack of ammunition and exhaustion forced Meagher to call back his brigade. Luckily, their enemies had enough as well and ceased fire around 9 P.M., so that the northerners could retreat "despite of the fatigue and excitement they had undergone, in high confidence and spirits."[10] At about the same time, Schack received orders to withdraw from his position at the right flank after his regiment had stood its ground for two hours without ammunition. Falling back to Nelson's Farm, the Germans marched on to Harrison's Landing where McClellan gathered his army. Also straggling in came the men of the 9th Massachusetts after the loss of Colonel Cass who had been mortally wounded that day. In one of the sadly ironic situations of the war, the most violent fighting had again occurred between the men of the Irish Brigade and their fellow immigrants in the Louisiana Tigers.

By the time McClellan reached safety under the heavy navy guns at Harrison's Landing, the Army of the Potomac had suffered some 10,000 casualties. Lee, whose losses amounted to twice that number, withdrew to Richmond after he had won his first important strategic victory that had saved the Confederacy. German and Irish regiments had proved their worth in battle, but ethnic support for the war had begun to wane during the grueling campaign. Irish newspapers were quick to criticize the appalling losses and point to the fact that Meagher's regiments had been thrown into almost every battle, while other brigades had stood by idly. In fact, the Irish Brigade had suffered terribly, losing some 20 percent of its original strength due to battle casualties and illness on the fatiguing marches. Always at the center of action, the 69th New York lost over 455 men and officers out of their original strength of 750. General Meagher subsequently went to New York to recruit for his brigade, but he had to face severe criticism from the home front for having slaughtered his troops.

The Union artillery had demonstrated its superior skills and the firepower on the Peninsula that would become an indispensable asset of the federal armies in the ongoing war. Just as they had in Missouri, German and other ethnic batteries contributed substantially to the dominance of this branch. The German 1st New York Battalion of Light Artillery under forty-eighter Major Albert Arndt was one of those units that played a prominent part during the Seven Days' Battles. Still this supremacy on the battlefield was not there from the beginning, and the vital cooperation of infantry and artillery developed only slowly. Wilhelm Albrecht, who had so little confidence in his officers, knew from his military education in Germany that the infantry had to protect the movements of the batteries, which otherwise could not escape fast enough in case of a counterattack. Serving in one of Arndt's batteries, Albrecht witnessed how regiments retreated without orders several times and left their vulnerable artillery behind. In the battle of Gaines's Mill, Albrecht later remembered, panicking federal soldiers fled to the rear through the lines of the artillery and left the guns "defenseless and exposed to the thickest infantry fire." The men endeavored to mount their guns and retreat under hails of bullets, but Albrecht was sure that "we would not have gotten far if not the few brave Zouaves had returned and thrown themselves against the enemy after they had realized the danger we were in." Less fortunate than the Germans, "The batteries to the right and left were taken while we were lucky to escape."[11]

While McClellan had failed to conquer Richmond and end the war, things had gone decidedly better for the Union in the West. In February, a rumpled general from Illinois with his Army of the Tennessee had brilliantly taken strategic Forts Henry and Donelson on the Tennessee and Cumberland Rivers. True to his motto to never let his enemy pause and recover, Ulysses S. Grant pressed on along the Tennessee after the retreating Confederates, securing Kentucky for the Union. Meanwhile, however, a newly organized Confederate army under General Albert Sidney Johnston moved north from Corinth, Mississippi, against Grant's advancing forces. In the early morning of April 6, Johnston hit the completely unsuspecting Union troops like a lightning bolt at Pittsburgh Landing. Two Union divisions under Generals William T. Sherman and Benjamin M. Prentiss took the first blow; the rebel onslaught routed and drove back both divisions for about two miles before officers succeeded in regrouping their regiments and forming defensive lines. Although taken by surprise, some regiments managed to withstand the poorly coordinated Confederate assaults with extraordinary bravery. Swedish Colonel Oscar Malmborg commanded the partly ethnic 55th Illinois Infantry, exposed to the attack in the very first line of Sherman's Division. Resisting gallantly for two hours before they had to fall back for lack of ammunition, Malmborg's men suffered more than eighty casualties. When his brigade commander was wounded, Malmborg took over and finally succeeded in forming a strong defensive line, organizing some 3,000 men from various regiments. Colonel David Stuart later expressed his obligation to the Swedish professional, "whose military education and experience were of every importance to me. Comprehending at a glance the purpose and object of every movement of the enemy, he was able to advise me promptly and intelligently as to the disposition of my men. He was cool, observant, discreet, and brave, and of infinite service to me."[12]

Crucial to the federal defense was a spot at the center of the heaviest fighting, called the Hornets' Nest. Arriving on the battlefield and personally rallying his troops, Grant ordered Prentiss to hold that position at all cost, while the rest of the army slowly retreated toward the river. In an effort to relieve Sherman and Prentiss, General John McClernand had already brought up his First Division from the rear. With two senior officers absent, the general passed command of the Third Brigade to Colonel Julius Raith who was just forming his 43rd Illinois Infantry to attack. "Although thus unexpectedly called upon to assume the functions of brigade commander," McClernand reported later, Raith at once took to "forming the line of battle in the face of an overwhelming foe." Reaching Shiloh Church, the whole division was soon engaged in the most murderous battle raging back and forth. Leading his brigade with "coolness, courage, and skill," Colonel Raith received a mortal wound "while encouraging his men by his heroic and daring example." McClernand's troops pressed on, while artillery fired with such vehemence that "Trees of considerable size were cut off or scathed by the round shot of opposing batteries." Although the division succeeded in wresting some ground from the enemy, McClernand soon discovered that the forward thrust had left his flank vulnerable. Without proper support on the left and outflanked on the right, McClernand decided to fall back under constant infantry and artillery fire to save his division from being surrounded. Unfortunately, the order did not reach Lieutenant Colonel Adolph Engelmann, who had taken over the Körner Regiment from Raith. Thus, unaware of the general backward movement, Engelmann's "gallant regiment still continued the conflict until it was surrounded, and cut its way through the enemy to the right and rear of my third line."[13]

Eventually, the federals could fortify their positions at the river landing under protection of heavy siege guns and the Union river fleet's gunboats. General Prentiss's division gallantly held the Hornet's Nest with high losses until he finally had to surrender in the late afternoon. Immediately before, Lieutenant Wilhelm Pfänder with his German veterans of the 1st Minnesota Battery had daringly saved several field guns from falling into enemy hands. Reinforced by General Don Carlos Buell's

Army of the Ohio, rushing to the scene from the other side of the river, the federal line never broke. General P. G. T. Beauregard, who had taken Confederate command after Johnston had been killed in the afternoon, reorganized his scattered troops, but it was too late for a second attack. Equally decimated and exhausted as Grant's men, the Confederates settled for a cold and rainy night continuously shelled by the Union artillery. The battlefield was strewn with dead and wounded, and soldiers on both sides could hear the moans of their countless injured comrades all through the seemingly endless night. One of the wounded was Dresden-born Private Paul Petasch of Malmborg's 55th Illinois, who received a bullet in his right knee and "lay on the battlefield without help for 36 hours."[14] Recovered from the field and brought to a hospital in Evansville, Petasch died a month later of typhoid. This single day had destroyed every idealistic notion about the war any soldier might still have harbored. Americans and immigrants alike had realized that war was hell and nothing else.

With Buell's fresh troops bolstering his front, Grant set out on Sunday morning, April 7, to retake the lost ground from the outworn enemy troops. Led by August Willich, the 32nd Indiana Infantry marched to glory that day. Arriving at Pittsburgh Landing with Buell's army, Willich was among the first to reach the field and take position for the attack. As his brigade commander later reported, "Nothing further was heard from him by me during the day, but his list of casualties shows that he was hotly engaged, and the testimony of distinguished officers, who witnessed the conduct of his command, justifies me in saying that officers and men gave proof of skill and courage worthy the heroes" of Indiana.[15] Indeed, Willich had not received specific orders as to where he should join in the Union attack that had already driven back the enemy lines to the Peach Orchard. There, Beauregard's troops had managed to reorganize and bring the northern offensive to a halt. "The regiment marched as fast as possible," Willich described their situation, and simply "took its course to the heaviest firing." Filing up behind the second line of battle, the forty-eighter noticed that despite heavy fighting, neither party was advancing or retreating. Eager to take the initiative, Willich obtained the commanding general's permission "to pass with the regiment to the front and make a bayonet charge." Advancing against Confederates led by Beauregard personally, Willich's Germans saved the day when they charged in closed ranks and at the point of the bayonet "succeeded, after short and heavy firing, to check the enemy's advance till reenforcements came up." Supported by most destructive artillery fire, the Union troops now fell on both flanks of the enemy, and finally "the whole of our force advanced again and threw the enemy back finally."[16] Having turned the battle, the 32nd Indiana's heroic charge was lauded by other commanders, among them the colonel of the 11th Indiana, whose front had just threatened to break. "Fortunately, and much to our relief," Colonel McGinnis testified, "at this critical moment the Thirty-second Indiana, Colonel Willich, came up on our left, and with their assistance the advancing enemy was compelled to retire."[17]

Finally, without much needed reinforcements, Beauregard found his fatigued army outnumbered and had to break off the battle.

It had been the bloodiest battle thus far on American soil. The Union victory drove the Confederates back to Corinth, while Grant had little more than regained his old positions after two days of most desperate fighting. Magnus Brucker served as surgeon in the nonethnic 23rd Indiana Infantry, participating in the counterattack on the second day in General Lew Wallace's division. Telling his family that "our division fought splendidly," Brucker wrote that while he was tending to the wounded on the field, "the bombs flew and whirled over my head, musket fire was heard all day like hail crackling on shingles; the battle was fought with the utmost exasperation on both sides."[18] The inconceivably high casualties at Shiloh also compelled August Achenbach, who had traveled to the battlefield and attended to the wounded, to enter the Union army and defend his country. Together with the other regimental surgeons, Achenbach and Brucker had a tremendous task to fulfill; the Union losses amounted to 13,000 killed, wounded, and missing, while the southerners had lost 10,700 men and officers. Brucker estimated that he alone cared for 400 soldiers during and after the battle, many of them Germans of the 32nd Indiana Infantry.

Among the largely inexperienced troops that faced the similarly green Confederates, several ethnic and partly ethnic regiments had distinguished themselves at Shiloh. Besides Engelmann's and Malmborg's soldiers, the 57th Illinois suffered badly in the afternoon of the first day, its Swedish Company from Bishop Hill losing sixteen men in the steadfast defense of the federal positions. As part of Buell's army, the 6th Kentucky with its four German companies participated in the initial attack on the second day and threw the Confederates back across a wheat field until stopped by superior enemy numbers. Soon caught in devastating crossfire, the regiment lost badly in their gallant charge. The partly German 9th Illinois Infantry under forty-eighter August Mersey participated prominently on both days of the battle and suffered the heaviest loss of any regiment in that battle. Part of General W. H. L. Wallace's Second Division, Mersey and his men fought the Confederate onslaught on the Union left near the river on Sunday morning, holding their ground for one and a half hours. Running out of ammunition and reduced to about half their strength, Wallace ordered Mersey "to retire to our camp, replenish the cartridge-boxes, clean the guns, and be in readiness for action as speedily as possible." In the afternoon then, the 9th was ordered to assist Sherman's division. "Here we again entered action," Mersey wrote after the battle, "our regiment numbering about 300 men, and for about an hour aided in checking the advance of the enemy's force, disputing the ground inch by inch, until compelled to retire on account of a flank movement of the rebels and a destructive artillery fire, in all which the enemy suffered terribly."[19] On Monday, the remainder of the regiment was stationed as reserve and order to enter the battlefield around 4 p.m. Fortunately, the enemy had already retired from their section of the front and Mersey's men were spared another bloody engagement. The 9th Illinois lost 61 killed, 300 wounded, and 5 missing out of 578 men present, according to Fox "the greatest loss in killed and wounded sustained by any infantry regiment during the war."[20]

Shiloh proved even to western soldiers hostile to subordination that discipline was paramount to military success. Losing almost 200 men and officers in its desperate break through the enemy lines, the 43rd Körner Regiment could only prevail in this situation through strict discipline and order in the ranks. Probably the most stunning feat of preserving discipline in battle was performed by "Papa" Willich who never lost control over his unconditionally loyal men. Rushing toward their enemies in the final charge, Willich found his soldiers firing prematurely from too great a distance where they could not do any damage. Consequently, the resolute professional officer "stopped the firing and practiced them in the manual of arms, which they executed as if on the parade ground, and then reopened deliberate and effective fire."[21] Such cold-blooded behavior in front of the enemy lines left a deep impact on friends and foes alike, and officers in Grant's army acknowledged the valor and skills of their immigrant comrades. Grieving over the loss of Julius Raith, McClernand promised that this "honored martyr in a just cause, will be mourned by his friends and adopted country."[22]

While Beauregard retreated south, the Union scored an even more important victory when another northern "fighting general" took New Madrid and Island No. 10. The capture of these strategic points by General John Pope opened the Mississippi all the way to Fort Pillow. Several western regiments in Pope's Army of the Mississippi distinguished themselves during this significant campaign, including Colonel Heg's 15th Wisconsin Infantry. The Scandinavians also played a major role in the subsequent capture of the strategic railroad hub of Union City east of the river in Tennessee. Because Confederate reinforcements could still be hauled through that supply center and threaten the federal grip on the Mississippi, Colonel Napoleon Bonaparte Buford set out to occupy the city and remove that menace. Apart from his own partly German 27th Illinois Infantry, Buford's brigade consisted of Heg's regiment, some cavalry, and Major Stohlbrand's Swedish Battery G of the 2nd Illinois Light Artillery. Still suffering from a concussion, Stohlbrand nevertheless followed his battery commanded by Captain Frederick Sparrestrom, "full of enthusiasm." Nearing the rebel camps outside Union City, the Illinoisans swiftly formed into line of battle and cleared a passage for Sparrestrom's guns. While Colonel Heg deployed his men to the flank to check approaching enemy cavalry, Sparrestrom wheeled his guns up a hill overlooking the camps and opened fire. Completely surprised, the rebel infantry had no time to form and gave up the city in a hurry. "The whistle of the departing engine was heard," Colonel Buford summed up the spectacle, "leaving three cars at the depot, and the stampede of infantry, cavalry, loose horses, and citizens was complete. The artillery moved forward, and the cavalry and infantry marched into the camps." In his report Buford, soon to be appointed brigadier general, spoke highly of his largely ethnic troops who had been "confined for fifteen days on the transports near this place; they marched 30 miles in a little less than twenty-four hours; they slept on the ground; they made no fire; they respected all private property; they obeyed all my orders with cheerful alacrity." Proudly, the Union commander closed, "When did troops behave better? They made but one complaint, and that was that the enemy would not stand. . . . With such troops any commander would feel sure of victory."[23]

After Shiloh, Grant moved south to conquer Corinth and Memphis, while a Union fleet under intrepid Admiral David Farragut took New Orleans. By late April the Union was near its war aim of controlling the Mississippi River and splitting the Confederacy in two. In desperate need of similar success in the East, President Lincoln relieved McClellan and made Pope commander of the newly created Army of Virginia. An infuriated Frémont immediately declared that he would not serve under Pope who was nine years his minor. Frustrated with Frémont, Lincoln removed the Pathfinder and conferred command of the First Army Corps on Franz Sigel, a major general since February. Placing the heavily immigrant corps under ethnic command was a significant decision, because it now could increase its visibility even more. By promoting Carl Schurz to brigadier general in April, Lincoln finally gave the ethnic leader the field command he had wanted since the beginning of the war. The First Corps now consisted of three divisions under General Robert C. Schenck from Ohio, General Steinwehr who had risen from brigade command in Blenker's Division, and newly appointed Carl Schurz. The regiments of the old Division Blenker now were scattered all over the First Corps. Ironically, General Milroy who had expressed so little sympathy for Blenker's Germans now led a brigade in their corps.[24] Unfortunately, Sigel's force, later renamed the Eleventh Corps und put under Schurz's leadership, would eventually hurt the image of German-American soldiers much more than they fairly deserved.

In August then, self-possessed John Pope suffered a humiliating defeat when Stonewall Jackson beat his army at exactly the same place where the first battle of Bull Run had taken place a year before. Convinced of his superiority, Pope believed Jackson to have retreated before his show of force and on August 29 sent Sigel's corps against the enemy at the Warrenton Turnpike. However, Jackson's troops were well prepared for battle and awaited the federal attack. Despite later claims of ineptitude, Sigel led his corps ably and gained initial success against Jackson's battle-hardened Virginians. Schimmelfennig's brigade even overran the famed "Stonewall Brigade" and pushed it beyond Cushing's Farm. Here, Major Franz Blessing's spearheading 74th Pennsylvania, together with the nonethnic 61st Ohio Infantry, was dangerously outflanked by the enemy, and "under a galling fire of grapeshot and canister, the regiment had to leave its position, which it did by making a flank movement to the left, forcing the enemy to withdraw from the woods." Retreating slowly before Confederate artillery and a counterattack by Jackson, the German regiments nevertheless had been able to wrest considerable ground from the enemy, and officers and men were sure to have won a victory that day. "Wearied and exhausted," Blessing reported, "we camped for the night on the same ground the enemy held the night previous." However, while Jackson received reinforcements from Longstreet and set up formidable defensive lines for the following day, Union commanders Fitz John Porter and McClellan would not cooperate with Pope out of disgust and hurt pride. Bravely attacking again on August 30, Sigel's isolated corps eventually could not prevail against Longstreet's fresh forces. Although exposed "all day to a tremendous shower of bomb-shell, canister, &c.," Blessing and his men still determinedly contested their ground and did not fall back "until the order for general retreat was given."[25] With Sigel's corps covering the beaten Army of Virginia against Longstreet's counteroffensive, Pope had to withdraw across the Bull Run to Centreville. In its first major engagement the "Dutch Corps" had demonstrated that it could fight and hold its own on the field, although the different attacks had not been well coordinated. The First Corps lost a total of 2,000 officers and men on those two days, including Colonel Johann Koltes who fell at the head of his brigade in an attack against enemy artillery.

Nobody could earnestly claim that the battle's outcome was the First Corps's fault. While ethnic papers praised Sigel's conduct and the near-victory of his soldiers, Americans were reluctant to agree because the troops had not been able to exploit their early success on the battlefield. However, the fact that several supporting commanders, among them General Phil Kearny, had failed to reinforce Sigel did not receive much public attention. Not surprisingly, many immigrants afterward grumbled about treachery on the part of American generals and ongoing discrimination against the German regiments. Lieutenant Cornelius Knoebel had stood in the thickest fight with his 74th Pennsylvania and told his family about the "long, hot battle" in which "under the command of General Sigel we beat back the enemy under much heavier losses that we had to endure ourselves. The dead enemy soldiers lay piled up on the battlefield." Even though the troops "commenced the battle again with fresh vehemence" the next day, a disgruntled Knoebel insisted that "we were beaten by treason and had to retire." Defiantly, German Americans rallied behind their idol and in turn accused the Americans of having abandoned the field in cowardice. John Dieden sent his cousin a newspaper article including an illustration of "General Franz Siegel [sic], as he personally leads a bayonet charge against the on storming rebels on the Second Bull Run battlefield, while the whole Union army is fleeing."[26]

Critical as always of poor military leadership, James Sullivan of the Iron Brigade backed the forty-eighter against Pope. "During the sixty days that Pope was in command," the Irish veteran was convinced, "the army had one uninterrupted series of disasters, and although they fought well and lost heavily, there was no talent to direct the men." Alluding to the mutual indictments after the battle, the Irish soldier in his memoirs told a story that probably did not happen but nevertheless could have been true given Sigel's irritable temperament. "It was said, but I did not see it," Sullivan writes, "that Pope, McDowell and Sigel quarreled on the battle-field, and that Sigel drew his pistol to shoot Pope, calling him a cowardly ignoramus, who was not qualified to hold the rank of corporal." Already before the battle, according to the Irish volunteer, Sigel had been "the only corps commander that had the confidence and respect of the men, for they believed he would fight."[27]

Throughout the rest of the year the renamed Eleventh Corps remained in the defenses of Washington around Centreville. Through frequent inspections and a close contact with his soldiers, Sigel maintained strict discipline and even won the respect of non-German soldiers under his command. One of them was Irish William McCarter, whose newly organized 116th Pennsylvania was temporarily attached to the "Dutch Corps" for some weeks before it became part of the Irish Brigade in October. McCarter had the chance of observing the general on several occasions and described Sigel as a typical "short, stout and healthy" German who had every regiment in his command "under strict military discipline." Most notably, McCarter added, by "his manners, talk and actions" General Sigel "left the impression on the minds of all the men that he was a good, skillful officer, capable of handling a large body of troops to the greatest advantage."[28]

Again, Lincoln was in search of an effective military leader able and willing to turn the tables. After Lee put even more pressure on the Union when he carried the war north in early September, the president reinstated McClellan to check the southern invasion. McClellan was still popular with immigrant and native American soldiers alike, and the army gladly set out on the great hunt to avenge the recent disgrace under Pope. Unfortunately, "Little Mac" lost the unique opportunity to attack and crush his enemy although he knew that Lee had dangerously split his forces. Fearing a trap, McClellan hesitated and instead let his opponent choose the ground of battle at Antietam Creek east of the town of Sharpsburg. The harbingers of the ensuing battle showed in the early morning of the September 16 when the slowly approaching Union army encountered heavy artillery fire from the Confederate positions near Sharpsburg. Major Arndt speedily brought up his guns and successfully silenced the enemy batteries, but was mortally wounded during that action. The artillery shelled the rebels effectively, allowing Sumner's Second Corps to line up at the Sharpsburg Turnpike, while the rest of McClellan's army deployed to their right and left during the day. On the following bloodiest single day in American history, several ethnic regiments would make heroic stands and suffer badly in repulsing Lee's invasion.

At daybreak of the 17th, General Hooker attacked the enemy's left flank and threw back Jackson's men from a cornfield along the Hagerstown Pike. However, Confederate General John Bell Hood came to the rescue and counterattacked. While Hooker's division withdrew and federal reinforcements checked the assault of Hood's Texans, Sumner sent his brigades against the Confederate center along a depression between the Hagerstown and Boonsboro Roads called the "Sunken Road." General D. H. Hill's troops had erected breastworks from wooden fence rails atop a descending ravine and expected the attack. At around 10:30 A.M., Meagher's brigade forded

Antietam Creek and deployed in one line at the edge of a cornfield facing the Sunken Road, which would soon turn into the "Bloody Lane." Getting rid of every unnecessary baggage except their cartridge boxes, the four regiments steadily marched through the field until they reached a rail fence just 300 yards "from which the enemy were drawn up in close column, exhibiting a double front, with their battle-flags defiantly displayed." Under harassing musket fire by the rebels' advance line, the Irish soldiers crossed the fence and again regrouped to attack. Despite their discouraging situation against strong and seemingly impenetrable enemy works, Meagher reported that "the officers and men of the brigade waved their swords and hats and gave the heartiest cheers for their general, George B. McClellan." Finally after a few volleys the Irish Brigade attacked with General Meagher at the head, who would confirm that "Never were men in higher spirits. Never did men with such alacrity and generosity of heart press forward and encounter the perils of the battle-field." The Confederates withdrew their skirmishers to the Sunken Road and met the Irishmen with a murderous volley as they reached the top of the ravine. "Boys, raise the colors and follow me!" Meagher shouted, knowing that he could rely "on the impetuosity and recklessness of Irish soldiers in a charge." Pressing forward against the enemies, the leading 63rd and 69th New York regiments lost some 60 percent in the first minutes of the engagement until their advance came to a halt. Realizing that they could not take the breastworks by storm, the brigade halted and delivered volley after volley while maintaining "every inch of the ground" for almost four hours. Reduced to some 500 men, Meagher's brigade finally fell back when General Caldwell's brigade relieved their position and continued to engage the southerners along the "Bloody Lane." The 69th New York had lost eight color-bearers shot down during the fierce battle.[29]

General Caldwell's brigade, among them the 7th New York Steuben Rifles, passed the Irish Brigade and succeeded in breaking through the enemy lines by a flanking movement. Enveloping the enemies along the Sunken Road, the brigade captured 300 men and six stands of colors. Pressing on, Caldwell reported that the Germans in the heat of the battle "wavered for a few minutes, but I rallied them and led them forward in person, and during the remainder of the battle they fought with the most determined bravery."[30] Another partly German regiment exhibited less determination to fight. Attacking the enemy lines to the right of the Bloody Lane with Max Weber's brigade, the 5th Maryland Infantry came up under command of its senior Captain Ernst Fähtz after Major Blumenberg had been wounded earlier in the battle. A former Austrian officer and forty-eighter, Fähtz nevertheless was not up to the task of leading a regiment, and the Marylanders broke after the first enemy volleys. Trying to rally the regiment, General Weber was wounded and carried from the field. Meanwhile, ferocious fighting raged to the far right of Weber's brigade where Sumner's Second Division under General John Sedgwick engaged the Confederates near a small church of the German Dunker sect. There, the Irish 69th Pennsylvania Infantry under its Colonel Joshua T. Owen was part of a brigade that was gripped by the panic to their left while under "a most terrific fire of infantry and artillery." Taking command during a temporary absence of the brigade commander, Owen could not prevent the line from faltering under the unremitting shower of musketry and artillery fire. Finally General Sumner gave the order to fall back and the brigade retreated with "some confusion upon the left," as Owen admitted.[31] To the rear, the colonel restored order and positioned the brigade in support of the reserve batteries until the end of the battle. Although forced to withdraw with the rest of the brigade, the Irishmen of the 69th had fought gallantly at Dunker Church, losing in total over ninety men and officers dead, wounded, or killed.

While the battle raged back and forth around places like the Dunker Church and the Bloody Lane that gained eternal notoriety that day, General Max Weber's former regiment was on its way to make its most important contribution to the war. Now under the command of Colonel von Vegesack, the Turners were part of a division in General William B. Franklin's Sixth Corps arriving from Rohrersville during the morning. Ordered to support Sumner's troops, General William F. Smith hurried his division into battle. Vegesack with his regiment valiantly attacked and stormed the hills between the Dunker Church and Roulette House that had been taken and lost by the Union troops several times before. With the assistance of his artillery, Vegesack kept the strategic position against heaviest enemy fire for the rest of the day. Brigade commander Colonel William Irwin especially mentioned the regiment's "unyielding courage," lauding the German Turners' exceptional feat of bravery. "The firmness of this regiment deserves very great praise," Irwin expressed his respect, adding that "Colonel Von Vegesack was under fire with his men constantly, and his calm courage gave an admirable example to them. Each of their stand of colors is rent by the balls and shells of the enemy, and their killed and wounded is 145."[32] The Union attacks never succeeded in destroying the enemy lines, although they forced the Confederates to fall back from their original positions. Around 4:30 P.M., in the afternoon, General Ambrose E. Burnside started the final assault at the Union's left flank. Pushing his Ninth Corps over a stone bridge across the Antietam, Burnside drove back the enemy's right to Sharpsburg. The 46th New York Frémont Rifles under their Colonel Joseph Gerhardt firmly pressed forward in the assault, leaving behind several other regiments. Just when the Confederate lines seemed to crumble, however, a division under General A. P. Hill arriving from Harper's Ferry turned against the federal left flank and delivered a devastating blow to Burnside's divisions. Some of Burnside's troops, which had already reached the town, were captured like Colonel August Moor's 28th Ohio Infantry. Hill's last counterattack closed the battle of Antietam. Both armies lost an aggregate 26,100 dead, wounded, and missing on that terrible day. As a consequence, Lee abandoned his invasion and led his severely damaged army back to Virginia. Equally traumatized, McClellan decided not to pursue Lee and let another chance pass by to destroy his enemy, for which he earned severe criticism.

Among the ethnic troops that had fought nobly around Sharpsburg, the Irish Brigade had once more "sustained its well-earned reputation," as General McClellan put it.[33] Even retiring from the Bloody Lane the regiments had moved as steadily as on drill. Recovering from their heavy losses, Meagher's brigade was reinforced by the 28th Massachusetts and 116th Pennsylvania Infantries. As Private McCarter remembered, the members of his regiment were proud to become "a portion of the famous Irish Brigade."[34] Ethnic visibility had clearly sharpened during the first year of the war, and the Irish Brigade had already entered on its way to glory.

ETHNIC REACTIONS TO EMANCIPATION AND CONSCRIPTION

Although he had prevented Frémont from freeing Missouri slaves the previous year, by 1862 President Lincoln was determined to end slavery. To lend a proclamation of emancipation the necessary authority, however, Lincoln needed a military victory. Antietam finally provided that opportunity, even if it was a Pyrrhic victory. By announcing emancipation on September 22, Lincoln profoundly altered the character of the Civil War and turned the fight against secession into a crusade for the destruction of slavery. On January 1, then, Lincoln declared that "all persons held as slaves" in the rebellious southern states "henceforward shall be free." He furthermore decreed that blacks "will be received into the armed service of the United States," thus laying the foundation for a military organization under almost exclusively white officers that would altogether number some 200,000 men and become known as the United States Colored Troops.[35]

In the opinion of those immigrants who had long argued for emancipation, the Second American Revolution had finally begun. Carl Schurz later confessed that he had already begun to loose faith in the president, as had other radical abolitionists. Reversing this premature judgment in his memoirs, Schurz acknowledged Lincoln's opinion "that if we would fail in battle, a declaration to free the slaves would achieve just as much as an edict by the Pope against the comet." While the forty-eighter in hindsight agreed with this conclusion, he claimed that Lincoln's course "at that time seemed intolerable to the impatient enemies of slavery." Schurz admitted freely "that I myself was among this class and I did not see the wisdom of this cautious policy until it bore fruit."[36] European radicals on both sides of the Atlantic welcomed Lincoln's proclamation as a necessary radicalization of the Union's war policy. In England, Karl Marx triumphantly wrote to his friend Friedrich Engels that this declaration was "the most important document in American history since the establishment of the Union, tantamount to the tearing tip of the old American Constitution."[37] August Börnstein, son of noted forty-eighter Heinrich Börnstein and editor of the steadfastly Republican *Anzeiger des Westens*, praised the proclamation by which "Mister Lincoln has turned our Army into an armed mass migration from the North to the South and every soldier in this Army to an emancipator, to a soldier of freedom . . . If we succeed in a military victory over the South, we will destroy slavery at the same time." Börnstein, who would later command black soldiers himself as a commissioned officer in the 4th United States Colored Infantry, predicted an active role of African-Americans in their own liberation: "No longer will the Negroes simply be the subjects of debates and the cause of all our problems, but themselves participate in the fight for their freedom."[38] The *Minnesota Staats Zeitung* from St. Paul reacted similarly after Lincoln had signed emancipation into reality in January, anticipating "if not $4\frac{1}{4}$ million new Union soldiers, then still many many thousands."[39]

Other immigrants had not pressed for emancipation as aggressively as men like Schurz or Börnstein, but welcomed it with equal fervor. Appointed brigadier general a few days earlier, Wladimir Krzyzanowski declared that "My happiness at this event was doubled and tripled when President Lincoln issued a proclamation forever prohibiting slavery in America."[40] Confronted daily with slavery and pro-southern sentiment in his western Missouri home, Adolph Frick from Baden had already before the war hoped for eventual abolition. Only a few days after the proclamation, Frick jubilantly told his mother and sister of Lincoln's bold step "to suppress the rebellion with all might." The immigrant was confident that the freeing of the slaves "will certainly deliver the final blow to those [slave] states."[41] Liberal Dietrich Gerstein had always detested slavery. Now he also hoped for emancipation to add new commitment to the war. "This rebellion has to be crushed," he told his family, "even if it cost the life of the last white man in the South and the sunny South has to be settled with free colored people."[42]

Gerstein had enlisted to fight against slavery from the start while most Union soldiers, including the majority of immigrants, had decidedly not. Many of them now felt betrayed, as numerous letters and articles in ethnic newspapers show. Several Irish and some German newspapers even argued that the constitution did not back emancipation. Even worse, waging war against slavery would only serve to prolong the conflict after already two years of bloody fighting. The Illinois *Wöchentliches Belleviller Volksblatt* demanded that "reconstruction of peace should not be put at risk because of the Negro."[43] The greater part of Irish Americans closed ranks in their opposition to an "abolition war." The publisher of the influential *Boston Pilot*, Patrick Donahoe, plainly held that of all Irish soldiers, "Not one volunteer in a hundred" had taken up arms "to liberate slaves."[44] Likewise, one German sergeant in the Potomac Army told the *Deutscher Anzeiger* that he and his comrades would only fight "for the Union and its re-establishment." Certainly no one he knew had ever wanted "to let oneself be shot to death for the Niggers."[45] Never the most enthusiastic supporters of the war, many Dutch immigrants thought similarly. "I think more highly of white than of black," C. Jongewaard confided in August 1863, "and with me many are tired of this war since long, but it probably will not end before others take over the helm. They declare openly they will not stop before the last black man is free."[46]

Worn out by the incredibly high battle casualties and distrustful of unqualified military leaders, many immigrants suspected emancipation to be a pretext that shrouded other goals. A Welsh immigrant in March 1863 accused both Democrats and Republicans of betraying the Union to the South, presuming "that the leaders of the North and South have an understanding and are working together to undermine government by the people under the excuse of destroying slavery."[47] According to a German soldier in the Confederate army, many northern soldiers, who had deserted and preferred captivity, "are weary of the war and say that their whole army is demoralized and that Lincoln's Proclamation has caused uproar" among the Union troops.[48]

Never accepting emancipation and its effects, many Irish believed that Lincoln added even more insult to injury when in November 1862 he finally removed revered General George McClellan from command and replaced him with Ambrose Burnside. Camping near Warrenton in Virginia, the Irish Brigade heard of the order when General Meagher read McClellan's farewell address to the Army of the Potomac. "It created among the troops universal feelings of the most profound sorrow, sadness and gloom," William McCarter recalled in his memoirs. A few days later the army lined up for several miles along the road McClellan was to take on his way back to Washington to bid farewell to "our beloved, honored, respected and noble commander." Cannon fired salutes and "Cheer upon cheer rent the air" as the general rode by, leaving the troops in desperation after so many hard-fought battles and losses.[49] The *Boston Pilot* was infuriated that "the general who made the grand army" would not lead this army any longer. Instead, McClellan "has been removed in disgrace," the newspaper fumed, and Irish Americans would not back the continuing of the war any longer.[50] Many Irish soldiers, politicians, and clergymen lost complete faith in Lincoln after the Emancipation Proclamation and the exchange of McClellan for Burnside. Officers in the Irish Brigade offered their resignation in protest and even ethnic idols like Michael Corcoran, who had returned to the army in August, shared the prevailing dislike of Lincoln's policy. Thomas Francis Meagher did not openly criticize emancipation, but in the following he and Corcoran encountered severe difficulties attempting to inspire their fellow Irishmen to enlist for the Union cause.

Like in the rest of society, Irish support for the war finally hit rock bottom when the new commanding general sent his army head-on against Lee's impenetrably entrenched troops at Fredericksburg in December. Among the troops suffering most dearly in that senseless operation was the Irish Brigade. In an order just before the battle that soon would become famous, Meagher told his men to carry green sprigs of boxwood as an Irish symbol on their caps. Attacking the enemy lines behind an insurmountable stone wall on Marye's Heights above the town, the brigade gallantly marched forward in a battle everybody knew could not be won. In what was to become "wholesale slaughter of human beings," according to Captain Conyngham, the Irish regiments within half an hour lost all but 250 men and officers out of 1,200 engaged that day.[51] Also badly decimated were the German 7th and 52nd New York Infantries. By nightfall of December 13, fourteen Union assaults against Marye's Heights had been bloodily beaten back, and Private McCarter said that "the Army of the Potomac was a defeated, dejected and demoralized mob."[52] Sadly disappointed by Burnside's blunder, Adolf Warberg called "shame upon the general who has sullied his hands with the blood of needlessly sacrificed soldiers."[53]

While growing war weariness ruled at the home front, firsthand contact with slavery on their campaigns in the South ultimately caused a change of heart among many Union soldiers regarding emancipation. Encountering slavery was a novel experience for immigrant and native-born northerners who, until their enlistment in the army, had only known their local environments. Confronted with the inhumane treatment and the degenerating effects of slavery on southern society, numerous opponents of abolition now realized the necessity of emancipation. A Dutch soldier, for example, after attending a black religious service in 1863, conceded that "The Negroes are not as stupid as people say they are. Those that say this should come and see the true state of these people who are slaves." Amazed by the slaves' ability to overcome their hardships through spiritual devotion, the immigrant asserted that "the Negroes put to shame the white and free people because there is not much religion here among the slave-owners."[54] The horrors of slavery also changed the mind of Colonel Marcus Spiegel, a forty-eighter from Germany and the highest-ranking Jewish officer in the Union army. Like other revolutionary veterans Spiegel had opposed the Republican Party since his arrival in America until his service with the nonethnic 67th and 120th Ohio regiments in the war. In January 1863, the immigrant confided to his wife that "I do not fight or want to fight for Lincoln's Negro proclamation one day longer." However, when his soldiers openly denounced Lincoln and the new war aims, Spiegel joined the emancipation crusade and called on his regiment to "Stand by the government right or wrong." With his mind set totally to Lincoln's course, Spiegel even joined the Republican Party and, shortly before his death on the battlefield, told his wife that "I am a strong abolitionist" in January 1864.[55] Other forty-eighters and antislavery commanders like Krzyzanowski passed on their enthusiasm for emancipation to their men. When Friedrich Hecker read the proclamation at battalion drill on January 3, 1863, Bräutigam noted in his diary that his speech "was greeted jubilantly" by the soldiers of the 82nd Illinois.[56]

Just how much freedom-loving Albert Krause had thought of the emancipation of the slaves when he joined the 116th New York Infantry in the summer of 1862 is not clear. First and foremost Krause fought for the Union as did most of his fellow immigrants. With emancipation officially proclaimed he confided to his family in February 1863 that "there is little hope for peace in the near future.... It is highly doubtful whether we will be victorious. But slavery simply has to end sooner or later after this affair that is delivering the coup de grace to this institution." Even if emancipation would eventually lengthen the war, as many feared, Krause nevertheless supported freeing the slaves and wished "Shame and disgrace to those who trade with human flesh!"[57] In the midst of general war weariness at the beginning of 1863, this letter is all the more telling of Krause's perspective on slavery. Still, many immigrants did not like the idea of risking their lives for the slaves or, even worse, fighting side by side with black soldiers. A son of German immigrants, Henry Kircher served in the ethnic 12th Missouri Infantry and in his diary repeatedly stated his dislike of black soldiers. He noted ironically that they still might become "tolerable soldiers [because] they possess all the necessary attributes, such as vanity, much greed and imagination."[58] This attitude shows the degree to which some ethnic Americans had taken in racist views. In perfect accord with many of his native Kentucky comrades, Gottfried Rentschler rejected the idea of black Union troops and uttered his disapproval "about the employment of Negroes as soldiers."[59]

August Börnstein was one of those immigrants who proved the opposite. Leading African-American soldiers in their fight for freedom, Börnstein was one of several hundred foreign-born officers from all European countries who joined the Colored Troops as noncommissioned and commissioned officers. Carl Uterhard and August Achenbach eventually became surgeons in black regiments after taking the necessary examinations. Eduard Reichhelm, who had run away to join Sigel's regiment in Missouri, later commanded black soldiers, as did Peter Karberg. In the most famous black regiment, the 54th Massachusetts Infantry, two immigrants served as officers, Surgeon Louis Radzinsky from Switzerland and Swedish Lieutenant Eric Wulf. Just like many American officers in the U. S. Colored Troops, immigrant officers for the most part did not join the black troops for purely philanthropic reasons. Foreign-born applicants, in particular, saw commissions in these regiments as alternative career venues. Because regulations forbade the appointment of black officers, German applicants in particular hoped for speedy advancement in the black regiments as opposed to other volunteer regiments. There were, to be sure, many immigrants who acted out of idealistic motivations. Börnstein was a dedicated abolitionist as was Colonel Ladislas Zsulavszky of the 82nd United States Colored Infantry, one of several cousins of Kossuth in the Union army. Believing in the soldierly and human qualities of the former slaves, the Hungarian forty-eighter told his men that "the eyes of the world are upon you—to you the friends of your long oppressed race look for the proof of that manliness which they hold to be just as much your gift from Almighty God as that of any white man." The commander continued urging the members of his black regiment to "unitedly strive to accomplish our glorious share in the crushing of this unholy rebellion."[60] Although never directly connected to the Colored Troops, Franz Sigel explicitly advocated the recruitment of African-Americans and demanded the same conditions for them as for white soldiers. In his straightforward style he linked the prevailing discrimination against black troops to the obstacles German immigrants had to surmount in the volunteer army. Endorsing a petition to appoint African-American officers, Sigel wrote to Secretary of War Edwin Stanton, "believing that difference of race, color or nationality should be no obstacle to the appointment or promotion to the rank of commissioned officer if the applicants are otherwise qualified to command."[61]

As in the white volunteer regiments, immigrants conspicuously filled many positions in black artillery regiments, where they could put to use their professional knowledge as drillmasters and commanders. The 6th Heavy Artillery's forty-nine noncommissioned officers, for example, included eleven Germans. Hermann Lieb, the former participant in the Paris street fights, had proven his valor in several battles as captain in the 8th Illinois Infantry before applying for a commission in the Colored Troops. As his former commander testified, the Swiss "was most conspicuous for able service and gallant conduct; that while he had known many brave men, he had known none braver than Herman Lieb."[62] As commander of the 5th U. S. Colored Heavy Artillery, Colonel Lieb lived up to his reputation. A strict and impartial disciplinarian and a professional commander, the officer earned the veneration of his men. One of their first tests as soldiers came in June 1863, when Lieb personally led his black recruits in the battle of Milliken's Bend in Louisiana. When a superior enemy force attacked the fortified post on the Mississippi, Lieb's men proved that they could fight as well as their white comrades in a murderous hand-to-hand melee. Finally, the Confederates had to retreat, "repulsed and defeated through the ability, skill and courage of General Lieb and the tenacious resistance made by his command."[63] When African-American soldiers entered the war, their discipline and soldierly conduct did not convert all skeptics who kept on arguing against the experience of arming slaves. Even after black troops had acquitted themselves nobly in their first battles, ethnic newspapers held on to their prejudicial views, calling black soldiers a "bunch of savages" and belittling their courage in battle as "nothing more than barbarity."[64]

There were sympathetic appraisals, to be sure. Already in 1862, Cincinnati had organized a black guard to defend the city against Confederate irregulars. Although the regiment, numbering 1,100 men, was disbanded after the threat ended late in 1862, the citizens backed the idea of having blacks fight for their protection. When freed slaves formed the first black regiments on the Sea Islands off the South Carolina Coast, Welsh immigrant James Griffiths attested to their worthiness. Writing to his family about impending emancipation in December 1862, Griffith noted that "There are many blacks from South Carolina in our Northern armies whom many said would be no use. But when they were given the chance to face their enemies they showed unflinching bravery and were as worthy of trust as anyone."[65] Serving with Michael Zimmer in the 9th Wisconsin Infantry, Adrian Schweizer witnessed the black troops' bravery in Arkansas in April 1864. When Confederates attacked a supply train near Camden, the immigrant asserted that "the Negro soldiers behaved well and proved that they can fight." Shortly after, the Southerners under Generals Kirby Smith and Price made another assault at Jenkin's Ferry that resulted in a veritable slaughter. Using their rifle butts and bayonets with deadly effect, Schweizer was impressed how "each regiment black or white fought like soldiers and drove back the threefold superiority." An English immigrant was equally impressed with the performance of black soldiers who in his opinion "fought like Tigers."[66] Some ethnic newspapers tried their best to present an unbiased picture of the Colored Troops. The *Minnesota Staats Zeitung* repeatedly reported the black soldiers' courage in detail. "Those who have always cried out against the arming of the Negro," the paper commented on the usefulness of African-American recruitment in June 1863, "in the face of general conscription may now be glad when the 'niggers' will spare them from being killed by their 'southern brothers.' "[67]

Always a careful observer of public opinion, Lincoln had known full well that he alienated many immigrants with his decree to free the slaves. He also knew that it was a time when countless Americans and immigrants did not want to carry on with a seemingly endless war and vehemently opposed conscription. Yet even the attentive president could not anticipate the violence that opposition to emancipation and a forced draft would eventually trigger.

When volunteer numbers trickled away in the face of continuing federal defeats, a general draft that included foreign-born citizens and immigrants who had applied for citizenship became inevitable.[68] Already in August 1862, the impending draft had caused German, Irish, and other immigrants to protest in several northern cities. Workers and small farmers especially opposed the substitute rule that allowed wealthy men to buy themselves out of conscription for $300. Especially for Irish-Americans, emancipation, distrust of the government, and the horrendous toll in human lives had made it hard if not impossible to believe that the war served any ethnic interest. Brutal attacks by Irish workers on black strike breakers and laborers in Cincinnati and Brooklyn showed their anxiety about the effects the war had on job competition. Such occurrences also reinforced the ubiquitous image of Irish riotousness that dated back to earlier brawls with blacks since the mid-1850s.

In July 1863, then, the first drawing of names for conscription sparked unparalleled violence in New York City that left over 1,000 dead and injured. On Monday morning, July 13, native-born as well as Irish and German workers in New York's shipyards, iron foundries, and other state and municipal shops went on a widespread strike to demonstrate against the injustice of the draft. Immigrant painters, carpenters, and other artisans joined protest marches alongside fire companies and even small entrepreneurs. However, the protest quickly got out of hand when elements who from the beginning aimed at more than mere strikes and peaceful rallies took over. As many of the German and native skilled workers and artisans returned home later on Monday, predominantly Irish-Catholic industrial and unskilled laborers from the city's numerous sweatshops gathered and by afternoon turned the protest into violent mutiny. Assailing federal offices, police stations, and the provost marshal's office, the rioters at first directed their fury against representatives of the state and the hated Republican Party. While many German citizens tried to stem the wave of violence, some of them accompanied the Irish mobs that roamed the streets for five days, looting and rampaging in their frenzied rage. Singling out African-Americans as the alleged instigators of the war and therefore of emancipation and conscription, the hordes turned their attention away from their original objectives. Longshoremen and other Irish laborers now gave expression to their detestation of blacks. Attacking blacks at random, the hooligan bands looted and burned a colored orphanage and even destroyed surrounding yards and fences. By Wednesday, the infuriated Irish had succeeded in forcibly driving blacks from whole parts of the city. Heavily assaulted, the city police could do little against the bloodthirsty masses running amok. In the barricaded streets of the Upper East Side factory district a regular war evolved between the insurgents and armed police and military forces. It was only after Secretary of War Stanton ordered 6,000 Union troops from Gettysburg north to the city that order was restored by Friday, July 17.[69]

During the riots, German and Jewish merchants and other shop proprietors had repeatedly fallen victim to the violent crowds. Telling his mother about the "terrible things" that had happened in New York, Emile Dupré from Brunswick described the burning and pillaging that reminded him of the turmoil during the Paris revolutions.[70] Another immigrant wrote that the city's mob by far surpassed the lowliest criminals of German cities. "These persons have committed every atrocity imaginable," Karl Wesslau wrote to his parents in Prussia, adding that "for 3 nights in a row the sky and the city were illuminated by the buildings on fire."[71] While some Germans noted that blacks were the most preferred victims of the mobs, none blamed Irishmen for starting the violence. In fact, although Irish-Americans had formed the core of the rioters, most Irish workers in the notorious Sixth and Fourteenth Wards of the city had refrained from participating in the unrest. There, Irish squads had even organized against the violence. Nevertheless, the riots severely damaged the public image of Irish immigrants, even if Irish firemen had risked their lives and assisted in getting the situation under control. To many Americans, Irish again were the violent hoodlums unfit for civilization. Opposition to the draft never ceded. All throughout the summer, protest continued in several other northern cities when Germans and Welsh immigrants, unable to raise the substitute payments, joined the Irish.

SEVEN

CHANCELLORSVILLE
TO MISSIONARY RIDGE:
HUMILIATION AND TRIUMPH

After its humiliating defeat at Fredericksburg, the Union army had received yet another commander. General Joseph "Fighting Joe" Hooker was a West Pointer with considerable experience who had shown aggressiveness in battle as well as in his open criticism of Burnside. Hooker soon devised a new strategy to deliver the final blow to Lee's Confederates. Boldly parting his army, Hooker planned on pinning down Lee in his Fredericksburg positions, while simultaneously outflanking him to the north across the Rappahannock to fall on his rear. Widely enveloping the Southerners via Kelly's Ford, the bulk of the Union army turned south again and reached Chancellorsville on April 30. By then, Lee had learned about Hooker's plans and rushed to intercept the federals. Leaving only a small portion of his troops in Fredericksburg, in an even more audacious move he divided the rest of his army once more and sent Jackson with 28,000 men against Hooker's main column. Thus the stage was set for a most important and tragic battle that would deprive the South of one of its most brilliant generals, and at the same time seal the public image of German troops and forever cement the myth of Irish bravery.

Full of confidence in their new commanding general, the soldiers of the Eleventh Corps were nevertheless sad to have lost Franz Sigel, who had resigned a third time, relinquishing command of the Eleventh Corps in March. Always quick to accuse officials and Army Chief of Staff Henry W. Halleck of discriminating against his German soldiers, a self-important Sigel finally had overstrained Lincoln and Stanton's nerves and had lost his corps for good. Command had devolved to General Oliver

O. Howard, a "temperance man and a pious Christian" from New England who banned drinking and swearing, enforced Sabbatarianism, and generally displayed little tact in dealing with the German majority in his corps.[1] Of his three division commanders, Schurz, von Steinwehr, and Francis Barlow, two were German, though, and thirteen of the twenty-seven infantry regiments were predominantly ethnic in makeup. The German regiments included many freethinkers and antireligious soldiers who viewed the distanced New Englander skeptically, all the more because he had replaced their forty-eighter idol. Anticipating difficulties "which would be apt to impair the efficiency of the corps," Carl Schurz even asked Howard to transfer his division to some other army, which Howard declined to do.[2] Nevertheless, spirits were high in the Eleventh Corps as the troops prepared for Hooker's campaign. Colonel Krzyzanowski, commanding the Second Brigade of Schurz's Third Division, was full of praise for his troops as the "best drilled and most soldierly" of all.[3] On April 10 the Corps paraded before President Lincoln and other Washington eminences, showing excellent discipline and drill, and performing the finest of band music. Then it was off to the great enveloping movement around Lee's army.

Marching south after they had crossed Kelly's Ford, Howard's troops formed the exposed right flank when Hooker ordered the army to halt. The Eleventh Corps, with Barlow's and Schurz's divisions in the first line and Steinwehr's in reserve, found itself halted in the densely forested area called the Wilderness. Expecting an attack, the commanders threw out pickets, dug trenches, and formed in line of battle along the road from Chancellorsville to Wilderness Tavern facing south. Learning that the Union right flank now hung in the air, Jackson rushed his troops through the thick brushwood right across the federal front. Although scouts detected this flanking movement and alerted Hooker and Howard, neither one reacted to the imminent danger.

In the afternoon of May 2, Jackson's veterans hit the Eleventh Corps with full force. Out on the federal line's far right, the partly German 153rd Pennsylvania Infantry under Colonel Charles Glanz received the initial blow that soon rolled up Colonel Leopold von Gilsa's brigade. Still able to fire a few rounds against the rebel onslaught alongside their comrades of the De Kalb Infantry, the Pennsylvanians tried to retreat in order, but soon broke and fled together with the 45th and 54th New York regiments. The wave of soldiers running in confusion quickly reached the neighboring division. The men of the 74th Pennsylvania were caught at their evening meals when the remnants of the First Division scampered through their ranks, hotly pursued by the yelling Confederates. Lieutenant Colonel Adolph von Hartung reported that his soldiers were "at once thrown in such disorder that a restoring of order was an utter impossibility. The first we ever knew of the enemy was that our men, while sitting on their knapsacks and ready to spring to their arms, were shot from the rear and flank." In his report the Saxon professional officer expressed his outrage about the commanding generals' lack to take adequate precautions against: "A surprise in broad daylight, a case not yet heard of in the history of any war." Hartung wrote that the shock had been "so complete that the men had not even time to take their arms before they were thrown in the wildest confusion. The different regiments on our right were in a few minutes all mixed up with the Seventy-fourth." While many of his soldiers and parts of their sister regiment, the 75th Pennsylvania, were captured by the pressing rebels, Hartung blamed General Howard for at least part of the general confusion. Attempting to preserve the most order possible, the lieutenant colonel rallied his troops and scattered parts of the other brigades in a rifle pit in the rear. Just at that moment, Howard arrived on the scene, crying, "Stop; face about; do not retreat any farther!" The German officer coldly asserted that "This was well said, but impossible to be done. The troops were entirely mixed up, the panic was great, the enemy pressed heavily, the rifle-pits in the rear was already glittering with bayonets, and occasional shots from behind were showing the greatness of the danger of trying to rally the troops in front of the pit."[4] Frankly disobeying the general's order, Hartung rushed the men into the trenches.

The Pennsylvania men formed along a defensive line established by Colonel Adolph Buschbeck and his brigade consisting of the 29th and 154th New York and the 27th and 73rd Pennsylvania Infantry regiments. When Hartung and Schurz, with the help of Buschbeck, had managed to restore discipline and confidence in the officers, the men of the Eleventh Corps calmly waited for the rebels and with determined resistance slowed down their attack. Division commander von Steinwehr found Buschbeck "defending this position with great firmness and gallantry" and ordered the colonel to hold it "as long as possible," realizing the importance of that line of defense. For one and a half hours the "Buschbeck line" held its ground against Jackson, allowing the artillery to draw back and organize with the rest of the Union army. Although the men fought with utmost courage they were soon overpowered by their enemies, falling upon both flanks and threatening to roll up the entire front. With almost one-third of his undersized force dead and wounded, Colonel Buschbeck was forced to withdraw his brigade toward the protecting woods in their rear. Retiring in exemplary order upon the colonel's command, the men even halted twice and fired at the advancing Confederates before they finally reached the lines of General Sickles's Third Corps. Severely decimated, Buschbeck nevertheless "formed his brigade in close column, and . . . offered to advance again to a bayonet charge."[5] Fortunately, they were spared another round with the enemy.

The Eleventh Corps had suffered dearly from Jackson's surprise attack. Never faltering, the 26th Wisconsin under Colonel Wilhelm Jacobs and Hecker's 82nd Illinois fought bravely near the Wilderness Church before falling back to Buschbeck's line. The price for their heroic stand was immense; both regiments lost an aggregate 359 men and officers (including Jacobs and Hecker, both wounded). This was their first time in battle, and the Wisconsin Germans' conduct was all the more laudable after they had lost their commander. The total number of casualties in Howard's

Corps that day ran to 2,400 killed, wounded, and missing. While the Union troops recovered from the devastating attack, an ever-aggressive Jackson planned a night attack to cut off the federal retreat. Setting out to reconnoiter his next exploit, the southern general was accidentally shot by his own men and died a few days later.[6]

The Irish Brigade had crossed the Rappahannock farther south at U.S. Ford with the Second Corps on April 30 to unite with the rest of the army. When General J. E. B. Stuart launched a second Confederate attack on May 3, Hancock's Division became vital in providing a retreat corridor and saving Hooker from near-certain destruction. Hurried to the center of the withdrawing Union line, the Irish Brigade assisted a lone battery in their effort to stem the enemy flooding across a clearing near the Chancellor House. The Fifth Maine Battery stood its ground stubbornly for about an hour against galling fire until every man but one corporal was killed or wounded, or had fled to the rear. It was then that the Irish Brigade performed probably its most daring feat in the war. After the lone remaining artillerist had fired a final round into the Confederate lines and Hancock had ordered retreat, the general told Mulholland and his 116th Pennsylvania "to bring out a sufficient number of men to haul the abandoned guns off the field, as they were in great danger of being captured by the enemy."[7] Mulholland reacted promptly and amidst hails of bullets his soldiers slung ropes around the cannons to haul them to safety. Lieutenant Edward Whiteford of the 88th New York was amazed at the accomplishment of his comrades who slung ropes around the cannons and drew "them out of stiff yellow clay, where the guns were stuck . . . under a galling fire of the enemy."[8] Colonel Mulholland would later receive the Congressional Medal of Honor for his daring courage that day, but the Irish Brigade never recovered after the battle. Having lost another hundred men in their heroic stand at the Chancellor House, General Meagher's troops now only numbered some 400 men fit for service. When his request to go on leave and start another recruitment campaign was denied, an angrily disappointed Meagher resigned. On May 19, the general assembled his small force and took leave. Conyngham recalled the touching scene when Meagher delivered a poignant speech followed by "vociferous cheers," and then shook his officers' hands to bid them farewell. "Then the general passed along the lines and shook each and every soldier by the hand . . . and during all this, many a manly eye was filled with tears."[9] Meagher left behind a decimated yet still dedicated command that was reorganized under Colonel Patrick Kelly of the 88th New York into three two-company battalions. Still, it would never continue its glorious history beyond Chancellorsville. As Meagher had sadly noted, "That brigade no longer exists."[10]

General Hooker finally managed to establish a defensive position in front of U.S. Ford during the following night, but the expected attack never came. Instead, Lee turned his main force against reinforcements Hooker had called up from Fredericksburg and completed his most brilliant victory. Hooker finally decided to fall back across the river and through pouring rain and relentless enemy fire moved his demoralized army back to its camps north of Fredericksburg. Another attempt to crush the Army of Northern Virginia had failed miserably, leaving the northern public puzzled and increasingly dissatisfied with Lincoln's military leadership. To make things even worse for the German soldiers, word immediately spread through the army that, in contrast to the Irish Brigade, the Eleventh Corps had collapsed and fled ingloriously before the rebels. As the men of the Iron Brigade had moved in to protect the federal retreat on May 4, James Sullivan recounted, "the first thing attracted our attention was a squad of Meagher's Irish Brigade who, with a great deal of Irish hullabaloo, were hauling off by the drag ropes, a couple of guns belonging to their battery." Trotting on, Sullivan and his comrades "struggled through the almost impenetrable undergrowth of the Wilderness and took position on the ground from which the Eleventh Corps had so disgracefully fallen back." Sullivan's fellow Irish immigrant Colonel Patrick R. Guiney, commanding the 9th Massachusetts Infantry, explicitly charged the Germans to have prevented "a great victory" with their cowardice. "The Dutch Corps ran," Guiney judged in disparagement.[11] Discharged from Hecker's 82nd Infantry only a few weeks earlier, Friedrich Bräutigam was back home in Illinois at the time of the battle. Army rumors quickly became national headlines and the veteran, who had so proudly joined the ethnic regiment, was shocked when he heard "of the cowardly conduct and the scandalous flight of the 11th Army Corps, and especially of Schurz's Division." Such terrible news, Bräutigam confided in his diary, "causes my mind to stand still; never had I expected this from the guardians of the German military honor." Although Bräutigam did not want to judge prematurely before he had detailed news, he could not "exonerate their behavior in the least." With their rout the soldiers of the Eleventh Corps and especially his former comrades in the 2nd Hecker Regiment had done irreparable damage to "the honor of the German name which until now has stood unblemished in the history of this pitiful brothers' war."[12]

Nativist voices in the American press were quick to turn the more or less orderly retreat of parts of the Eleventh Corps into a blunder by unreliable foreigners. Singling out Carl Schurz as the most visible German-American, the *New York Times* harshly condemned the general and his troops as "retreating and cowardly poltroons." To "the disgrace of the Eleventh Corps," the *Times* clamored, "the division of General Schurz, which was the first assailed, almost instantly gave way." Further distorting the facts of the battle, the paper asserted that "Threats, entreaties and orders of commanders were of no avail. Thousands of these cowards threw down their guns and soon streamed down the road toward headquarters."[13] The *New York Herald* used equally derisive words when it wrote about "the disastrous and disgraceful giving way of General Schurz's Division," whose members "fled like so many sheep before a pack of wolves."[14] Echoing the two papers' accusations, other journals fell upon Schurz and his "Flying Dutchmen" and blamed them for the failure of the entire campaign. Schurz embodied Germanness to most Americans, and they identified him with the Eleventh Corps after he had led it twice during Sigel's absence.[15]

With American papers slandering German-American honor and integrity in such an offensive way, the ethnic press rushed to a counteroffensive in uncommon harmony. Accusing the American press of "stinking nativism," German newspapers closed ranks to publicly defend the conduct of the German soldiers and demand retribution. General Schimmelfennig also protested against the treatment of his division. In an official communication he wrote that his officers and men, "filled with indignation, come to me, with newspapers in their hands, and ask if such be the rewards they may expect for the sufferings they have endured and the bravery they have displayed." Recounting the facts of the battle, Schimmelfennig pointed to the conduct of his division in particular, closing with "I am an old soldier. To this hour I have been proud to command the brave men of this brigade; but I am sure that unless these infamous falsehoods be retracted and reparations made, their good-will and soldierly spirit will be broken, and I shall no longer be at the head of the same brave men whom I have had heretofore the honor to lead."[16] Like Schimmelfennig, several officers offered to resign after being so wickedly indicted with cowardice. Some eventually did, like Colonel Jacobs who subsequently laid down his command of the 26th Wisconsin together with Major Henry Bätz.[17]

Personally insulted and abused as a scapegoat, Schurz felt compelled to act as an attorney for his fellow immigrants—and, of course, himself. The forty-eighter complained to Secretary of War Edwin Stanton that "The conduct of the Eleventh Corps, and especially of my division, has been so outrageously and so persistently misrepresented by the press throughout the country, and officers, as well as men, have had and still have to suffer so much abuse and insult at the hands of the rest of the army." Understanding fully well the mental strain such unfounded accusations caused among soldiers in wartime, Schurz continued to argue, "It is a very hard thing for soldiers to be universally stigmatized as cowards, and apt to demoralize them more than a defeat."[18] Already in his official battle report Schurz had pointed to the fact that Hooker had been at fault in leaving the whole Eleventh Corps hanging entirely in the air when an attack was imminent. Their position at the unprotected far right flank, he elaborated in his highly detailed report, had been untenable. Schurz declared, "because I know it: these men are no cowards. I have seen most of them fight before this, and they fought as bravely as any."[19] For weeks to come Schurz pounded his superiors and the war department with letters in which he demanded either the publication of his battle report or a court of inquiry to straighten out his division's role in the battle. Not even an official exculpation by General Howard served to reconcile Americans with Schurz and his Germans. Nothing German soldiers would achieve during the rest of the war could restore their reputation after the tragedy of Chancellorsville. The American public had reached their verdict and declared German soldiers cowards. Even though several newspapers afterward revised their premature criticism and several American officers came to the defense of the Eleventh Corps, public opinion stuck to the image of the flying Dutchmen. In response, German

Americans all over the country rallied in protest meetings to oppose prejudice and injustice. Many Germans even expressed their strong belief that Franz Sigel would never have abandoned his corps in the face of an attack the way Howard had. When neither Lincoln nor Stanton came to their defense, many Germans who already disagreed with emancipation completely lost faith in the government.

Irish voices also rose in the wake of Chancellorsville, censuring the neglect of the Irish Brigade and the war department's refusal to let Meagher replenish his troops sounded strikingly similar to the ethnic German pleas in defense of Sigel and Schurz. Those who had criticized Meagher for having his brigade slaughtered for his personal glory for the most part remained silent after the general had resigned. In combination with their increasing opposition to the draft these Irish claims caused a backlash in public opinion, however. Annoyed, many Americans fell back into their old habits of stamping Irish immigrants as a general nuisance to society.[20] Judging from ethnic newspapers and immigrant letters, both German and Irish support for the war had reached an all-time low after Chancellorsville.

Why, then, did immigrants continue to fight for the Union and an ungrateful society instead of deserting in great numbers? For many Irish soldiers the reason was most probably the motivation to stand by their own national flag of Ireland. A sense of pride in their ethnic cause and an obligation to their Irish fighting reputation made them carry on. After all, they had followed the appeals of Meagher and Corcoran rather than those of a Republican president. Still, as the riots in New York City would show all too clearly, the impending draft prevented new enlistees from coming forward, and it was the Irish veterans who continued the war. In the German soldiers' case, at least part of the answer lies in the sense of duty and discipline Schimmelfennig and Schurz talked about. Germans had for the most part volunteered to save their adopted country, not to serve an arrogant society ignorant of their ethnic values and traditions. Immigrants in all their disappointment and hurt pride repeatedly affirmed that they were willing to continue their fight for the Union in spite of corrupt politicians, stupid generals, and an ignorant public demeaning their efforts. They still had able and trustworthy leaders, and redemption could only come through stubborn disregard of all the defamation and by proving their worth on the battlefield. When Howard reconsidered Schurz's request for transferal from the Army of the Potomac two weeks after Chancellorsville, the general utterly refused to leave. Because he and his officers had been called cowards, Schurz explained, "If we go now, will it not have the appearance as if we were shaken off by the Army of the Potomac? Would it not to a certainty confirm the slanders circulated about me? Would it not seem as if I voluntarily accepted the responsibility for the disaster of May 2?" Instead, the proud forty-eighter insisted to remain and enable the German soldiers to "stand right here until the mist that hangs over the events of the 2d of May is cleared up." Howard, who had never openly blamed the Germans for what had happened, respected Schurz's opinion and withdrew his request formally.[21]

Schurz's wish for redemption was granted when Robert E. Lee's Army of Northern Virginia started out to invade the northern homeland a second time. Bolstered by his smashing victory in May, Lee had again seized the offensive and quickly marched his 75,000 men through Maryland into Pennsylvania. Morale ran high among the southern troops and Lee was convinced that this time he would force the northerners to their knees. Under yet another commander, Major General George G. Meade, the Army of the Potomac went after the intruders in hasty pursuit. On their forced marches under a burning July sun along the eastern Appalachians, the Germans in the Eleventh Corps knew fully well that the nation's eyes were upon them.

Running into the advance guards of A. P. Hill's Confederates at the small town of Gettysburg, General John Buford and his cavalry division started the battle on July 1. Meanwhile the Iron Brigade came marching up the Baltimore Pike in the vanguard of General John F. Reynolds's First Corps. When the 6th Wisconsin approached Gettysburg "and our lads straightened up to pass through it in good style," James Sullivan recalled, "all at once hell broke loose" in their front. The Wisconsin regiment had arrived just in time to assist Buford's dismounted troopers who had already fended off several infantry attacks. "The band swung out to one side and began 'Yankee Doodle' in double quick time and 'Forward, double quick,' sang out the colonel, and the decisive battle of the war had begun."[22] As usual the Iron Brigade rushed at the foe and captured two enemy regiments. Holding the high ground on Seminary Ridge against superior numbers, the brigade suffered extremely high casualties, among them fearless Sullivan who was shot in the shoulder and taken to a hospital in town. While the Confederates fell back after several unsuccessful attacks, Howard arrived with the Eleventh Corps and took control of the federal operations after Reynolds had been killed by a sharpshooter. Taking over command of the corps, Schurz deployed his division now under Alexander Schimmelfennig and that of Barlow to the north to strengthen the Union right flank, while Steinwehr's Division together with Wiedrich's battery entrenched on Cemetery Hill on the south side of the town. Advancing through Gettysburg at the head of Schimmelfennig's First Division, the 74th Pennsylvania was thrown out as skirmishers and passed beyond the town into the open field. There, according to First Lieutenant Emil Knoebel, the regiment "at once received artillery fire with bombs and solid shots. One shell whirled passed my head so close that the blast nearly threw me to the ground and knocked off my cap." The rest of the divisions then rushed up and joined the First Corps in their fight. With the bulk of the army still several miles away, Schurz again met with bad luck when in the afternoon an overpowering attack crashed against his line. Once more parts of the Eleventh Corps broke, soon to be chased through Gettysburg by General Ewell's rebel troops. As Knoebel recalled, "After we had been exposed to heavy artillery fire for about one hour the enemy infantry attacked with such superior numbers and such vehemence that we were forced to withdraw. An effort to halt and fight had to be abandoned because the enemy threatened to surround us." Retreating through the Gettysburg streets, all of a sudden Knoebel and his regiment were cut off from their brigade and had to surrender. "Never in my entire life will I forget the feeling I had when I had to hand over my saber."[23] Brought to the rear, Knoebel and his comrades of the 74th did not participate in the rest of the battle. In the meantime the federal rout had come to a halt at the advance lines of their reserve division. The First Corps, dangerously exposed by the broken front to their right, also withdrew and met their comrades on Cemetery Hill where they organized for a second stand. When Meade brought up the rest of the army in the late afternoon, the hills and ridges south of Gettysburg became the Union's new and ultimately impenetrable position.

The Eleventh Corps had again failed to stem a Confederate attack and they soon experienced renewed criticism. Having his wound treated in the hospital, Sullivan was among the first who heard "that the Eleventh Corps had broke and run and the rebs were driving our fellows through the town." Like his comrades, Sullivan "was mad as the devil to think that all our hard fighting that morning had went for nothing, and here was over two hundred of our brigade all smashed to pieces." Freely cursing the "Flying Moon" Corps, Sullivan and the other patients, however, laid most of the blame on the "bible thumping hypocrite" General Howard.[24] Losing thousands in wounded and captured, the troops under Schurz had actually offered brave resistance before parts had collapsed and fled. Indeed, von Gilsa's brigade made a valiant stand against enfilading infantry and artillery fire before it retreated to a second line in good order. Likewise, Schimmelfennig's two brigades under Colonels von Amsberg and Wladimir Krzyzanowski fought bravely alongside the First Corps and for the most part did not participate in the rout. The 45th "Platt Deutsch" and the half-German 119th New York Regiments in particular suffered heavily holding the Confederates at bay. Considering the fate of the corps on the first day of Gettysburg, historian Lonn assumes that "because it was still suffering from the humiliation of the reproaches after Chancellorsville, the Eleventh Corps did not measure up to its best."[25] This conclusion seems doubtful, given the resolutions made by Schurz and other German officers to restore their honor. Far more probably, physical limitations after the exhausting ten-mile march may have prevented the soldiers from mounting a more rigorous defense. The loss of several officers, among them Colonel Franz Mahler of the 75th Pennsylvania and division commander Barlow, further demoralized the troops. Nevertheless, their will to fight was not broken and the men demonstrated soldierly qualities during the rest of the battle. On July 2, the Eleventh Corps valiantly defended its fortified positions on Cemetery Hill against powerful Confederate attacks. Only von Gilsa's Brigade once more received the full impact of the enemy onslaught, just as it had at Chancellorsville. Shortly thrown in confusion by superior forces, the brigade soon rallied and fought on credibly.

Replenished to 530 men, the Irish Brigade had arrived with the Second Corps near Gettysburg in the evening of July 1 and on the next morning took up position at the center of the Union line along Cemetery Ridge. Once again, the Irishmen made a remarkable stand when Confederates broke through the dangerously advanced federal line to their left. As the yelling rebels came pouring through a wheat field and a neighboring peach orchard, in a solemn ceremony admired by onlookers, Father Corby mounted a rock and offered absolution of their sins to his kneeling soldiers. About 5 P.M., General Caldwell—now in command of the division—ordered a counterattack to throw back the Confederates. Though few in number, the Irish Brigade advanced in picture-book-style past the foot of Little Round Top into the Wheatfield. A Confederate officer described the scene "of gaily dressed Union forces in the wheat field whose almost perfect line was preserved, though enfiladed by our own fire from the woods, decimating the front line, whose gaps were promptly filled by each file-closer."[26] The Irish Brigade charged into the woods, capturing a number of southern soldiers and engaging in a fierce hand-to-hand melee. Fighting for about an hour, the federals finally withdrew through the Wheatfield under galling fire and regrouped at Little Round Top. They reached their lines at Cemetery Hill covered by darkness and spent an uneasy night throwing up earthworks and preparing for another fight. Fortunately, the decimated brigade was spared the drama of the coming day. The remaining 328 Irish men and officers nevertheless knew what was going on while they were crouching in their trenches "under probably the heaviest artillery fire ever heard."[27] Another Irish regiment would win undying fame on the last day at Gettysburg.

On July 3, after a two-hour long artillery barrage Lee ordered a frontal assault against what he perceived to be the weakest point of the enemy positions. Led by Virginian General George Pickett, 12,000 southerners delivered their spine-chilling rebel yell as they emerged out of the woods opposing Cemetery Ridge and charged against the entrenched Union soldiers along a mile-wide front. The southerners had to cross an open field over three-quarters of a mile in length against steady and terribly effective musket and cannon fire. Enough of them made it, however, to reach the breastworks on Cemetery Ridge and break through the federal lines. Now they met with determined resistance by Brigadier General Alexander Webb's Philadelphia Brigade of the Second Corps. Among Webb's troops was the Irish 69th Pennsylvania Infantry, which quickly formed a right angle to open a new front against the intruding rebels. Colonel Owen O'Kane's men soon found themselves in a brutal clinch, stabbing and clubbing their enemies with bayonets and rifle butts. Finally the Irish soldiers, together with reinforcements called from the rear, brought the rebel assault to a standstill, and repulsed it, sealing the Confederates' fate in that battle. In less than twenty minutes, the regiment had lost 129 men and officers, including Colonel O'Kane and Lieutenant Colonel Martin Tschudy mortally wounded. Also bearing its share in the final action at Gettysburg, the Garibaldi Guard under Captain Heinrich Dietrich, a forty-eighter from Germany, fought with equal valor in the lines of the Second Corps. The regiment distinguished itself when it retook an abandoned battery of the 5th U.S. Artillery under maddening enemy fire and brought it safely to the rear. Reduced to a mere four companies numbering 320 men before the battle, the Garibaldians lost another ninety-five casualties at Gettysburg.[28]

Pickett's futile charge marked ultimate Confederate defeat after three days' ferocious fighting. Although 23,000 northern soldiers had been killed, wounded, or captured, the Union had finally won a major victory and averted a vital threat to its capital. The Army of Northern Virginia would never recover from its 20,500 casualties, and from now on Lee was on the defensive. "In the early morning of July 4 we could see that the enemy was beaten," captured Lieutenant Knoebel wrote. "Hastily [Lee] retreated, leaving behind thousands of wounded. Every barn, every house, every stable was filled with wounded men, yes, hundreds of them lay strewn in the woods."[29] Amidst the confusion during the Confederate retreat back south Knoebel managed to escape together with two comrades and rejoined the federal army.

As historian Ella Lonn has remarked, all the various nationalities represented in the Army of the Potomac participated in that momentous battle.[30] Although the engagement had gotten off to a bad start on the first day, during the following two days the ethnic soldiers fought with determination and bravery. Colonel Freudenberg was wounded when his New Yorkers charged through the Wheatfield together with Kelly's Irishmen. The federal batteries of Dilger and Wiedrich had been instrumental in holding Cemetery Hill throughout the three days' fighting against repeated attempts to storm them. Caspar Trepp's Swiss sharpshooters fought on every part of the federal front and conducted valuable reconnoitering services, while Colonel de Trobriand's Frenchmen withstood the Confederate attack against the left flank on July 2. Most importantly, in the eyes of many immigrants the Eleventh Corps had won back its honor at Gettysburg. Suffering heavily, Schurz's troops had lost a total of 3,800 men and officers, most of them captured. Again delivering a most detailed battle report, Schurz was convinced that his portrayal of events at Gettysburg "bears ample testimony that my men in that battle fought with bravery, and never yielded without necessity."[31] Still, nativist attacks against his division and German troops in general did not subside. A week after the battle General Howard finally responded publicly to the unremitting indictments of cowardice. Issuing General Orders No. 18, Howard officially acknowledged his troops' achievements. "The Eleventh Corps, as a corps, has done well," Howard declared, "well in marching, well in fighting; the Sacrifices it has made shall not be forgotten. In the retrospect, your general feels satisfied."[32]

Returning south to Virginia after Gettysburg, the Eleventh Corps was broken up in August when Halleck ordered its First Division, including Schimmelfennig's brigade, to South Carolina. Schimmelfennig himself had requested a transfer of his brigade away from the Army of the Potomac after continuing accusations against German troops. In late September, Steinwehr and Schurz's Divisions were ordered to Tennessee together with the Twelfth Army Corps. In an extraordinary logistical operation, 20,000 troops moved some 1,200 miles and reached their destination at Bridgeport on the Tennessee River safely within only a week. Finally the "Dutch Corps" had left the Army of the Potomac and vanished from the headlines of the national press.

Encamped in winter quarters at Fredericksburg in January 1863, August Horstmann mused about the futile operations against Lee's army whereas the federal armies had been victorious in the New Year's battle at Murfreesboro, Tennessee, "where our German General Rosencranz totally defeated the southerners." Born in Ohio of German descent, Major General William S. Rosecrans had indeed won a significant strategic victory with his Army of the Cumberland when he battled Confederate General Braxton Bragg at Stones River for three days and drove his army from central Tennessee. "More such success in the West will end the war sooner than this obdurate campaign in Virginia," Horstmann trusted.[33] While the war was running a depressingly fruitless course in Virginia, many immigrants turned their attention to the successful campaigns in the west where their countrymen contributed to hard-fought victories. Actually, in the battle of Stones River it had been American regiments in General Phil Sheridan's Division that broke before the Confederate onslaught, while the German 2nd and 15th Missouri, the Swiss Rifles, doggedly stood their ground.[34]

The success in the West Horstmann hoped for came in July when General Grant finally conquered the last Confederate citadel on the Mississippi. Towering over the river atop steep bluffs, the fortified city of Vicksburg had withstood several assaults by the Union. Its heavy artillery easily swept the river and the surrounding swamps made it impossible for the Union army to take Vicksburg from the north. In the spring of 1863, Grant decided to circumvent the city west of the Mississippi, cross the river to the south, and attack it from the rear. It was the same kind of bold decision as Hooker's at Chancellorsville, but this time the operation was successful. While Admiral David Dixon Porter daringly ran the gantlet below the Confederate river batteries, Colonel Benjamin Grierson set out from La Grange in Tennessee on a 600-mile cavalry raid that diverted the attention from the actual campaign. Meanwhile, Porter's ships steamed down the Mississippi to Grand Gulf, south of Vicksburg, and battered the fort into submission. Then Grant arrived out of the swamps with his Army of the Tennessee consisting of the Fifteenth, Seventeenth, and Eighteenth Army Corps. As part of General Frederick Steele's Division, the 3rd Missouri Infantry reached the rendezvous point on May 3. "We immediately boarded the ships and crossed the Mississippi," Johann Buegel wrote, "and our troops took possession of Grand Gulf. The garrison was captured and the fort leveled."[35] The rest of the army followed over the coming three days and Grant headed northeast. After preventing southern reinforcements under Joseph E. Johnston from relieving Vicksburg in the battle of Jackson, Grant turned west toward the formidable defenses held by General John C. Pemberton. Driving in Pemberton's army at the costly battle of Champion's Hill, the three corps marched up in full force in front of the impressive trenches and artillery works guarding Vicksburg.

Together with the rest of the division, the 3rd Missouri went into position on the federal right flank on Walnut Hill near the river, and Johann Buegel described the unnerving situation in the trenches "where we were exposed to the enemy's musket and cannon fire." Daily harassed by snipers and artillery, the soldiers lived dangerously and "Lieutenant Fischer of our Company F was wounded because he could not run very fast. By then the enemy had retreated into his earth works and was firmly entrenched." From a riverbank fort, the rebel batteries constantly raked the federal positions. To evade the incessant hail of shells, the Union soldiers endeavored to entrench as best they could. "To protect ourselves somewhat from the opposing guns we had dug holes in the side of the hill. As soon as the battery started to shell us, everyone slipped into his hole like mice." This did not help much, though. Many of Buegel's comrades were killed during the coming weeks. As the German's diary reads, "On the morning of 22 May a shell tore the head from our color bearer's body (an Irish) as he was reading the newspaper in his hole. Thus, we were not safe for a minute." Later on the same day Grant ordered a frontal attack against Pemberton's defenses. As Buegel recalled, his brigade set out to cross several hills and open fields "controlled by the enemy with guns and rifles" to the point where they could form into lines of battle. The open spaces they had to cover were some 300 to 400 feet wide, and the soldiers darted across in small groups. "Understandably, many fell under these circumstances." Reaching its destination at the foot of a hill, General Steele's Division formed for the attack. Two brigades stormed the hill but were repulsed and it seemed to Buegel that everyone reaching the crest was killed. Finally, his First Brigade set out for a third desperate attempt, "but the enemy doubled his fire and it was impossible to do a step forward or back. Luckily, at least we were hidden behind a ravine or hills so that the enemy could not fire into our flanks." Eventually, the Missourians broke off the attack and sought cover until nightfall when they managed to withdraw into their trenches. Angrily, Buegel concluded, "It was murder and slaughter, and it is a miracle that not all of the division was annihilated on that battlefield. What had been gained? Absolutely nothing. But we had to mourn the loss of some 1,000 men killed."[36] The 3rd Missouri suffered forty-three casualties, most of them dead. Also participating prominently was Hugo Wangelin's 12th Missouri. Losing 108 men and officers in that futile assault against impregnable defensive works, Wangelin later criticized the action as a totally unnecessary sacrifice of human lives.[37]

After this defeat Grant changed his strategy and laid siege to the city. "Strong fortresses were erected along the whole line and furnished with heavy guns," Buegel recalled, which kept up a cannonade across the whole front around the clock. Impressed by the army's firepower, Buegel described how Porter's flotilla on the Mississippi "threw red hot shells into the enemy's works by day and night causing massive destruction."[38] A most effective artilleryman who had exhibited his skills in several of the Western battles, Klemens Landgräber earned high reputation among the American regiments as the "Flying Dutchman," for his ability in swiftly moving and accurately operating his battery. In the beleaguered city, meanwhile, conditions deteriorated rapidly in the humid summer heat and after forty-seven days Pemberton surrendered the key to the Mississippi on July 4. A triumphant federal army occupied the city, and the North rejoiced over the second crucial victory within a few days. "The Father of Waters again goes unvexed to the sea," President Lincoln sighed, hoping that finally "Peace does not appear so distant as it did."[39]

News of the victory at Vicksburg finally brought the war in the West into every newspaper around the Union and made Grant a national hero. The presence of countless immigrant soldiers before Vicksburg and in the grueling western campaigns that followed, however, still went largely unnoticed. Ethnic regiments in the western theater of the war never received the same public attention as the larger immigrant organizations in the Army of the Potomac. Especially after Franz Sigel had gone east there was no ethnic leader left to promote the visibility of immigrants in the western armies, and when the remnants of the Eleventh Corps were transferred to Grant's army in the fall, nobody in the east seemed to care anymore.

All the same, ethnic regiments and immigrants in mixed units rendered valuable contributions to the winning of the war in the two years from Vicksburg to Appomattox. The achievements of victorious leaders like Osterhaus and Willich soothed the maltreated ethnic consciousness. Largely German brigades in the West served under Hugo Wangelin, Wladimir Krzyzanowski, Adolph Engelmann, and Bernhardt Laiboldt, whom Kaufmann claims to have been "known throughout the Western army."[40] Another highly commended fighting unit, Hans Heg's Scandinavian Regiment, would soon distinguish itself once more in the slaughter of another battle.

Following a sound strategy, General Rosecrans had marched his three army corps southeast from central Tennessee in June and on September 9 took the railroad center of Chattanooga, the gateway to the lower Confederacy situated on the Tennessee River at the entrance to a valley between Lookout Mountain and Missionary Ridge. Crossing the rugged Cumberland Mountains, Rosecrans succeeded in maneuvering the Confederate Army of Tennessee under Braxton Bragg out of central Tennessee without a single battle. However, in pursuing Bragg's scattered forces into Georgia Rosecrans had critically dispersed his own army. While the federal troops were still hacking their way through rough and densely forested terrain, Bragg hit them in an impenetrable wilderness around a creek named the "River of Death" by the Cherokee. Out of utter confusion as to the whereabouts of their forces, neither commander was able to bring on a concentrated attack. With the battle raging back and forth, soldiers got lost in the thick woods broken by occasional rolling fields, and casualties mounted in the ghastly fight.

On September 19, fighting evolved along Chickamauga Creek between General George H. Thomas's Fourteenth Corps and the Confederates. General Alexander

McDowell McCook had hurried the Twentieth Corps up from Alpine through Lookout Valley and formed his three divisions in line at the southern right wing of the Union army. August Willich's Brigade soon made contact. What followed was one of the gallant charges that made Willich and his troops so famous. Skillfully forming the regiments in line of battle, Willich brought up his artillery and, "having sufficiently shaken the enemy's infantry line, I ordered a bayonet charge, and took the Eighty-ninth Illinois into a line with the Forty-ninth Ohio and Thirty-second Indiana, keeping the Fifteenth Ohio in reserve. The charge was executed in splendid order, and with such an energy that everything was swept before it for about a mile."[41] Rushing forward against the staggering Confederates, the regiments swarmed over the enemy lines and captured an entire battery. In their enthusiastic thrust the attackers advanced so far, indeed, that Willich feared to lose connection with the rest of the army. The forty-eighter halted his brigade, secured its new position, and waited for reinforcements.

To the far right, another division had also engaged the enemy. Part of Colonel Hans Heg's Brigade, the Scandinavians of the 15th Wisconsin soon found themselves in the thickest of battle. Captain Mons Grinager in his report described how the soldiers had to grapple with unfavorable ground, advancing "through some heavy underbrush till our right rested on a corn-field about three-quarters of a mile from the road." On they went up a hill, "and on ascending the top the enemy's skirmishers opened fire on us, but with little effect." Driving in the skirmish line, the Wisconsin men soon ran head-on into stronger enemy formations, and "the engagement now became general." Grinager and his men managed to hold their position for some time against heavy pressure and fired steadily until they had to fall back a few paces to evade dangerous crossfire "from infantry on our right and a rebel battery on our left. This position we held for some time, and had fired about 10 or 12 rounds, when we were ordered to fix bayonets and charge the line immediately in our front."[42] Dashing gallantly forward, the sturdy Scandinavians found their right flank again exposed to crossfire and had to withdraw. Crossing an open field under heavy fire, the regiment immediately turned around to retake their old positions at a log hut now occupied by the southerners. After a first unsuccessful attempt to traverse the field, the 15th finally managed to gain and hold the lost ground together with several pieces of artillery. During this remarkable and largely independent action the regiment lost seven officers dead and wounded, including Colonel Ole C. Johnson and brigade commander Heg.

Meanwhile, August Willich had in vain hoped for reinforcements while the Confederates brought up massive numbers of troops in his front. Then finally the counterattack hit his lines, and a "shower of canister and columns of infantry streamed at once into our front and both flanks." Willich's skirmishers fell back to the second line, which for a moment was thrown into confusion, but quickly recovered to breast the assault. With great discipline the brigade "formed one solid line, sending death into the enemy's masses, who immediately fell back from the front, and there did not answer with a single round."[43] Keeping up their accurate fire, the brigade slowly withdrew to the federal line of battle and went into bivouac for the night. When darkness fell on that day, the firing ceased and troops on both sides struggled to reorganize during an uncomfortable night in which no commander would allow campfires.

While Rosecrans rearranged his lines during the night, across the creek General Longstreet had arrived and reinforced Bragg. Battle was renewed the next morning, when due to a fatal misunderstanding and Rosecrans' ignorance of the exact where-abouts of his troops a gap opened along the lines of Sheridan's and Davis's Divisions inviting the Confederates to strike hard. Exchanging artillery salvos with the enemy, Willich witnessed the critical error at the front line. For some time, his men had been watching clouds of dust rising from the woods that indicated Longstreet's prepara-tions for a major offensive in their front. "Just when it was on the point of breaking forth," Willich later described the puzzling situation at that moment, "One or two of our divisions on the right of our breastworks left this portion of the battle-field under higher orders, each regiment cheering as they left, which cheering did not at all cheer us, who kept the position under a heavy fire." Soon after the federal divisions had departed and moved to another position, according to Willich "the storm broke loose."[44] The Confederates hit right into the gap and hammered at their enemies desperately trying to close the breach. Willich and several others tried to resist the onslaught, among them Colonel Laiboldt with his brigade consisting of the ethnic 2nd and 15th Missouri and the 44th and 73rd Illinois Regiments. With the lines around them breaking, Laiboldt rallied his regiments and counterattacked "in rear of the flying troops, and . . . the regiments, with charged bayonets, rushed into the thicket of woods," parting them even farther from their division. The routed Union soldiers fled to the rear first in small groups, but soon in a whirling stream, stum-bling through Laiboldt's lines. Amidst this general confusion the brigade could not sustain itself. His regiments were thrown into confusion by the fleeing troops and soon his brigade stood isolated against "the scathing fire of the enemy in front, as also a fire in the flank." Laiboldt and his officers tried to calm and steady their men but finally allowed them to fall back to a safer position against a steep slope, where finally "I succeeded in collecting the remaining portion."[45] During the short and terrible encounter, his brigade had virtually ceased to exist.

The ensuing chaos led Rosecrans to believe his whole force to be on the verge of annihilation. Ordering a general retreat, the general hurried back to Chattanooga with the greater part of the army, while General Thomas with his corps went into history as the "Rock of Chickamauga."[46] Forming a strong line on top of a protruding hill named Horseshoe Ridge, Thomas fought back Bragg's repeated assaults until nightfall and thus prevented the Confederates from destroying the fleeing federal army. Remaining on the field was Willich who with his brigade came up to Thomas's positions. His divisional commander later evaluated the importance of Willich's decision for the federal rear guard actions: "By having Willich in reserve," General Richard W. Johnson wrote, Thomas "was enabled to engage the enemy in four different directions, and by his prompt movements he saved the troops from annihilation and capture."[47] When Rosecrans finally told Thomas to retreat to safety, Willich together with another brigade under Russian-born General Basil Turchin brought up the rear and covered the Fourteenth Corps's withdrawal. Willich placed his artillery along the main route to Chattanooga, "permitted all troops to pass, and followed as rear guard, driving many stragglers before us, and reached camp unmolested at 12 P.M."[48]

Once again ethnic soldiers had stood in a major battle, and once again many of them had conducted themselves nobly. Although forced to retreat eventually, the men of the 15th Wisconsin and the 32nd Indiana as well as the ethnic Missourians could be proud of their record on these two days of merciless mayhem. Another battle-hardened ethnic regiment that exhibited its usual coolness was "Die Neuner" from Ohio. Led by Colonel Gustav Kämmerling after Robert McCook had been appointed brigadier general, the German Ohioans delivered two memorable charges during the battle. Escorting the ammunition train of the Fourteenth Corps's Third Division, the Ninth arrived on the scene of the battle late on the first day, and the brigade commander would later recall that Kämmerling chafed "like a wounded tiger that he had been behind at the opening." The Rhinelander professional at once ordered his men to line up in front of the enemy, and "Away they went."[49] Followed by the rest of the brigade, the *Neuner* drove the enemy before them and gallantly recaptured a battery of artillery, which they held until it was taken to the rear. On the second day of the battle, Colonel Ferdinand Van Derveer's Brigade participated in the defense of Horseshoe Ridge, and here again "the Ninth Ohio made a gallant charge down the hill into the midst of the enemy, scattering them like chaff, and then returning to their position on the hill."[50] Laiboldt, Kämmerling, and other ethnic commanders received due praise from their superiors. About the man who did so much to prevent utter devastation, General Johnson later wrote, that "This gallant old veteran," August Willich, with his command had been "always in the right place, and by his individual daring rendered the country great service."[51]

His soldiers called Willich "Papa" for good reason. In his report the affectionate commander told how he cared for the welfare of his troops upon their return to Chattanooga. After drawing rations for the brigade, he and his officers tried to calm the men's "sore feelings over the apparent non-success of our fighting, marching, and suffering, and over the great havoc death had worked in the ranks of our friends and brothers in arms." Praising the bravery and self-denial of his soldiers, the dedicated forty-eighter elevated the battle to a struggle for humanity and universal liberty. His men had "again and again proven that they are true sons of the Republic, who value life only so long as it is the life of freemen, and who are determined to make the neck of every power, slaveratic [sic] or monarchical, bend before the commonwealth of the freemen of the United States of America." Those in the Union who clamored for a lenient course toward the rebellion and demanded peace negotiations he called outright traitors who tried to make the fallen soldiers' "glorious deaths useless for the cause of humanity."[52]

In the killing fields around the River of Death the Union had suffered over 16,000 casualties out of their effective strength of a good 58,000 troops. Sending over 66,000 men into battle, the Confederates lost almost 18,500 killed, wounded, and missing. Several regiments contesting the dense forests and open fields competed for the highest losses. The Scandinavians counted 167 casualties or 63 percent of their number engaged, and the regiment only lived on because two companies arrived from detached service after the battle. Lieutenant Colonel Franz Erdelmeyer reported a total of 122 for the 32nd Indiana, including five officers. The Swiss Rifles lost a hundred men and officers killed, wounded, or captured, the partly German 6th Kentucky Infantry 118. For all these regiments it was the heaviest loss in a single battle during the entire war. Suffering hideously on both days of the battle, General Willich's Brigade had faded away to 800 men from their original strength of 3,500. With a view to these terrible casualties, Willich criticized the hasty recruitment of green regiments on the home front to replenish the army. Like Meagher, the German officer instead saw the benefits of filling the depleted ranks of veteran regiments with recruits. "Then . . . the new troops would have been veterans in a short time. Now the veterans day by day die out."[53] Rosecrans's promising campaign had ended in embarrassing defeat. The Confederates closed in on Chattanooga, occupying the west bank of the Tennessee, Lookout Mountain, and Missionary Ridge. Under siege by late fall, the federal troops trapped in the city and the surrounding works and trenches had to endure cold weather as well as increasing lack of food and supplies. Realizing the gravity of the situation, Halleck made several significant decisions. He relieved Rosecrans, called in Grant to break the deadlock, and reinforced the beleaguered forces by transferring troops West—including the remnants of the Eleventh Corps.

Grant went to work immediately; by the end of October he had reopened the supply lines and set out to break the Confederate stranglehold. Ethnic troops again played important parts in the following campaign that eventually secured all of Tennessee for the Union. In the famous "Midnight Battle" of Wauhatchie and the subsequent storming of Orchard Knob and Lookout Mountain in the "Battle above the Clouds," the Germans and Scandinavians had their share in driving the Confederates from their fortifications east of Chattanooga and regaining the offensive in the cold Tennessee winter. Then on November 25, the Union won one of its most incredible victories when August Willich and his brigade disobeyed orders and charged the enemy lines up on Missionary Ridge. Originally, Grant had only told his troops to take the rifle pits at the foot of the ridge, but Willich together with several other brigades pressed on. With "Chickamauga" as their battle cry, the federals swept over the breastworks, overran a second line of skirmishers, and reached the summit before their commanding generals even knew what was going on. Various regiments entered in a veritable race up the slope and threw the stunned rebels out of their works, sending them down the other side in a wild rout. The men of the 15th Missouri were second to plant their Swiss flag on the crest, and had the deep satisfaction of witnessing Bragg and his troops spurring their horses down the ridge to prevent capture.[54]

The Union breakout completed at Missionary Ridge opened the door to Georgia and eventually to the eastern seaboard. Ignoring calls for negotiations by the Democrats who nominated George McClellan for presidential candidate in 1864, Lincoln unerringly continued his course of subduing the enemy. In appointing General U.S. "Unconditional Surrender" Grant to commander in chief of all Union forces, Lincoln made an unmistakable statement that he would not rest until southern capitulation. After the crucial victories at Gettysburg and Vicksburg, a growing number of immigrants had again turned to Lincoln and approved his military policy. "One or two such victorious battles," Adolph Frick wrote to his family, "and the unworthy rebellion is deprived of all its power [and] its armies are wiped out."[55] Equally confident of eventual Union triumph August Horstmann predicted in September 1863 that "the final and decisive battle will be fought in southern Virginia or in upper North Carolina, and if we prevail then the whole South with its knights and slavery will lie at our feet; then the curse of tyranny will be avenged."[56]

Called to Washington in March 1864, Grant took command of all Union forces and gave the war its final and decisive turn. Ordering several simultaneous offensive campaigns the new general in chief set out to annihilate southern resistance and brought forth the first total war. While Sherman marched southeast with the consolidated western armies to conquer Atlanta, Grant himself took over the Army of the Potomac to battle it out with Lee once and for all. In a series of violent clashes from the Wilderness to Cold Harbor Grant battered the still defiant Army of Northern Virginia south to Petersburg where Lee dug in for his last stand. During these last campaigns in the east, most ethnic regiments had already melted down to mere shadows of their original splendid and colorful appearances. Others had received so many new recruits that they hardly resembled their initial ethnic makeup anymore. Decimated and exhausted, the Irish Brigade under Colonel Nugent could not reclaim their former glory and performed poorly in several engagements. After one of the battles around Petersburg in August, Division Commander General Barlow even wrote that the Irish soldiers had "behaved disgracefully," when they "crowded off to our right into the shelter of some woods."[57] Yet the Irishmen continued to fight to the last, as did their compatriots in Corcoran's Legion. General Corcoran had been killed in Virginia in December 1863, but his memory lived on in the bravery of his troops. At Cold Harbor and Petersburg, the 164th and 170th New York Infantries lost dreadfully while exhibiting the highest gallantry.

While Grant besieged Petersburg, Sherman set off from Atlanta on his ravaging march to the Atlantic Coast that ended with his presenting occupied Savannah to Lincoln for Christmas. When in February 1865 the indomitable stronghold of

Charleston finally surrendered, it was General Alexander Schimmelfennig and his troops who first entered the city where the war had begun almost four years earlier. August Valentin Kautz had dreamed of conquering Richmond since he first had caught "a glimpse of the spires of the rebel capitol" during the Peninsula campaign. When Lee could not hold off Grant anymore and abandoned Petersburg and Richmond in early April, Kautz's wish was granted. At the head of his division, the general occupied the deserted city on April 3. "We did not make much noise over the entry," the immigrant would later write, "but there was not a soldier in the command who did not feel the greatest possible pride over the event."[58] Six days later Lee's capitulation at Appomattox Courthouse marked the beginning of the end of the American Civil War. Together with the rest of the ethnic soldiers in the Army of the Potomac, the handful of the Irish Brigade was there. As a former slave and Union soldier from Virginia would later claim, the Confederates had finally given in because "them Dutch an Irish was too much fer 'em."[59]

EPILOGUE: THE AFTERMATH OF WAR

Marching down Pennsylvania Avenue in the Grand Review of the Union armies on May 22, 1865, every surviving member of the Irish Brigade sported a sprig of green on their coats in honor of their general's already famous order before the battle of Fredericksburg. When the remnants of Meagher's proud organization participated in another parade in New York in July, a broken Thomas Francis Meagher stood by and watched in civilian clothes. The last remaining Irish idol after Corcoran had been killed and Shields had resigned, Meagher had taken a new command of two makeshift brigades in December 1863, but soon fell from grace with Halleck and Grant. Personal quarrels and his incessant drinking problem led to Meagher's discharge in February 1865, and his request to take part in the New York parade in uniform was denied.[1] Over the coming decades, veterans and historians cultivated the gallant history of the Irish Brigade and stressed their glorious deeds, covering up the humiliating end of Meagher's career. The witty, recklessly daring Irish soldier who went into battle singing—albeit out of tune—became the dominant picture of the ethnic soldier in the Civil War.

While the country struggled with the legacy of that terrible war and entered into a period of uneasy reunification, ethnic groups tried to find their position in the new society. As immigrants had hoped to achieve social recognition by joining the army, they began to point to their achievements in the preceding national conflict and their upright motivations. In their effort to forge a favorable public image, Irish Americans stressed their bravery in battle, while at the same time concealing the virulent campaigns against Lincoln before the war and their misbehavior on the home front. Scandinavian Americans, on the other hand, were quick to point to their early Republicanism and the fact that they had unanimously voted for Lincoln in 1860.[2] While Swedes and Norwegians had a valid point, many Germans went to great lengths in claiming the same honor and often distorting the facts. Disregarding their own divisiveness, German veterans and, later, historians spouted memoirs and historical accounts fortifying ethnic myths. According to these authors, it had been the Germans who had swung the election in 1860 and with their undaunted patriotism in the following year saved Missouri for the Union against overwhelming odds. Another standard interpretation was that "the Germans had always been the most sincere enemies of slavery."[3] A similar claim was made by a former Swiss officer in Berdan's Sharpshooters. "It is beautiful to fight for an idea that is to bring freedom to all men," Rudolf Aschmann wrote in his memoirs. Doubtlessly inflating the number of Swiss abolitionists, Aschmann in hindsight expected his fellow immigrants to have agreed: "Most of the Swiss may have found this the cause for their participation in the great work."[4]

Courage in battle and a noble role in victory were most important in refining ethnic public memory. Americans agreed that the Irish had no problem in pointing to their role, and they acknowledged the participation of other ethnic groups. Still angry about the accusations against the Eleventh Corps, German Americans felt compelled to disprove their tarnished image as poor soldiers. Defiantly, German accounts made much of ethnic professionalism and agreed "that the Germans were the best soldiers."[5] Former officer Gustav Tafel challenged every unprejudiced citizen to admit that it had been the "Germans' willingness to make sacrifices" that made "final victory possible."[6]

However, nineteenth century Americans—just as much as Europeans—strongly believed in racial and ethnic predestination. Therefore, certain stereotypes were accepted as inherited ethnic traits that determined a group's character. Interestingly, many later authors have accepted these stereotypes based on inherent racial traits as true. Perhaps relying too much on contemporary sources and prejudicial commentaries, historian Bell I. Wiley in his groundbreaking study of the Union soldier came to the conclusion that what "the Teutons lacked in quickness and glamour was more than offset by their patience and steadiness." Accepting "neatness, precision and respect for authority" as typical German characteristics, on the other hand, Wiley attested that the German element in the Union army "was of infinite aid in molding a mob of individualists into an organized fighting force." Overall, Wiley held that "the Germans were good soldiers" in spite of the accusations made against them. Wiley also agreed with the prevailing image of the Irish soldiers, whose "pugnaciousness and the excessive fondness of many of them for strong drink sometimes made them difficult to discipline, but their troublesomeness was counterbalanced by their ready humor, sparkling repartee and matchless buoyancy." Admitting that some Irish soldiers acted cowardly and betrayed the general bravery of their ethnic group, Wiley nevertheless asserted that "the sons of old Erin were among the most desperate and dependable of fighters." This, he assumed, came from their motivation to enlist. Contrary to the idealistic Germans, Wiley was sure, Irish recruits had come forward for the "sheer love of combat."[7] Certainly, Meagher, Corcoran, and many of their followers would have strongly contested that opinion.

In his judgment, Wiley drew largely on the findings of Ella Lonn, who had done much to cement the image of ethnic soldiers. "From Yorktown to Appomattox," Lonn had concluded, "the Irishman was full of fun as well as full of fight. He was always cheerful and never disobeyed an order in battle." Totally disregarding their advantage in language, furthermore, Lonn was convinced that it was the Irish ability "to manage people" that had earned them more promotions to low-ranking office than Germans. As to German ethnicity, Lonn held them as a group to have been "patient, philosophical, plodding men" who were rather slow in response but "stable and solid in battle." Lonn refuted the charges made against German soldiers after Chancellorsville and Gettysburg, but she likewise criticized the Prussian elitism among German officers, which in turn led to prejudice among American soldiers. True to their sluggish and obedient nature, Lonn found Germans to be lacking the "dash and verve" of the Irish. With little consideration of the great majority of ethnic soldiers in American regiments, Lonn finally ascertained that German soldiers were only able to fight in large masses, "with little individuality."[8] August Willich, "Flying Dutchman" Klemens Landgräber, and many other German officers and soldiers might not have liked such a verdict.

Trying to find other ethnic classifications, Ella Lonn attributed "steadfastness, persistence, patience, obedience, and endurance" to the pious Scandinavian Protestants as well as "élan and whirlwind vigor" to the fiery Hungarian soldiers. Keeping with predominant stereotypes, Lonn further reduced ethnic qualities to "the readiness and idealism of the Poles in coming forward promptly; the pertinacity and loyalty of the English, who fought for a country which most of them had not adopted; the stern steadfastness of the Scotch; and the quiet courage of the Swiss, who contributed their special skill in marksmanship."[9]

All claims for ethnic distinctiveness and exclusiveness notwithstanding, differences in group and individual behavior may not have been as fundamental as contemporary observers, ethnic spokesmen, and even historians have asserted. Most significantly, there was no monopoly on cowardice; while Germans fled in panic at Chancellorsville, American regiments broke and ran at Stones River. On the other hand, daring valor was not the exclusive privilege of Irish soldiers. Scandinavian, German, and other soldiers performed heroic deeds in battle in the same way when they retook captured batteries under deadly fire or executed memorable bayonet charges. In his Civil War roll of honor, Fox not only named the units of the Irish Brigade, the 164th and 170th New York Regiments of Corcoran's Legion as well as the Irish 9th Massachusetts and 69th Pennsylvania Infantry, but also several German units. August Willich's 32nd Indiana appears in this list of regiments sustaining the heaviest battle losses as well as Hecker's

82nd Illinois, the 52nd New York, 26th Wisconsin, and the 12th Missouri Infantry together with the mixed ethnic Swiss Rifles. In addition, Fox lists the 79th New York Highlanders as well as several partly ethnic regiments, such as 5th and 6th Kentucky Regiments.[10] As they came forward for much the same reasons to join the Union army, ethnic and immigrant soldiers shared courage and cowardice, genius in battle and poor leadership. They endured fatiguing marches and relaxed sociably in their camps, and the various forms of socializing when they enjoyed periods between campaigns in many cases served to increase mutual interest between ethnic and native-born soldiers.

Most importantly, immigrants were never behind their nonethnic comrades in their devotion to the country. Even during times of shame and defeat, desertion in ethnic regiments did not surpass that of other units. When enlistment terms expired in late 1863 and early 1864 and soldiers had to decide whether or not to reenlist, many immigrants had a tougher choice than most native-born Americans. However, despite prejudice after the draft riots and the stigma of alleged cowardice, the majority of Irish and German veterans signed up for another term when called to do so. Almost all members of the Irish Brigade, for example, reenlisted in January 1864, although high bounties and the opportunity to go on leave may have played more important roles for many than continuing patriotism and determination for Union.[11] In other cases, it was the influence and charisma of their ethnic leaders that induced immigrants to reenlist. When Colonel Krzyzanowski urged the men in his brigade to reenlist in 1864, he recalled that "my own regiment, the 58th New York Infantry, sent a delegation to me declaring that they would reenlist only if they were assured that I would remain in command."[12] Still, many immigrants did not waver in their conviction. An English corporal wrote after his reenlistment that he would fight on "not only for my Country and my Children but for Liberty all over the World." If the Union would not be able to safeguard liberty in America, George Cadman feared, "What hope would there be for the cause of Human Progress anywhere else?"[13] Captain August Horstmann, whose parents had criticized him for reenlisting and continuing to risk his life, defended his decision in equally glowing words. "Dear parents," Horstmann pleaded,

> Men of *Principle* cannot endure for 3 years such greatest hardships as only imagination can conceive—without ever receiving the satisfaction of witnessing the fortunate or unfortunate outcome of their labors. If you fight for *Principle* and ideas, you must not stop at half way! This is the opinion of our government, of the people, and my own! Believe me that this war will be carried out to the end, the rebellion will fail, slavery will end [and] equal human rights will prevail in *all of America*. . . .[14]

The Union army was no mere band of mercenaries (as southerners liked to believe), but a highly literate group of citizen-soldiers who had made conscious decisions.[15]

Ulysses Grant may not purposely have included immigrants when in his memoirs he wrote that "our armies were composed of men who were able to read, men who knew what they were fighting for."[16] However, his assertion was valid for the foreign-born soldiers as well. Also, like their Anglo-American comrades, ethnic volunteers knew specifically whom they were not fighting for—incompetent officers, corrupt politicians, and prejudiced society. Ethnic soldiers were equally quick to criticize ethnic officers as to snub Americans. At the same time, many were proud of their units and did not care if they were ethnic ones or not—as long as they were good ones. When James Sullivan in the fall of 1862 ran into a soldier of another Wisconsin regiment who bragged about military success in the West, while the Army of the Potomac was suffering consecutive defeats, the Irishman finally "admonished him by an Iron Brigade rap between the eyes and at it we went, and that time the Army of the Potomac came out victorious."[17] Ironically, it was actions like these that produced further prejudice against Sullivan and his fellow Irishmen.

Even if nativism was far from extinct after the war and not all immigrants had found their hopes of recognition through military service fulfilled, the Civil War was instrumental in forging a new consciousness for most foreign-born citizens. Many Americans were willing to acknowledge the participation of immigrants in saving the Union and to accept them into a multicultural society, especially in the face of a new wave of immigration from eastern and southeastern Europe, which reinforced American xenophobia against allegedly inferior racial traits. By the end of the century, the Irish St. Patrick's Day was already understood as an American holiday. Some ethnic leaders entered highly respected careers after the war. Peter Kiolbassa was instrumental in forging ethnic Polish politics in Chicago where "Honest Pete" became known as an outstanding city treasurer. Carl Schurz, who in 1864 had again campaigned for Lincoln, went on to become Senator from Missouri and even Secretary of the Interior under President Grant. His fellow forty-eighter, Franz Sigel, also continued his influential role as a publisher and ethnic politician in New York. A friend of Schurz and Sigel, Hungarian General Stahel was made consul to Japan and China and afterwards became a figure of some public prominence in New York.

At the same time, most former revolutionaries had not forgotten what they had been fighting for in their old countries. Many immigrants had followed attentively when Poles again rose to fight for their independence in 1863. Too young to have been an active forty-eighter, a Silesian lieutenant nevertheless identified with the insurrectionists when he wrote that "I wish they can gain their liberty, the best right for which a nation can fight."[18] The immigrant even hinted at the possibility of actively participating in the rebellion. Several freedom fighters returned to their native Ireland where in 1867 the Fenians made another attempt at overthrowing English rule. Other immigrants joined the Mexican Revolution under Benito Juarez, although the majority may have acted out of professional and mercenary reasons rather than the spirit of 1848. Several German forty-eighters also returned to Europe and participated in the Franco-Prussian War that finally brought about national unity in 1871. Americans, who had sympathetically watched the nationalist movement in Germany, now expressed their respect for the founding of a unified German Nation.

The national idea had been the great common goal for immigrants and native Americans alike in fighting for the Union. As the vast majority of foreign-born volunteers had served and assimilated in nonethnic and mixed regiments, they had contributed to the creation of a truly national army that laid the foundation for a multicultural postwar society. Deeply relieved about the conquest of the Mississippi in August 1863, Abraham Lincoln certainly made no ethnic distinctions when he wrote: "The job was a great national one; and let none be banned who bore an honorable part in it. . . . It is hard to say that anything has been more bravely and well done than at Antietam, Murfreesborough, Gettysburg, and on many fields of lesser note. . . . Thanks to all. For the great Republic—for the principle it lives by, and keeps alive—for man's vast future—thanks to all."[19]

NOTES

PREFACE AND ACKNOWLEDGMENTS

1. Philip Taylor, *The Distant Magnet. European Emigration to the U.S.A.* (New York: Harper & Row, 1971), 19; Dudley Baines, *Emigration from Europe, 1815–1930* (Cambridge: Cambridge University Press, 1995), 1–2.

2. Ella Lonn, *Foreigners in the Union Army and Navy* (Baton Rouge, LA: Louisiana State University Press, 1951), 577–582. Lonn's numbers are mostly based on Benjamin A. Gould, *Investigations in the Military and Anthropological Statistics of the American Soldier* (New York: Hurd and Houghton, 1869), 27–28; see also Miecislaus Haiman, *Polish Past in America, 1608–1865* (Chicago, IL: The Polish Roman Catholic Union Archives and Museum, 1939), 109–112.

3. Wilhelm Kaufmann, *Die Deutschen im Amerikanischen Bürgerkriege* (München/Berlin: R. Oldenbourg, 1911). For this book, the English version translated and edited by Steven Rowan and Don Heinrich Tolzmann has been used: *The Germans in the American Civil War* (Carlisle, PA: John Kallmann, 1999).

4. Kaufmann, *Germans*, 77; Lonn, *Foreigners*, 577–578. This number has been accepted as the most accurate in following studies, such as William L. Burton, *Melting Pot Soldiers: The Union's Ethnic Regiments* (Ames, IA: Iowa State University Press, 1988), 110.

5. Ezra Warner, *Generals in Blue: The Lives of the Union Commanders* (Baton Rouge, LA: Louisiana State University Press, 1964), 596–604.

6. Translated from *Westliche Post* (St. Louis), May 8, 1861. Translations from foreign-language sources have been marked accordingly throughout the book.

7. Ella Lonn, *Foreigners in the Confederacy* (Chapel Hill, NC: University of North Carolina Press, 1940), 220.

CHAPTER ONE

1. Translated from Hagen Schulze, *Staat und Nation* (February 1995), 150–155. For concise overviews of the European and transatlantic migration movements, see Baines, *Emigration*; Taylor, *Distant Magnet*; John Bodnar, *The Transplanted. A History of Immigrants in Urban America* (Bloomington, IN: Indiana University Press, 1985), 1–23; Ronald Takaki, *A Different Mirror: A History of Multicultural America* (Boston, MA: Little, Brown & Company, 1993); Leslie Page Moch, *Moving Europeans: Migration in Western Europe Since 1650* (Bloomington and Indianapolis, IA: Indiana University Press, 1992).

2. Bodnar, *Transplanted*, 54.

3. William Van Vugt, *Britain to America: Mid-Nineteenth-Century Immigrants to the United States* (Urbana and Chicago, IL: University of Illinois Press, 1999), 9.

4. On Irish emigration in the nineteenth century, see Roger Daniels, *Coming to America: A History of Immigration and Ethnicity in American Life* (New York: HarperCollins, 1990), 125–145; P. J. Drudy, ed., *The Irish in America: Emigration, Assimilation, and Impact* (Cambridge, MA: Cambridge University Press, 1985); Patrick J. Blessing, "Irish," *Harvard Encyclopedia of American Ethnic Groups*, edited by Stephan Thernstrom et al. (Cambridge, MA: Cambridge University Press, 1980): 524–545; Kerby A. Miller, *Emigrants and Exiles: Ireland and the Irish Exodus to North America* (New York: Oxford University Press, 1985). Much valuable in-depth information on the Irish emigration during the Great Famine years provides Oliver MacDonagh, "The Irish Famine Emigration to the United States," *Perspectives in American History*, 10(1976): 357–446.

5. The following studies deal with various aspects of British nineteenth-century emigration: Gordon Donaldson, "Scots," *Harvard Encyclopedia*, 908–916; Thomas M. Devine, ed., *Scottish Emigration and Scottish Society* (Edinburgh: John Donald Publishers, 1992); Rowland Berthoff, "Welsh." *Harvard Encyclopedia*, 1011–1017; Charlotte J. Erickson, "English," ibid., 319–336.

6. Erickson, "English," 325–326; William Van Vugt places the number of British emigrants to the United States between 1845 and 1855 alone at "closer to a million than the half-million counted by the authorities." Van Vugt, *Britain to America*, 17.

7. On Nordic emigration from the Scandinavian countries and Finland, see Ulf Beijbom, "Swedes," *Harvard Encyclopedia*, 971–981; Hans Norman and Harald Runblom, *Transatlantic Connections: Nordic Migration to the New World After 1800* (Oslo: Norwegian University Press, 1987); A. William Hoglund, "Finns," *Harvard Encyclopedia*, 362–370; Dorothy Burton Skårdal, "Danes," ibid., 273–282; Peter A. Munch, "Norwegians," ibid., 750–761.

8. For histories of the Napoleonic Wars and their aftermath, see especially Eric J. Hobsbawm, *The Age of Revolution 1789–1848* (New York: Vintage Books, 1996); David S. Mason, *Revolutionary Europe, 1789–1989: Liberty, Equality, Solidarity* (Lanham, MD: Rowman & Littlefield, 2005).

9. Heinrich Heine, *The Complete Poems of Heinrich Heine*, edited by Hal Draper (Boston, MA: Suhrkamp, 1982), 484.

10. There is abounding literature on the 1848 Revolutions in Europe. Overviews provide R. J. W. Evans, ed., *The Revolutions in Europe 1848–1849: From Reform to Reaction* (Oxford: Oxford University Press, 2000); Michael Broers, *Europe After Napoleon: Revolution, Reaction and Romanticism, 1814–1848* (Manchester: Manchester University Press, 1996). The following case studies deal with events in the several affected countries and the forty-eighter movement:

Bruce Levine, *The Spirit of 1848: German Immigrants, Labor Conflict, and the Coming of the Civil War* (Urbana, IL: University of Illinois Press, 1992); Wolfgang Hochbruck, Ulrich Bachteler, and Henning Zimmermann, eds., *Achtundvierziger/Forty-Eighters* (Münster: Westfälisches Dampfboot, 2000); A. E. Zucker, ed., *The Forty-Eighters: Political Refugees of the German Revolution of 1848* (New York: Columbia University Press, 1950); György Spira, *The Nationality Issue in the Hungary of 1848–49* (Budapest: Akadémiai Kiadó, 1992); Istvan Deak, *The Lawful Revolution: Louis Kossuth and the Hungarians, 1848–1849* (London: Phoenix Press, 2001); Herbert Mitgang, "Garibaldi And Lincoln," *Civil War Chronicles* 2, 1(Summer 1992): 4–13.

11. Hermann Lieb and Emil Dietzsch, *Kaiser Wilhelm I. Der Schöpfer des Neuen Deutschen Reiches* (Chicago, IL: Belford, Clarke & Company, 1888), 288.

12. Heine, *Complete Poems*, 646.

13. Sándor Szillassy, "America and the Hungarian Revolution of 1848–49," *Slavonic and East European Review* 44, 102(January 1966): 180–196; Gary R. Forney, *Thomas Francis Meagher. Irish Rebel, American Yankee, Montana Pioneer* (Philadelphia, PA: Xlibris, 2003), 58–59.

14. On Hungarian and Polish forty-eighter emigration, see Paula Benkart, "Hungarians," *Harvard Encyclopedia*, 462–471; Victor Greene, "Poles," ibid., 787–803; Andrzej Brozek, "The Roots of Polish Migration to Texas," *Polish-American Studies* 30(1–2) (January–June 1973): 20–35.

15. James S. Pula, *The Memoirs of Wladimir Krzyzanowski* (San Francisco, CA: R & E Research Associates, 1978), 9. Krzyzanowski had already left Poland in 1846.

16. Karen Johnson Freeze, "Czechs," *Harvard Encyclopedia*, 261–272; Frederick C. Luebke, "Austrians," ibid., 164–171; Kaufmann, *Germans*, 280.

17. Patrice Louis René Higonnet, "French," *Harvard Encyclopedia*, 379–388.

18. Humbert S. Nelli, "Italians," *Harvard Encyclopedia*, 545–560; Robert P. Swierenga, "Dutch," ibid., 284–295; Leo Schelbert, "Swiss," ibid., 981–986; Pierre-Henri Laurent, "Belgians" ibid., 179–181.

19. For the complex subject of German emigration see the still valuable standard work of Mack Walker, *Germany and the Emigration, 1816–1866* (Cambridge, MA: Harvard University Press, 1964); Kathleen Neils Conzen, "Germans," *Harvard Encyclopedia*, 405–425.

20. *Military Autobiography* by U. G. Scheller-de Buol. LR CT 1864 D 89. Record Group (hereafter cited as RG) 94, National Archives, Washington, DC (hereafter cited as NA).

21. Defense statement by Ladislas Zulavsky, proceedings of General Court-Martial, December 1, 1864, case of L. L. Zulavsky, OO 280, RG 153, NA.

22. Kaufmann, *Germans*, 289.

23. Translated from Gustav Struve, *Diesseits und jenseits des Oceans* (Coburg: F. Streit, 1863), 1.

24. *Schlegel's German-American Families in the United States* (New York: The American Historical Society, 1916–1917), Vol. 2, 162.

25. Kaufmann, *Germans*, 318.

CHAPTER TWO

1. Irish made up 38.9 percent of the immigrants in 1860, Germans 30.8 percent. Daniels, *Coming to America*, 127–150; Conzen, "Germans," 406–416.

2. Forney, *Thomas Francis Meagher*, 63.

3. Daniels, *Coming to America*, 131–137; Takaki, *Different Mirror*, 154–160.

4. Conzen, "Germans," 413–421; Hartmut Keil, ed., *German Workers' Culture in the United States 1850 to 1920* (Washington, DC: Smithsonian Institution Press, 1988), 6–17; Daniels, *Coming To America*, 161–162.

5. Translated from Heinrich Börnstein, *Fünfundsiebzig Jahre in der Alten und Neuen Welt* (Leipzig: Otto Wigand, 1881), 257.

6. Theodore Stempfel, *Fünfzig Jahre unermüdlichen Strebens in Indianapolis* (Indianapolis, IN: German-American Center, 1991), 21.

7. American nativism rooted in eighteenth-century xenophobic fears that European monarchical and Papal influences would undermine republican freedom, and propaganda to protect the "noble Saxon blood" against inferior "Celtic" traits continued well into the nineteenth century. Only few enlightened Americans, among them Abraham Lincoln, thought differently. Stephen Steinberg, *The Ethnic Myth: Race, Ethnicity, and Class in America* (Boston, MA: Beacon Press, 1989), 11–12; John Higham, *Strangers in the Land: Patterns of American Nativism, 1860–1925* (New York: Atheneum, 1973), 5–11.

8. Higonnet, "French," 383–384.

9. Nels Hokanson, *Swedish Immigrants in Lincoln's Time* (New York: Arno Press, 1979), 48.

10. Erickson, "English," 320; Donaldson, "Scots," 912–915.

11. Both quoted in Hokanson, *Swedish Immigrants*, 19–20.

12. Adolf E. Schroeder and Carla Schulz Geisberg, eds., *Hold Dear, as Always: Jette, a German Immigrant Life in Letters* (Columbia, MO: University of Missouri Press, 1988), 178.

13. Aled Jones and Bill Jones, "*Y Drych* and American Welsh Identities 1851–1951," *North American Journal of Welsh Studies* 1(1) (Winter 2001), 46.

14. Translated from Helbich and Kamphoefner, *Deutsche*, 331.

15. Forney, *Thomas Francis Meagher*, 77.

16. Quoted in Hokanson, *Swedish Immigrants*, 28. For a discussion of immigrants in the South, see Lonn, *Confederacy*, 1–32, 481.

17. Quoted in Mark Wyman, *Immigrants in the Valley: Irish, German, and Americans in the Upper Mississippi Valley, 1830–1860* (Chicago, IL: Nelson Hall, 1984), 217.

18. Körner quoted in Wyman, *Immigrants*, 218.

19. Translated from Carl Schurz, *Lebenserinnerungen* (Berlin: Georg Reimer, 1906–1912), Vol. 3, 120.

20. Van Vugt, *Britain to America*, 143–144.

21. Quoted in Schroeder and Geisberg, *Hold Dear*, 164.

22. Quoted in Hokanson, *Swedish Immigrants*, 32.

23. Stephen B. Oates, *To Purge This Land with Blood: A Biography of John Brown* (Amherst, MA: University of Massachusetts Press, 1984), 148. By the time Brown finally staged his campaign against Harper's Ferry in 1859, he had no more immigrants among his men.

24. Translated from Helbich and Kamphoefner, *Deutsche*, 352.

25. Ibid., 331.

26. Quoted in Hokanson, *Swedish Immigrants*, 32.

27. Translated from Schurz, *Lebenserinnerungen*, Vol. 2, 56. Frémont had earned the nickname "Pathfinder of the West" for his daring expeditions.

28. Quoted in Carl Wittke, *The Irish in America* (Baton Rouge, LA: Louisiana State University Press, 1956), 130.

29. Translated from Schurz, *Lebenserinnerungen*, Vol. 3, 141–142.

30. Ibid., 186.

31. Translated from *Belleviller Zeitung*, November 15, 1860.

32. Translated from Freeport *Deutscher Anzeiger*, November 7, 1860.

33. Quoted in Schroeder and Geisberg, *Hold Dear*, 176.

34. Translated from Helbich and Kamphoefner, *Deutsche*, 354.

35. Walter D. Kamphoefner, " 'Auch unser Deutschland muss einmal frei warden.' The Immigrant Civil War Experience as a Mirror on Political Conditions in Germany," *Transatlantic Images and Perceptions: Germany and America Since 1776*, edited by David E. Barclay and Elisabeth Glaser-Schmidt (Cambridge: Cambridge University Press, 1997), 95.

36. *Hemlandet*, November 7, 1860, quoted in Lonn, *Union*, 62–63.

37. Quoted in Susannah Ural Bruce, *The Harp and the Eagle. Irish-American Volunteers and the Union Army, 1861–1865* (New York: New York University Press, 2006), 42.

38. Quoted in Bruce, *Harp and Eagle*, 43.

39. For thorough discussions of ethnic voting in 1860, see William E. Gienapp, "Who Voted for Lincoln?" *Abraham Lincoln and the American Political Tradition*, edited by John L. Thomas (Amherst, MA: University of Massachusetts Press, 1986), 50–97; Frederick C. Luebke, ed., *Ethnic Voters and the Election of Lincoln* (Lincoln, NE: University of Nebraska Press, 1971).

40. Alan Conway, ed., *The Welsh in America. Letters from the Immigrants* (Minneapolis, MN: University of Minnesota Press, 1961), 284–285.

41. Translated from Schurz, *Lebenserinnerungen*, Vol. 2, 34–35.

42. Translated from Max Burgheim, *Cincinnati in Wort und Bild* (Cincinnati, OH: The Burgheim Publishing Company, 1891), 152.

43. Translated from *Wisconsin Banner* (Milwaukee), February 4, 1850.

44. On the *Latin Farmers* in Illinois, see Kaufmann, *Germans*, 277–278; Oswald Garrison Villard, "The 'Latin Peasants' of Belleville, Illinois," *Journal of the Illinois State Historical Society* 35(1942): 7–20.

45. U. G. Scheller to F. Wanner, Swiss Consul in Havre, February 4, 1859, Archives of the Swiss Consulate in Le Havre, E. 2200.51, Schweizerisches Bundesarchiv, Bern.

46. Translated from Schurz, *Lebenserinnerungen*, Vol. 2, 1.

47. Translated from Börnstein, *Fünfundsiebzig Jahre*, 250.

48. Translated from *Oldenburgischer Volksfreund*, April 3, 1850.

49. Jacob Rader Marcus, ed., *Memoirs of American Jews, 1775–1865* (3 Vols., Philadelphia, PA: The Jewish Publication Society of America, 1956), Vol. 3, 58–59.

50. Quoted in Susanne Martha Schick, " 'For God, Mac, and Country:' The Political Worlds of Midwestern Germans during the Civil War Era" (Ph.D. dissertation, University of Illinois Urbana-Champaign, 1989), 41.

51. Military Autobiography by U. G. Scheller-de Buol.

CHAPTER THREE

1. Quoted in Lonn, *Union*, 68–69.

2. Ibid., 52.

3. Quoted Wittke, *Irish*, 131.

4. Meagher quoted in John M. Hearne and Rory T. Cornish, eds., *Thomas Francis Meagher: The Making of an Irish American* (Dublin: Irish Academic Press, 2005), 145.

5. Quoted in Burton, *Melting Pot Soldiers*, 35.

6. Lonn, *Union*, 87; Blessing, "Irish," 536.

7. Translated from *Belleviller Zeitung*, April 11, 1861.

8. Translated from Schurz, *Lebenserinnerungen*, Vol. 2, 175.

9. Ibid.

10. Translated from *Belleviller Zeitung*, April 18, 1861.

11. Translated from *Anzeiger des Westens* (St. Louis), April 19, 1861.

12. Quoted in Lonn, *Union*, 59.

13. Ibid., 59.

14. Translated from *Westliche Post* (St. Louis), May 8, 1861. A friend of Karl Marx, German emigrant Fritz Anneke was one of the first to call the Civil War "The Second War for Liberty." Fritz Anneke, *Der Zweite Freiheitskampf der Vereinigten Staaten von Amerika* (Frankfurt am Main: J. D. Sauerlander, 1861).

15. Quoted in Lonn, *Union*, 51–52.

16. Translated from Gustav Tafel, *Die Neuner* (Cincinnati, OH: S. Rosenthal & Co, 1897), 99.

17. Burton, *Melting Pot Soldiers*, 36.

18. Quoted in Lonn, *Union*, 57.

19. Ibid., 54.

20. Translated from Schurz, *Lebenserinnerungen*, Vol. 3, 200.

21. Lonn, *Union*, 44–46.

22. Translated from Jürgen Macha, Marlene Nikolay-Panter, and Wolfgang Herborn, eds. *Wir verlangen nicht mehr nach Deutschland. Auswandererbriefe und Dokumente der Sammlung Joseph Scheben (1825–1938)* (Frankfurt: Peter Lang, 2003), 328–329.

23. Translated from Macha et al., *Auswandererbriefe*, 4.

24. Translated from Helbich and Kamphoefner, *Deutsche*, 419.

25. Quoted in Ralph H. Bowen, ed., *A Frontier Family in Minnesota: Letters of Theodore and Sophie Bost, 1851–1920* (Minneapolis, MN: University of Minnesota Press, 1981), 181.

26. Translated from Helbich and Kamphoefner, *Deutsche*, 369.

27. Ibid., 180.

28. Translated from Andrea Wolf, *Kriegstagebücher des 19. Jahrhunderts: Entstehung-Sprache-Edition* (Frankfurt/Main: Peter Lang, 2005), 215.

29. Quoted in Lonn, *Union*, 51.

30. Translated from *Westliche Post* (St. Louis), January 11, 1860. The German name of the "Unabhängiges schwarzes Jäger-Corps" derived from the regiment's black uniforms and caused considerable confusion among Southerners who mistook it for a unit of black soldiers.

31. Translated from Börnstein, *Fündundsiebzig Jahre*, 280.

32. Stephen D. Engle, *Yankee Dutchman: The Life of Franz Sigel* (Fayetteville, AR: The University of Arkansas Press, 1993), 52–54; Kaufmann, *Germans*, 318. Kaufmann falsely mentions Salomon as commander of the 3rd Infantry.

33. Translated from Wolf, *Kriegstagebücher*, 212. Originally a misnomer derived from the mispronunciation of "Deutsch" for Pennsylvania Germans, "Dutch" had become a common synonym for all German-speaking immigrant groups, and Americans throughout the Civil War would use that term to insult foreigners. See Christian B. Keller, "Pennsylvania and Virginia Germans during the Civil War," *Virginia Magazine of History and Biography*, 109, 1(2001): 41.

34. Quoted in Schroeder and Geisberg, *Hold Dear*, 177.

35. Translated from Wolf, *Kriegstagebücher*, 213.

36. Quoted in Schroeder and Geisberg, *Hold Dear*, 182.

37. Ibid.

38. Translated from *Westliche Post* (St. Louis), May 29, 1861.

39. Translated from Helbich and Kamphoefner, *Deutsche*, 393.

40. Joseph Kugler to Secretary of War, March 8, 1866. Personal Papers, Medical Officers and Physicians, Joseph Kugler, RG 94, NA.

41. For thorough discussions of the American military tradition see Russell F. Weigley, *History of the United States Army* (New York: Macmillan, 1967) and Marcus Cunliffe, *Soldiers and Civilians: The Martial Spirit in America, 1775–1865* (Boston, MA: Little, Brown & Company, 1968).

42. Corcoran quoted in Bruce, *Harp and Eagle*, 45.

43. Meagher quoted in Forney, *Thomas Francis Meagher*, 88.

44. Burton, *Melting Pot Soldiers*, 80, 112, 161–165; Engle, *Yankee Dutchman*, 38.

45. Translated from Lonn, *Union*, 69.

46. Quoted in Lonn, *Union*, 71.

47. Quoted in Hearne and Cornish, *Meagher*, 145.

48. Meagher quoted in Hearne and Cornish, *Meagher*, 149.

49. Meagher quoted in Forney, *Thomas Francis Meagher*, 89.

50. Burton, *Melting Pot Soldiers*, illustration facing p. 60.

51. Translated from Louisville *Anzeiger*, October 11, 1861.

52. Translated from Börnstein, *Fünfundsiebzig Jahre*, 249. Lonn oversimplifies a bit when she assumes that generally "the Germans felt a special compulsion to maintain the unity of their adopted country in its integrity because of the evil effects from disunion under which they had suffered in their homeland." Lonn, *Union*, 67.

53. Wolf, *Kriegstagebücher*, 26–27.

54. Kaufmann, *Germans*, 107, 319.

55. Burton, *Melting Pot Soldiers*, 96.

56. Ibid., 94–97.

57. Ibid., 146–147.

58. Harry Simonhoff, *Jewish Participants in the Civil War* (New York: Arco Publishing Company, 1963), 36–46; Burton, *Melting Pot Soldiers*, 143–144.

59. William F. Fox, *Regimental Losses in the American Civil War, 1861–1865* (Albany, NY: Albany Publishing Company, 1889), 399.

60. Schick, "For God, Mac, and Country," 135–137.

61. Simonhoff, *Jewish Participants*, 25–26.

62. Lonn, *Union*, 112.

63. Burton, *Melting Pot Soldiers*, 105–106.

64. Kaufmann, *Germans*, 328.

65. Report of Brig.-Gen. A. Asboth, *The War of the Rebellion: A Compilation of the Official Records of the Union and Confederate Armies* (Washington, DC: Government Printing Office, 1880–1901), ser. I, Vol. 8, 243 (hereafter cited as *OR*).

66. For a comprehensive history of the 15th Missouri, see Donald Allendorf, *Long Road to Liberty. The Odyssey of a German Regiment in the Yankee Army: The 15th Missouri Volunteer Infantry* (Kent: Kent State University Press, 2006).

67. James I. Robertson, *Soldiers Blue and Gray* (Columbia, SC: University of South Carolina Press, 1998), 23.

68. Report of Col. John D. Stevenson, *OR*, I, 17, 372.

69. Kaufmann, *Germans*, 281–282.

70. Burton, *Melting Pot Soldiers*, 101–102.

71. Kaufmann, *Germans*, 321; Burton, *Melting Pot Soldiers*, 99–101.

72. Fox, *Losses*, 277.

73. Report of Maj.-Gen. Benjamin Butler, *OR*, I, 6, 506.

74. Report of Col. Michael T. Donohoe, *OR*, I, 21, 337.

75. Thomas O'Connor, *Civil War Boston: Home Front and Battlefield* (Boston, MA: Northeastern University Press, 1997), 73–75; Fox, *Losses*, 157.

76. Report of Col. Thomas Cass, *OR*, I, 11/1, 720.

77. David Porter Conyngham, *The Irish Brigade and its Campaigns* (Glasgow: Cameron and Ferguson, 1866), 28–29.

78. McIvor quoted in Burton, *Melting Pot Soldiers*, 118.

79. George B. McClellan, *McClellans Own Story: The War for the Union* (New York: Charles L. Webster & Company, 1887), 142–143.

80. Report of Capt. John Hamilton, *OR*, I, 53, 24.

81. Lonn, *Union*, 651.

82. Kaufmann, *Germans*, 304.

83. Burton, *Melting Pot Soldiers*, 162.

84. Fox, *Losses*, 210.

85. Burton, *Melting Pot Soldiers*, illustration facing p. 67.

86. Translated from *Morgenblatt für gebildete Leser* (New York), August 13, 1862, 781.

87. Translated from Schurz, *Lebenserinnerungen*, Vol. 2, 178.

88. Lonn, *Union*, 164–169.

89. Quoted in Lonn, *Union*, 71–72.

90. Kaufmann, *Germans*, 271.

91. Lonn, *Union*, 96.

92. Report of Lieut.-Col. C. G. Freudenberg, *OR*, I, 29/1, 267.

93. Fox, *Losses*, 199.

94. Bertram Wallace Korn, *American Jewry and the Civil War* (1951, reprint Philadelphia, PA: The Jewish Publication Society, 2001), 99–101; Simonhoff, *Jewish Participants*, 36–46.

95. Burton, *Melting Pot Soldiers*, 90–91.

96. Willemien M. Schenkeveld, "The 'Colony' and the Union: Dutch-American Reactions to the Civil War," *The Dutch in North America. Their Immigration and Cultural Continuity*, edited by Rob Kroes and Henk-Otto Neuschäfer (Amsterdam: VU University Press, 1991), 254.

97. Report of Col. Thomas W. Egan, *OR*, I, 29/1, 760.

98. Henry J. Hunt to Capt. G. Stoneman, *OR*, I, 2, 769.

99. Henry J. Hunt to Col. George D. Ruggles, *OR*, I, 40/6, 1244.

100. Alf Åberg, *Svenskarna under stjärnbaneret* (Stockholm: Natur och Kultur, 1994), 113.

101. Kaufmann, *Germans*, 284–285.

102. Lonn, *Union*, 152, 156–157.

103. Burton, *Melting Pot Soldiers*, 93.

104. Ibid., 44–45.

105. Translated from Wolf, *Kriegstagebücher* 219.

106. Burton, *Melting Pot Soldiers*, 110; Kaufmann, *Germans*, 102. Upholding German-American consciousness, Kaufmann may have included more than the "purely" German regiments in his count so that the number of 36,000 very probably must even be lower.

107. Translated from Schurz, *Lebenserinnerungen*, Vol. 3, 147.

108. Joseph A. Wytrwal, *Poles in American History and Tradition* (Detroit, MI: Endurance Press, 1969), 65. Kaufmann calls Blandowski the "first German-born officer to fall before the enemy." Kaufmann, *Germans*, 279.

109. Col. Richard Ballinger to Adjutant General's Office, June 10, 1863. Letters Received by the Adjutant General's Office of Colored Troops (hereafter cited as LR AGO CT) 1863 B 37, RG 94, NA.

110. For Sigel's military career and his falling out with Halleck, see Engle, *Yankee Dutchman*, 81–208.

111. Kaufmann, *Germans*, 273–274, 276.

112. Ibid., 173.

113. *Schlegel's German-American Families in the United States*, 3 Vols. (New York: The American Historical Society, 1916–1917), 164.

114. Kaufmann, *Germans*, 303.

115. Translated from Helbich and Kamphoefner, *Deutsche*, 177; Engle, *Yankee Dutchman*, 83–84.

CHAPTER FOUR

1. Ernest [*sic*] Hoffman [*sic*] to Hon. B. Gratz Brown, December 7, 1864. Personal Papers Ernest [*sic*] Hoffman [*sic*], RG 94, NA.

2. Translated from Wolf, *Kriegstagebücher*, 215.

3. Quoted in James I. Robertson, *Tenting Tonight: The Soldier's Life* (Alexandria, LA: Time Life Books, 1984), 24.

4. Pula, *Krzyzanowski*, 42–43.

5. Translated from Helbich and Kamphoefner, *Deutsche*, 256.

6. Translated from Wolfgang Helbich, Walter D. Kamphoefner, and Ulrike Sommer, eds. *Briefe aus Amerika: Deutsche Auswanderer schreiben aus der Neuen Welt* (München: C. H. Beck, 1988), 381.

7. Quoted in James M. McPherson, *What They Fought For, 1861–1865* (Baton Rouge, LA: Louisiana State University Press, 1994), 31–32.

8. Lawrence Kohl and Margaret C. Rich, eds. *Irish Green and Union Blue: The Civil War Letters of Peter Welsh* (New York: Fordham University Press, 1986), 103.

9. Quartermaster Joseph Tully quoted in Bruce, *Harp and Eagle*, 60.

10. Kevin O'Brien, ed., *My Life in the Irish Brigade. The Civil War Memoirs of Private William McCarter, 116th Pennsylvania Infantry* (New York: Da Capo Press, 2003), 221.

11. William J. K. Beaudot and Lance J. Herdegen, eds., *An Irishman in the Iron Brigade. The Civil War Memoirs of James P. Sullivan, Sergt., Company K, 6th Wisconsin Volunteers* (New York: Fordham University Press, 1993), 1.

12. Charlotte J. Erickson, *Invisible Immigrants: The Adaptation of English and Scottish Immigrants in 19th-Century America* (London: Weidenfeld and Nicolson, 1972), 348–349.

13. P. Weinmann to Bureau of USCT, LR AGO CT 1863 W 165, RG 94, NA.

14. Defense statement of L[adislas] L. Zulavsky [*sic*], General Court Martial File (GCM) OO 280, RG 153, NA.

15. Franz Wilhelmi, "Letter from Franz Wilhelmi, February 25, 1862" *Arkansas Historical Quarterly* 6(1947), 233.

16. Translated from Minnesota *Staats Zeitung* (St. Paul), April 27, 1861.

17. Quoted in Lonn, *Union*, 75.

18. Marcus, *Memoirs*, 230–231.

19. Translated from Macha et al., *Auswandererbriefe*, 329.

20. Translated from Helbich and Kamphoefner, *Deutsche*, 148.

21. Lonn, *Union*, 75.

22. Translated from Helbich and Kamphoefner, *Deutsche*, 166–167.

23. Ibid., 186.

24. Pula, *Krzyzanowski*, 33–34.

25. Translated from Helbich and Kamphoefner, *Deutsche*, 370.

26. Quoted in Conway, *Welsh*, 285–288.

27. Ibid., 289–290.

28. Quoted in Hokanson, *Swedish Immigrants*, 77.

29. Translated from Helbich and Kamphoefner, *Deutsche*, 334.

30. Ibid., 322–323.

31. Ibid., 152.

32. Robert C. Goodell and P. A. M. Taylor, "A German Immigrant in the Union Army: Selected Letters of Valentin Bechler," *Journal of American Studies* 4(February 1971): 145–162, 161.

33. Translated from Helbich and Kamphoefner, *Deutsche*, 441.

34. Kaufmann, *Germans*, 284.

35. Translated from Macha et al., *Auswandererbriefe*, 75; Hokanson, *Swedish Immigrants*, 144.n.2.

36. Report of Col. H. E. McCullough, *OR*, I, 9, 705.

37. Report of Lieut. C. D. McRae, *OR*, I, 9, 614.

38. Kaufmann, *Germans*, 90–91.

39. Ferdinand Ohlenburger to Secretary of the Interior, April 25, 1897. Civil War Pension Files, Ferdinand Ohlenburger, RG 15, NA.

40. Col. Chr. Thielemann to Col. William Hoffman, *OR*, II, 5, 287.

41. W. R. Holloway to Secretary of War Edwin M. Stanton, *OR*, III, 3, 766.

42. Wilhelm von Bechtold to Hon. Mr. Watson, June 21, 1864. LR AGO CT 1864 V 37, RG 94, NA.

43. Translated from Schurz, *Lebenserinnerungen*, Vol. 2, 261.

44. Translated from Helbich and Kamphoefner, *Deutsche*, 214.

45. Hokanson, *Swedish Immigrants*, 115.

46. Dietrich F. Tiedemann to Governor [Richard Yates], April 20, 1861. Civil War Records 9th Regiment, Company C. Illinois State Archives, Springfield.

47. Illinois *Staats Zeitung*, May 20, 1861.

48. St. Paul *Press*, October 15, 1861, cited in Hokanson, *Swedish Immigrants*, 120.n.6.

49. Kaufmann, *Germans*, 284.

50. Translated from Wolf, *Kriegstagebücher*, 215.

51. Translated from Helbich and Kamphoefner, *Deutsche*, 363.

52. Andrew cited in O'Connor, *Civil War Boston*, 186; report of Lieut. Col. Madison M. Cannon, *OR*, I, 44/1, 231. See also Lonn, *Union*, 155, 316.

53. Report of Col. Bernard F. Mullen, *OR*, I, 20/1, 612.

54. Hokanson, *Swedish Immigrants*, 216.

55. Translated from Wolf, *Kriegstagebücher*, 212.

56. *Ninth Reunion of the 37th Regiment O.V.V.I. St. Marys, Ohio, Tuesday and Wednesday September 10 and 11, 1889* (Toledo, OH: Montgomery & Vrooman, 1890), 69.

57. Translated from Helbich and Kamphoefner, *Deutsche*, 184.

58. Lonn, *Union*, 133; Hokanson, *Swedish Immigrants*, 114, 214; Conway, *Welsh*, 297.

59. Stempfel, *Fünfzig Jahre*, 24.

60. Service Records Charles Bornarth, 7th Minnesota Infantry, RG 94, NA.

61. Translated from Helbich and Kamphoefner, *Deutsche*, 276.

62. Ibid., 251.

63. Ibid., 346–347.

64. Charles Nordhoff, *The Communistic Societies of the United States* (1875, reprint New York: Dover, 1966), 206–214.

65. *OR*, III, 3, 336. McPherson has noted that even some Quakers left behind their pacifism and enlisted in the Union army. McPherson, *What They Fought For*, 34.

66. Lonn, *Union*, 66.

67. "Curriculum Vitae of Augustus Henry Achenbach Act. Ass. Surg. U.S.A.," Personal Papers, Medical Officers and Physicians, Augustus Achenbach, RG 94, NA.

68. Mattson quoted in Lonn, *Union*, 77.

CHAPTER FIVE

1. Kaufmann, *Germans*, 93.

2. Report of Capt. James Kelly, *OR*, I, 2, 372; Fox, *Losses*, 210.

3. Report of Col. Louis Blenker, *OR*, I, 2, 426–428. There has been some confusion regarding the question of who actually covered the Union retreat. Praising Colonel Max Einstein, Simonhoff tells that his 27th Pennsylvania covered the retreat, while Kaufmann says that he was absent. Simonhoff, *Jewish Participants*, 24; Kaufmann, *Germans*, 95. Blenker himself reported "that the Twenty-seventh Regiment Pennsylvania Volunteers . . . which was on guard duty in Centreville village at headquarters and under order to escort Colonel Miles' train, retired from Centreville at about 11 o'clock without any orders from me." *OR*, I, 2, 428.

4. Quoted in Forney, *Thomas Francis Meagher*, 91.

5. Hearne and Cornish, *Meagher*, 139, 149.

6. William Corby, *Memoirs of Chaplain Life: Three Years With the Irish Brigade in the Army of the Potomac*, edited by Lawrence Frederick Kohl (New York: Fordham University Press, 1992), 28.

7. Translated from Kaufmann, *Germans*, 97.

8. General Order No. 31, February 9, 1862, translated from Helbich and Kamphoefner, *Deutsche*, 72.

9. McClellan, *Story*, 141–142.

10. Ibid., 142.

11. Corby, *Memoirs*, 75.

12. St. Clair A. Mulholland, *The Story of the 116th Regiment*, edited by Lawrence Frederick Kohl (New York: Fordham University Press, 1996), 13.

13. McClellan, *Story*, 142

14. Translated from Wilhelm A. Fritsch, *Aus Amerika* (Stargard i. Pom.: Wilhelm Prange, n.d.), 29; see also Gerald F. Linderman, *Embattled Courage: The Experience of Combat in the American Civil War* (New York: The Free Press, 1989), 37.

15. Translated from Helbich and Kamphoefner, *Deutsche*, 425.

16. Ibid., 112.

17. August V. Kautz, "Reminiscences of the Civil War," transcribed by Mrs. Austin Kautz (1936), 3, August V. Kautz Papers, Manuscript Division, Library of Congress.

18. Quoted in Conway, *Welsh*, 291–292.

19. Translated from Schurz, *Lebenserinnerungen*, Vol. 2, 178.

20. Translated from Otto Heusinger, *Amerikanische Kriegsbilder* (Leipzig: Friedrich Wilhelm Grunow, 1869), 13–14.

21. Kaufmann frankly asserted that the appointment of Blenker to division commander "negatively influenced the role that our people were called to play in the Civil War." Kaufmann, *Germans*, 102.

22. Translated from *Morgenblatt für gebildete Leser* (New York), August 6, 1863, 752.

23. Translated from Helbich and Kamphoefner, *Deutsche*, 117.

24. *New York Times*, August 15, 1861.

25. Diary of August V. Kautz, December 20, 1862, *August V. Kautz Papers*, Manuscript Division, Library of Congress.

26. Quoted in Lonn, *Union*, 588.

27. Translated from Helbich and Kamphoefner, *Deutsche*, 257.

28. Ibid., 149.

29. Translated from Fritsch, *Aus Amerika*, 31.

30. Translated from Helbich and Kamphoefner, *Deutsche*, 167.

31. Translated from Wolf, *Kriegstagebücher*, 120, 207, 209.

32. Ibid., 205–206.

33. Ibid., 220–221.

34. Burton, *Melting Pot Soldiers*, 163–164; see also *OR*, I, 5, 561.

35. Report of Col. F. Sigel, *OR*, I, 3, 18.

36. Report of Brig.-Gen. N. Lyon, *OR*, I, 3, 18.

37. Report of Brig.-Gen. J. M. Schofield, *OR*, I, 3, 94.

38. Translated from Wolf, *Kriegstagebücher*, 213.

39. Report of Maj. John A. Halderman, *OR*, I, 82–83; Fox, *Losses*, 522.

40. Report of Brig.-Gen. J. M. Schofield, *OR*, I, 3, 94–95. See also Engle, *Yankee Dutchman*, 78–79.

41. Quoted in Schroeder and Geisberg, *Hold Dear*, 184–185.

42. Meagher quoted in Forney, *Thomas Francis Meagher*, 92.

43. Translated from Wolf, *Kriegstagebücher*, 216.

44. Translated from Jörg Nagler, *Fremont contra Lincoln* (Frankfurt: Peter Lang, 1984), 23–24.

45. Translated from Schurz, *Lebenserinnerungen*, Vol. 3, 210.

46. Translated from Wolf, *Kriegstagebücher*, 216.

47. Nagler, *Fremont Contra Lincoln*, 26–27, 37–42.

48. Halleck quoted in Engle, *Yankee Dutchman*, 95.

49. Quoted in Carl Wittke, *The German-Language Press in America* (Lexington, KY: University of Kentucky Press, 1957), 150.

50. "Franz Wilhelmi," 233.

51. Earl J. Hess, "The Obscurity of August Mersey: A German-American in the Civil War," *Illinois Historical Journal*, 79(Summer 1986), 130.

52. Translated from Helbich and Kamphoefner, *Deutsche*, 222.

53. Quoted in Lonn, *Union*, 600–601.

54. Ibid., 596

55. Meagher quoted in Daniel M. Callaghan, *Thomas Francis Meagher and the Irish Brigade in the Civil War* (Jefferson, NC: McFarland & Company, 2006), 47.

56. Joseph R. Reinhart, ed., *Two Germans in the Civil War. The Diary of John Daeuble and the Letters of Gottfried Rentschler, 6th Kentucky Volunteer Infantry* (Knoxville, TN: The University of Tennessee Press, 2004), 67, XXIXf.

57. Helbich and Kamphoefner, *Deutsche*, 72–74.

58. Schick, "For God, Mac, and Country," 71.

59. Translated from Helbich and Kamphoefner, *Deutsche*, 225–226.

60. O'Brien, *McCarter*, 70–71; see also Conyngham, *Irish Brigade*, 183–187.

61. Carl Uterhart to Major E. Grosskopff, June 14, 1865, Letters Received, 9th USC Heavy Artillery. Regimental Papers USCT. RG 94, NA.

62. Translated from Helbich and Kamphoefner, *Deutsche*, 144.

63. Ibid., 185.

64. Milwaukee *Seebote* quoted in Schick, "For God, Mac, and Country," 71.

65. Translated from Helbich and Kamphoefner, *Deutsche*, 201.

66. O'Brien, *McCarter*, 77.

67. Jerome Mushkat, ed., *A Citizen Soldier's Civil War: The Letters of Brevet Major General Alvin C. Voris* (DeKalb, IL: Northern Illinois University Press, 2002), 141.

68. Reinhart, *Two Germans*, 68.

69. Quoted in Burton, *Melting Pot Soldiers*, 69.

70. Joshua Chamberlain, *The Passing of the Armies* (New York: G. P. Putnam, 1915), 276.

71. Butler quoted in Lonn, *Union*, 359–360.

72. Beaudot and Herdegen, *Sullivan*, 93.

73. Kaufmann never fails to call the members of the 15th Missouri Infantry "German Swiss," as he generally tries to incorporate as many ethnicities in his own melting pot of "Germans" to stress this ethnic group's participation in the war. Kaufmann, *Germans*, 138.

74. Jay Monaghan, *Civil War on the Western Border, 1854–1865* (New York: Bonanza Books, 1955), 241.

75. Report of Brig.-Gen. A. Asboth, *OR*, I, 8, 192.

76. Dabney H. Maury to General Samuel R. Curtis, *OR*, I, 8, 195.

77. H. Z. Curtis to Capt. D. H. Maury, *OR*, II, 3, 399.

78. Maurice Marcoot quoted in Allendorf, *Long Road*, 42.

79. Report of Lieut. August Fischer, *OR*, I, 13, 78.

80. Translated from Helbich and Kamphoefner, *Deutsche*, 372; Fox, *Losses*, 429.

81. Albert Tracy to Maj.-Gen. John C. Fremont, *OR*, I, 15, 35.

82. On Blenker's March to the Shenandoah, see David L. Valuska and Christian B. Keller, *Damn Dutch: Pennsylvania Germans at Gettysburg* (Mechanicsburg, PA: Stackpole Books, 2004), 29–32.

83. Milroy quoted in James S. Pula, *The History of a German-Polish Civil War Brigade* (San Francisco, CA: R & E Research Associates, 1976), 17.

84. Brig.-Gen. W. S. Rosecrans to E. M. Stanton, *OR*, I, 12/3, 81.

85. George Suckley to Col. Albert Tracy, *OR*, I, 15, 30.

86. Translated from Helbich and Kamphoefner, *Deutsche*, 182–183.

87. Report of Col. Wladimir Krzyzanowski, *OR*, I, 15, 672.

88. Translated from Åberg, *Svenskarna*, 113.

89. Report of Capt. Michael Wiedrich, *OR*, I, 15, 670.

90. Report of Col. Eugene A. Kozlay, *OR*, I, 15, 671.

91. Translated from Helbich and Kamphoefner, *Deutsche*, 182.

CHAPTER SIX

1. Paul Jones, *The Irish Brigade* (Washington and New York: Robert B. Luce, 1969), 106.

2. Report of Brig. Gen. Thomas F. Meagher, *OR*, I, 11/1, 776–777.

3. Report of Col. Paul Frank, *OR*, I, 11/1, 784.

4. Report of Brig. Gen. Thomas F. Meagher, *OR*, I, 11/1, 775–776.

5. Ibid.; Report of Col. Paul Frank, *OR*, I, 11/1, 784.

6. Report of Brig. Gen. Thomas F. Meagher, *OR*, I, 11/2, 70–71; Fox, *Losses*, 157.

7. Report of Brig. Gen. John C. Caldwell, *OR*, I, 11/2, 61–62.

8. Report of Brig. Gen. Thomas F. Meagher, *OR*, I, 11/2, 72–73.

9. Quoted in Callaghan, *Irish Brigade*, 85.

10. Report of Brig. Gen. Thomas F. Meagher, *OR*, I, 11/2, 74.

11. Translated from Helbich and Kamphoefner, *Deutsche*, 169.

12. Report of Col. David Stuart, *OR*, I, 10/1, 259–260.

13. Report of Maj. Gen. John A. McClernand, *OR*, I, 10/1, 115.

14. Translated from Helbich and Kamphoefner, *Deutsche*, 365–366.

15. Report of Col. William H. Gibson, *OR*, I, 10/1, 315.

16. Report of Col. August Willich, *OR*, I, 10/1, 317.

17. Report of Col. George F. McGinnis, *OR*, I, 10/1, 190–191.

18. Translated from Helbich and Kamphoefner, *Deutsche*, 309.

19. Report of Col. August Mersey, *OR*, I, 10/1, 155–156.

20. Fox, *Losses*, 354.

21. Report of Col. August Willich, *OR*, I, 10/1, 318.

22. Report of Maj. Gen. John A. McClernand, *OR*, I, 10/1, 121.

23. Report of Col. Napoleon B. Buford, *OR*, I, 8, 116–118.

24. Valuska and Keller, *Damn Dutch*, 33–34.

25. Report of Maj. Franz Blessing, *OR*, I, 16, 310–311.

26. Translated from Helbich and Kamphoefner, *Deutsche*, 210, 356–357. See also Engle, *Yankee Dutchman*, 140–148.

27. Beaudot and Herdegen, *Sullivan*, 55, 44.

28. O'Brien, *McCarter*, 9.

29. Report of Brig. Gen. Thomas Francis Meagher, *OR*, I, 19/1, 293–295.

30. Report of Brig. Gen. John C. Caldwell, *OR*, I, 19/1, 285–287.

31. Report of Col. Joshua T. Owen, *OR*, I, 19/1, 318–319.

32. Report of Col. William H. Irwin, *OR*, I, 19/1, 410–411.

33. Report of Maj. Gen. George B. McClellan, *OR*, I, 19/1, 58.

34. O'Brien, *McCarter*, 15.

35. Mario M. Cuomo and Harold Holzer, eds., *Lincoln on Democracy* (New York: HarperCollins, 1990), 271–272.

36. Translated from Schurz, *Lebenserinnerungen*, Vol. 2, 242.

37. Karl Marx and Friedrich Engels, *Collected Works, Vol. 19: 1861–64* (London: Lawrence & Wishart, 1984), 248.

38. Translated from *Anzeiger des Westens* (St. Louis), 1, October 6, 1862.

39. Translated from Minnesota *Staats Zeitung* (St. Paul), January 10, 1863.

40. Pula, *Krzyzanowski*, 45.

41. Translated from Helbich and Kamphoefner, *Deutsche*, 400.

42. Ibid., 335.

43. Translated from *Wöchentliches Belleviller Volksblatt*, September 30, 1863.

44. Bruce, *Harp and Eagle*, 136–139; Donahoe cited in O'Connor, *Civil War Boston*, 73.

45. Schick, "For God, Mac, and Country," 151–152. On Union soldiers' reactions to emancipation and altered war aims in general, see McPherson, *What They Fought For*, 117–130.

46. Quoted in Schenkeveld, "Colony," 249.

47. Quoted in Conway, *Welsh*, 299–300.

48. Translated from Helbich and Kamphoefner, *Deutsche*, 455.

49. O'Brien, *McCarter*, 67–68.

50. Quoted in Bruce, *Harp and Eagle*, 141.

51. Conyngham, *Irish Brigade*, 168.

52. O'Brien, *McCarter*, 186.

53. Translated from Åberg, *Svenskarna*, 130

54. Quoted in Schenkeveld, "Colony," 251.

55. Frank L. Byrne and J. P. Soman, eds., *Your True Marcus: The Civil War Letters of a Jewish Colonel* (Kent, OH: Kent State University Press, 1985), vii; McPherson, *What They Fought For*, 65–66.

56. Translated from Wolf, *Kriegstagebücher*, 195.

57. Translated from Helbich and Kamphoefner, *Deutsche*, 258.

58. Earl J. Hess, ed., *A German in the Yankee Fatherland—The Civil War Letters of Henry A. Kircher* (Kent, OH: Kent State University Press, 1983), 92.

59. Quoted in Reinhart, *Two Germans*, 68.

60. General Order no. 16, by command of Col. L. L. Zulavsky [*sic*], in Ira Berlin, Joseph P. Reidy, and Leslie S. Rowland, eds., *Freedom: A Documentary History of Emancipation, 1861–1867. Series 2: The Black Military Experience* (Cambridge, MA: Cambridge University Press, 1982), 599–600. On the nativity of commissioned officers in the U.S. Colored Troops, see Joseph T. Glatthaar, *Forged in Battle: The Civil War Alliance of Black Soldiers and White Officers* (New York: Meridian, 1990), 265–267.

61. Louis H. Douglass, et al., to Secretary of War, in Berlin, et al., *Military Experience*, 341.

62. Report by Commissioner of Pensions, Pension File Herman Lieb, RG 15, NA.

63. David Cornwell, "Dan Caverno. A True Tale of American Life on the Farm, in a Country Store, and in the Volunteer Army," 128, Civil War Miscellaneous Collection, U.S. Army Military History Institute, Carlisle, PA.

64. Translated from *Wöchentliches Belleviller Volksblatt*, July 15, 1863.

65. Quoted in Conway, *Welsh*, 291–292.

66. Translated from Wolf, *Kriegstagebücher*, 210; J. P. Geraghty cited in Van Vugt, *Britain to America*, 145.

67. Translated from Minnesota *Staats Zeitung* (St. Paul), June 6, 1863.

68. *OR*, III, 3, 198–199.

69. For details about the New York City Draft Riots and Irish participation, see Bruce, *Harp and Eagle*, 178–180; and Iver Bernstein, *The New York Draft Riots: Their Significance for American Society and Politics in the Age of the Civil War* (New York: Oxford University Press, 1990), 17–42.

70. Translated from Helbich and Kamphoefner, *Deutsche*, 120.

71. Ibid., 130.

CHAPTER SEVEN

1. Kaufmann, *Germans*, 199.

2. *OR*, I, 25/1, 659. Schurz never officially explained the difficulties he expected.

3. Quoted in James S. Pula, *For Liberty and Justice: The Life and Times of Wladimir Krzyzanowski* (Chicago, IL: The Polish-American Congress Charitable Foundation, 1978), 74.

4. Report of Lieut. Col. Adolph von Hartung, *OR*, I, 25/1, 665–666.

5. Report of Brig. Gen. Adolph von Steinwehr, *OR*, I, 25/1, 645–646.

6. Fox, *Losses*, 399.

7. Report of Maj. St. Clair A. Mulholland, *OR*, I, 25/1, 328.

8. Report of Lieut. Edward Whiteford, *OR*, I, 25/1, 327–328; see also Callaghan, *Irish Brigade*, 148–151.

9. Conyngham, *Irish Brigade*, 200–201.

10. Meagher quoted in Callaghan, *Irish Brigade*, 152

11. Beaudot and Herdegen, *Sullivan*, 79; Christian G. Samito, ed., *Commanding Boston's Irish Ninth: The Civil War Letters of Colonel Patrick R. Guiney, Ninth Massachusetts Infantry* (New York: Fordham University Press, 1998), 187–188.

12. Translated from Wolf, *Kriegstagebücher*, 202.

13. *New York Times*, May 5, 1863.

14. *New York Herald*, May 5, 1863.

15. Engle, *Yankee Dutchman*, xiii, 157–161; Pula, *Liberty*, 119. Today, historians generally agree that the misfortune that befell the Eleventh Corps at Chancellorsville was not the fault of the German soldiers but resulted from their position at the exposed right wing of the army and the total surprise of Hooker and Howard. Much credit is due to historian Christian Keller who in his latest book exhaustively analyses the role of the Eleventh Corps at Chancellorsville and resulting nativism: Christian B. Keller, *Chancellorsville and the Germans: Nativism, Ethnicity, and Civil War Memory* (New York: Fordham University Press, 2007).

16. Report of Brig. Gen. Alexander Schimmelfennig, *OR*, I, 25/1, 662–663.

17. Kaufmann, *Germans*, 277, 299.

18. C. Schurz to Secretary of War, *OR*, I, 25/1, 658–659.

19. Report of Maj. Gen. C. Schurz, *OR*, I, 25/1, 651–658. Schurz nevertheless admitted later that parts of his division had lost their nerves in front of the Confederate onslaught. Schurz, *Lebenserinnerungen*, Vol. 2, 277–278.

20. Bruce, *Harp and Eagle*, 158–160.

21. *OR*, I, 25/1, 659–660.

22. Beaudot and Herdegen, *Sullivan*, 94.

23. Translated from Helbich and Kamphoefner, *Deutsche*, 211.

24. Beaudot and Herdegen, *Sullivan*, 97–98.

25. Lonn, *Union*, 523.

26. Quoted in Callaghan, *Irish Brigade*, 159.

27. Report of Col. Patrick Kelly, *OR*, I, 27/1, 386.

28. Bruce, *Harp and Eagle*, 168–172; Lonn, *Union*, 528; Kaufmann, *Germans*, 284.

29. Translated from Helbich and Kamphoefner, *Deutsche*, 211–212.

30. Lonn, *Union*, 522.

31. Report of Maj. Gen. Carl Schurz, *OR*, I, 27/1, 731–732.

32. General Orders No. 18, *OR*, I, 27/1, 712.

33. Translated from Helbich and Kamphoefner, *Deutsche*, 185.

34. According to Allendorf, there were "no criticisms of ethnic fighting abilities following the battle along the Stones River." Allendorf, *Long Road*, 105.

35. Translated from Wolf, *Kriegstagebücher*, 226.

36. Ibid., 227–278.

37. Kaufmann, *Germans*, 376.n.27; Lonn, *Union*, 529.

38. Translated from Wolf, *Kriegstagebücher*, 228.

39. Cuomo and Holzer, *Lincoln*, 291.

40. Kaufmann, *Germans*, 305.

41. Report of Brig. Gen. August Willich, *OR*, I, 30/1, 538–539.

42. Report of Capt. Mons Grinager, *OR*, I, 30/1, 533–534.

43. Report of Brig. Gen. August Willich, *OR*, I, 30/1, 539–540.

44. Ibid.

45. Report of Col. Bernard Laiboldt, *OR*, I, 30/1, 589–591.

46. Lonn, *Union*, 531.

47. Report of Brig. Gen. Richard W. Johnson, *OR*, I, 30/1, 535–536.

48. Report of Brig. Gen. August Willich, *OR*, I, 30/1, 541.

49. Report of Col. Ferdinand Van Derveer, *OR*, I, 30/1, 428.

50. Ibid., 430.

51. Report of Brig. Gen. Richard W. Johnson, *OR*, I, 30/1, 536.

52. Report of Brig. Gen. August Willich, *OR*, I, 30/1, 541–542.

53. Ibid., 542.

54. Lonn, *Union*, 532–537; Allendorf, *Long Road*, 138–157.

55. Translated from Helbich and Kamphoefner, *Deutsche*, 403.

56. Ibid., 186.

57. *OR*, I, 42, 247–248.

58. Kautz, "Reminiscences," 105

59. Charles L. Perdue, Jr., Thomas E. Barden, and Robert K. Phillips, eds., *Weevils in the Wheat: Interviews with Virginia Ex-Slaves* (Charlottesville, VA: University Press of Virginia, 1992), 29.

EPILOGUE: THE AFTERMATH OF WAR

1. Forney, *Thomas Francis Meagher*, 133; Callaghan, *Irish Brigade*, 178.

2. Orm Øverland, *Immigrant Minds, American Identities: Making the United States Home, 1870–1930* (Urbana, IL: University of Illinois Press, 2000), 14, 27–28.

3. Translated from Rudolf Cronau, *Drei Jahrhunderte Deutschen Lebens in Amerika* (Berlin: Dietrich Reimer, 1924), 310–311.

4. Aschmann quoted in Lonn, *Union*, 79.

5. Translated from Joseph Eiboeck, *Die Deutschen von Iowa und deren Errungenschaften: Eine Geschichte des Staates, dessen deutschen Pioniere und ihrer Nachkommen* (Des Moines: Iowa Staats-Anzeiger, 1900), 84.

6. Gustav Tafel, "Geschichte der Deutschen Cincinnati's im Bürgerkriege," *Cincinnati und sein Deutschthum* (Cincinnati, OH: Queen City Publishing Company, 1901): 99.

7. Bell I. Wiley, *The Life of Billy Yank: The Common Soldier of the Union* (Indianapolis, IN: Bobbs-Merrill, 1952), 308.

8. Lonn, *Union*, 645–650.

9. Ibid., 652. Subsequent studies sometimes picked up the entrenched characterizations, such Robertson, *Soldiers*, 28; Hokanson, *Swedish Immigrants*, 73.

10. See respective entries in Fox, *Losses*, 122–415.

11. Bruce, *Harp and Eagle*, 194.

12. Pula, *Krzyzanowski*, 51.

13. Quoted in McPherson, *What They Fought For*, 31.

14. Translated from Helbich and Kamphoefner, *Deutsche*, 190.

15. Unusual in military history up to the nineteenth century, more than 90 percent of the Union army and over 80 percent of the Confederate soldiers were literate. The volunteers came from "the world's most politicized and democratic society," as James McPherson has noted. McPherson, *What They Fought For*, 4.

16. Ulysses S. Grant, *Personal Memoirs* (New York: Webster, 1885–1886.), Vol. 2, 531.

17. Beaudot and Herdegen, *Sullivan*, 65.

18. Translated from Helbich and Kamphoefner, *Deutsche*, 165.

19. Cuomo and Holzer, *Lincoln*, 291–292.

BIBLIOGRAPHICAL ESSAY

Although the Civil War remains one of the most closely examined periods in American history, there is still a remarkable dearth of published primary sources that tell of the foreign-born participants' experience in this conflict. This is especially true for ethnic groups other than German and Irish, who have received increasing attention over the recent years. The stories of other immigrants like Hungarians, Poles, French, Italians, and Scandinavians for the most part remain yet inaccessible to a wider audience. Still, there is a long tradition of ethnic literature on the war historians can resort to. It has to be critically analyzed, though.

In the first decades following the war several immigrant officers published memoirs and narrative accounts of the war years, usually aimed at emphasizing their own and their ethnic groups' achievements. Good examples are Otto Heusinger's *Amerikanische Kriegsbilder* (1869), which proudly recalled the German participation in the war, and David Porter Conyngham's fairly unbiased *The Irish Brigade and its Campaigns* (1866). A year later, veteran Michael H. MacNamara published an account of his Massachusetts regiment, *The Irish Ninth in Bivouac and Battle* (1867).

When increasing nativism set in with renewed mass immigration from eastern and southern Europe, German-American authors closed ranks in defending ethnic German cultural and military achievements. Albert Bernhardt Faust, *The German Element in the United States* (1909) and Frederick Franklin Schrader, *The Germans in the Making of America* (1924), were among the most influential representatives of this filiopietistic and apologetic literature. The first historical work to deal exclusively with the German soldiers in the Civil War was Wilhelm Kaufmann's *Die Deutschen im Amerikanischen Bürgerkriege* (1911). Kaufmann compiled much valuable firsthand biographical information on German-speaking participants. However, Kaufmann lacked critical historical analysis and in the fashion of his time employed an ethnocentric perspective that frequently confused—probably purposely—Polish, Hungarian, and other immigrants with Germans. Steven Rowan has undertaken the creditable task of translating and editing Kaufmann's work: *The Germans in the American Civil War* (1999). In addition to Kaufmann's work, Joseph G. Rosengarten's *The German Soldier in the Wars of the United States* (1886) provides background information based on official statistics. Another early work was Eugene Pivány, *Hungarians in the Civil War* (1913).

Rising interest in the war by a generation of professional historians coming of age since the late 1930s produced the first studies on ethnic Americans, which included discussions of their role in the Civil War. Mainly interesting for their biographical information are Miecislaus Haiman, *Polish Past in America 1608–1865* (1939) and Edmund Vasvary, *Lincoln's Hungarian Heroes: The Participation of Hungarians in the Civil War, 1861–1865* (1939). Both contain minor historical flaws but are still basic works for the study of these ethnic groups in the mid-nineteenth century. The following year historian Ella Lonn had published her landmark study on *Foreigners in the Confederacy* (1940), doing away with the widely held southern prejudice that no immigrants had fought in the Confederate armies. Lonn contributed another seminal work with her *Foreigners in the Union Army and Navy* (1951). Lonn discussed numbers and percentages of the various immigrant groups in their role in the war and placed major emphasis on the comparison of Irish and German soldiers as the most numerous groups. Also, she portrayed the ambiguous role of Germans in the political process in greater detail than had her predecessors. Unfortunately her conservative and prejudiced differentiation of rigid and inflexible ethnic-national groups prevented Lonn from creating a truly revisionist study. Still, Lonn's work remains the logical starting point for anyone examining the ethnic participation in the Civil War. Probably her greatest contribution was her meticulous research of ethnic and partly ethnic Civil War units and her compilation of a vast number of accessible published secondary sources. Lonn's work has been critically updated by William L. Burton, *Melting Pot Soldiers: The Union's Ethnic Regiments* (1988). Burton for the first time gave insight in the political process of ethnic recruitment and wartime politics, leaving behind the traditional and emotional questions of who had contributed most to the northern cause.

Over the past decades, the historiography of the Civil War has profited from a revival of ethnic studies in general. Good, if overtly uncritical, examples for the study of a single ethnic group are Nels Hokanson, *Swedish Immigrants in Lincoln's Time* (1979), and Alf Åberg, *Svenskarna under stjärnbaneret. Insatser under nordamerikanska inbördeskriget 1861–1865* (1994). The latest addition to the literature on Irish

Americans in the Civil War Era that may well become the standard work on the subject is Susannah Ural Bruce's, *The Harp and the Eagle. Irish-American Volunteers and the Union Army, 1861–1865* (2006). In her well-documented work Bruce examines closely the various social, political, and military aspects of the Irish-American experience during that epoch.

Several biographies of some of the Civil War's ethnic protagonists have enriched the subject. Two books on Irish general Thomas Francis Meagher, Gary R. Forney's *Thomas Francis Meagher: Irish Rebel, American Yankee, Montana Pioneer* (2003), and John M. Hearne and Rory T. Cornish's *Thomas Francis Meagher: The Making of an Irish American* (2005) not only evaluate his endeavors for the Irish-American cause and his military achievements, but also reveal the public criticism he earned for allegedly slaughtering his brigade, and his at times excessive drinking. A highly readable biography of Carl Schurz, Hans L. Trefousse's *Carl Schurz: A Biography* (1982) remains the standard work on the most influential forty-eighter. Schurz's controversial fellow revolutionary, Franz Sigel, is treated by Stephen D. Engle, *Yankee Dutchman: The Life of Franz Sigel* (1993). Engle at times seems overtly critical of his subject when he sets out on the difficult task to portray the most enigmatic German-American idol of the nineteenth century. Interestingly enough, the recent biography of Sigel's superior, John F. Marszalek's *Commander of all Lincoln's Armies: A Life of General Henry W. Halleck* (2004), never mentions the personal quarrels between Halleck and Sigel, although the thoroughly researched book closely analyses Halleck's troubled physical and mental health, which influenced his erratic relationships with the German and others.

Illuminating publications of primary sources include James S. Pula, *The Memoirs of Wladimir Krzyzanowski* (1978), Frank L. Byrne and Jean Powers Soman, *Your True Marcus: The Civil War Letters of a Jewish Colonel* (1985), and Eugene C. Miller, *Der Turner Soldat; A Turner Soldier in the Civil War; Germany to Antietam* (1988). Together with a growing number of recently published sources, these often underrated works offer insight into the feelings and motivations of immigrant volunteers. Valuable edited publications of Irish memoirs and diaries are William J. K. Beaudot and Lance J. Herdegen, eds., *An Irishman in the Iron Brigade: The Civil War Memoirs of James P. Sullivan, Sergt., Company K, 6th Wisconsin Volunteers* (1993) and Kevin O'Brien, ed., *My Life in the Irish Brigade: The Civil War Memoirs of Private William McCarter, 116th Pennsylvania Infantry* (2003). The thoughts and experiences of an Irish regimental commander come to life in Christian G. Samito's, *Commanding Boston's Irish Ninth: The Civil War Letters of Colonel Patrick R. Guiney, Ninth Massachusetts Infantry* (1998). A recent contribution that tells much about the situation of immigrants in the Border States is Joseph R. Reinhart, ed., *Two Germans in the Civil War. The Diary of John Daeuble and the Letters of Gottfried Rentschler, 6th Kentucky Volunteer Infantry* (2004). Reinhart brings to life another German regiment in his *Willich's Gallant Dutchmen: Civil War letters from the 32nd Indiana Infantry* (2006).

James M. McPherson in his examination of Union Civil War soldiers' motivations and experiences, *What They Fought For, 1861–1865* (1994), lists only a few immigrant letters and diaries but places them in a larger context. One of the most important collections of sources is Wolfgang Helbich and Walter D. Kamphoefner's *Deutsche im Amerikanischen Bürgerkrieg: Briefe von Front und Farm, 1861–1865* (2002). Helbich and Kamphoefner have edited over 300 letters by German immigrants, an indispensable work that in its scope and richness remains a singular achievement. Throughout this book I have used translated excerpts of these German letters vividly illustrating how immigrants experienced the conflict and reflected on their roles in it. To the benefit of English-speaking audiences, a translated version of the whole collection is available as *Germans in the Civil War: The Letters They Wrote Home*, translated by Susan Carter Vogel (2006). In addition to these works, general collections of immigrant letters also yield information on ethnic life in the field and on the home front, such as Ralph H. Bowen's *A Frontier Family in Minnesota: Letters of Theodore and Sophie Bost, 1851–1920* (1981) on Swiss immigrants, and Alan Conway's *The Welsh in America. Letters from the Immigrants* (1961).

Another important contribution to the understanding of the ethnic side of the war are the various regimental histories published in recent years, such as Donald Allendorf, *Long Road to Liberty: The Odyssey of a German Regiment in the Yankee Army: The 15th Missouri Volunteer Infantry* (2006), Michael Bacarella, *Lincoln's Foreign Legion: The 39th New York Infantry, The Garibaldi Guard* (1996), and Eric Benjaminson's article on "A Regiment of Immigrants: The 82nd Illinois Volunteer Infantry and the Letters of Captain Rudolph Mueller," in the *Journal of the Illinois State Historical Society*, 94 (2001). Pioneers in the study of ethnic regiments were James S. Pula, *The History of a German-Polish Civil War Brigade* (1976) on the 48th New York Infantry and Earl J. Hess, "The 12th Missouri Infantry: A Socio-Military Profile of A Union Regiment" published in the *Missouri Historical Review*, 76(1) (1981). Several books have traced the history of the most famous of all ethnic units, such as Paul Jones's well-written but unfortunately not annotated narrative *The Irish Brigade* (1969), and Daniel M. Callaghan's critical account on *Thomas Francis Meagher and the Irish Brigade in the Civil War* (2006). Until now, no comprehensive studies of the other ethnic organizations, like Blenker's Brigade or the Eleventh Corps, exist. Only in recent years have historians undertaken to reevaluate critical aspects of the ethnic participation in the Civil War, such as the oft-mentioned cowardice of the Eleventh Corps at Chancellorsville. Drawing on virtually every source available, Christian B. Keller in his superb work, *Chancellorsville and the Germans: Nativism, Ethnicity, and Civil War Memory* (2007), has ultimately laid to rest the negative image of the German-American soldiers.

Much has been written about the most influential and divisive group of immigrants, the forty-eighters. A timeless classic remain Carl Schurz's, *Reminiscences of Carl Schurz* (1907–1908). Although highly self-centered, Schurz in his memoirs presents an accurate sketch of the forty-eighters' influence on American society. Biographical accounts of leading forty-eighters include A. E. Zucker, *The Forty-Eighters: Political Refugees of the German Revolution of 1848* (1950), and Carl Wittke, *Refugees of Revolution: The German Forty-Eighters in America* (1952). Recent works have critically analyzed the forty-eighter movement, such as Charlotte Brancaforte, *The German Forty-Eighters in the United States* (1989), and Bruce Levine, *The Spirit of 1848: German Immigrants, Labor Conflict, and the Coming of the Civil War* (1992).

INDEX

abolitionists, 24, 38, 43, 73, 74, 75–76, 100, 128

Achenbach, August, 85–86, 121, 132

African-Americans, 18, 20, 38, 129, 135; as soldiers, 132, 133

Albert, Anselm, 66, 98, 109

Albrecht, Wilhelm, 73, 95, 118

Andrew, John A., 53, 81

Anglo-Americans, in ethnic regiments, 39–41, 49, 52, 53, 55, 56; reactions to war, 33, 38, 41–42; motivations for enlistment, 85–86, 160

Anneke, Fritz, 37, 48

Antietam, battle of, 125–27

Anzeiger des Westens, 30, 35, 101, 128

Appomattox, 150, 156

Army of Northern Virginia, 115, 141, 144, 147, 155

Army of the Potomac, 71, 91, 94, 103, 113, 117, 129, 130, 131, 143, 144, 148, 150, 155, 161

Army of Virginia, 112, 123, 124

Arndt, Albert, 118, 125

Asboth, Alexander, 13, 50, 66, 107

Aschmann, Rudolf, 158

assimilation, 18, 19, 20–21, 48, 64, 104

atrocities, 108–9

Austria, 5, 6, 7, 8, 109; emigrants from, 10; immigrants from, 19, 25

Backof, Franz, 62, 97, 107

Baden, Grand Duchy of, 6, 7, 8, 12, 45, 57, 62, 65, 80

Baltimore, 22, 37, 49, 73; 27th Pennsylvania attacked in, 51

Barlow, Francis, 138, 145, 155

Beauregard, Pierre G. T., 88, 120–21, 122

beer, 19, 93, 103

Belgium, 6; emigrants from, 11; immigrants from, 61

Belleville, 29, 46, 49, 65, 80

Belleviller Zeitung, 27, 34, 35

Benedictine Order, 85

Berlin, Carl, 62

Bishop Hill (Illinois), 21, 79, 121

Blair, Francis P., 40

Blandowski, Konstantin, 64–65

Blenker, Ludwig, 57–58, 59, 60, 66, 87, 97, 104, 105, 109; at Cross Keys, 110–11; at first Bull Run, 88–89; criticized, 93–94; death of, 112; commands division, 90–91, 103

Blenker's Division, 91, 92, 103, 109, 111, 123; dissolved, 112; staff, 93–94

Blessing, Franz, 123–24

Blumenberg, Leopold, 14, 49, 126

Bohemia, 8, 10; immigrants from 19, 23, 25, 79

Bohlen, Heinrich, 51, 90, 110, 111

Bondi, August, 14, 25

Börnstein, August, 128–29, 132

Börnstein, Heinrich, xii, 10, 19, 29, 45, 64, 73, 128; commands 2nd Missouri Infantry, 40, 49, 65; newspaper editor, 30, 35

Bost, Theodore, 38

Boston Pilot, 18, 28, 34, 129, 130

Boston, 17, 29, 30, 81; ethnic regiments from, 43, 53

bounties, 45, 48, 70, 73, 81, 160

Bragg, Braxton, 148, 150, 152

Bräutigam, Friedrich August, 46, 131, 141

Britain, 6

British immigrants, 20–21, 24, 27, 43; on slavery and emancipation, 22, 24, 38, 74; in 1860 election, 28; in the South, 22; recruitment among, 61. *See also under various nationalities*

Brown, John, 14, 25

Brucker, Magnus, 75, 121

Bruns, Jette, 21, 24, 27, 40, 41, 99

Buchanan, James, 26

Buegel, Johann, 38, 40, 41, 69–70; and ethnic pride, 82, 98; on officers, 63, 96; on Frémont, 100; on Vicksburg campaign, 148–50; reenlists, 80

Buell, Don Carlos, 119–20

Buford, John, 144

Bull Run, 54, 57, 92, 96, 100; first battle of, 88–90; second battle of, 123–24

Bullenhaar, Hermann, 38

Burke, John, 54

Burnside, Ambrose E., 127, 130, 131, 137

Burton, William, 37, 49, 63, 97

Buschbeck, Adolph, 51, 110, 111, 139

Butler, Benjamin, 106

Cahill, Thomas W., 52

Caldwell, John C., 117, 126, 146

Cameron, James, 56, 88

Carthage, battle of, 97–98, 99

Cass, Thomas, 43, 53, 116, 117

Catholics, 14, 17, 18, 20, 23, 24; and slavery, 22, 38, 75

Cederström, Jakob, 36

Chancellorsville, 46, 51, 62, 137, 145, 148; battle of, 138–40; nativism after, 51, 141–43, 159

Chicago, 20, 21, 25, 27, 46, 62, 80, 100; ethnic regiments from, 43, 45, 57

Chickamauga, 50, 67; battle of, 150–53

Cincinnati *Volksfreund*, 31

Cincinnati, 17, 19, 29, 31, 33, 47, 82; ethnic regiments from, 43, 45, 47

Cluseret, Gustave Paul, 11, 36, 109, 110

Connecticut, 59; ethnic regiments from, 52; 9th Infantry, 52; 3rd Light Artillery, 63

conscription, 42; Confederate, 76–77, opposition to, 48, 134, 143. *See also* draft riots

Conyngham, David, 103, 130, 140

Cooney, Peter Paul, 78, 81

Corby, William, 90, 92, 146

Corcoran Legion, 54, 155, 159

Corcoran, Michael, 44, 52, 53, 67, 71, 90, 130, 143, 159; at first Bull Run, 88–89; captured, 54, 89; court-martial of, 42; death of, 155

corruption, 29–30

Courrier des États-Unis, 37, 55

Crawshaw, Titus, 71

Cross Keys, 62; battle of, 110–12

Curtis, Sam, 107
Czechs, 10
"damned Dutch," 40, 41
d'Epineuil, Lionel Jobert, 55
de Casale, Francesco Secchi, 20, 44
de Trobriand, Philippe Régis, 55–56, 147

Demokrat (Davenport), 100
Dengler, Adolf, 80, 98
Denmark, 5, 7, 36; immigrants from, 20, 49, 56
Deutscher Anzeiger, 27, 129
Dickel, Christian F., 57, 91
Dieckmann, Julius, 91
Dieden, John, 25, 27
Dilger, Hubert, 62, 147
discipline, 91, 92, 94, 96, 99, 112, 122, 133, 138, 143
Donohoe, Michael T., 53
draft riots, 48, 160; New York City, 134–35, 143
Dupré, Emile, 92–93, 135
d'Utassy (Strasser), Frederic George, 55, 79, 88
Dutch, 61, 129
education, 1, 2–3, 11

Einstein, Max, 51, 82, 89
election: of 1856, 26, 64; of 1860, 26, 27–28, 31
Eleventh Corps, 51, 104, 123, 125, 137, 154, 158; at Chancellorsville, 138–41; at Gettysburg, 144–45, 147
Emancipation Proclamation, 128, 130
emancipation, 133; as motivation to enlist, 73–75, 129; Frémont's proclamation, 100
Emigranten, 21, 33, 35
emigrants, 10; diversity of, 11–12
emigration, 1–12; Civil War and, 12; conscription and, 11; economic reasons for, 4, 11; numbers, xi–xii, 3, 4, 5, 10–12, 13; overpopulation and 1, 2, 4, 5, 6, 10,

11; poverty and, 3; reasons for, 1, 4, 9–11, 22, 42. *See also specific countries*
Engelmann, Adolph, 119, 121, 150
Engels, Friedrich, 7, 13, 128
England, 3, 9, 12, 13, 18, 29, 45, 71
English Americans, 20–21, 28, 41; argue for emancipation, 22; in German regiments, 51; patriotism of, 33, 36; recruitment among, 60–61
enlistment, 43–45; and religion, 81–82; motivations for, xiii, 44–45, 64, 69–86, 131, 160; of ethnic companies, 79–80, 83
Erickson, Charlotte, 20
ethnic identity, 18, 20, 21, 26, 44, 53, 60, 64
ethnic militias, 39, 42–43, 51, 52, 53, 58, 79–80
ethnic newspapers, 21, 33, 34, 35, 42, 87, 118, 124, 143; defend slavery, 37; on black troops, 133–34
ethnic officers, xii, 92; behavior of, 87, 103; criticized by Americans, 94; denied advancement, 94; drinking among, 54; in black regiments, 31, 71; lobbying among, 51, 60–61; on Frémont's staff, 99–100; oppose Fugitive Slave Law, 74; professionalism of, 42, 47, 51, 57, 87, 93, 133; traditional views of, 94–95; worth of, 79, 93, 122
ethnic organizations, 18, 19, 21, 23, 29, 39, 42, 43, 80
ethnic politics, 23–28
ethnic regiments, xii, 72, 159–60; and ethnic pride, 82–83; formation of, 40–64; loose ethnic character, 54, 55, 63–64, 155; mixed ethnicity in, 52, 83; number of, 63; uniforms of, 58, 87, 91. *See also respective regiments and various nationalities*
ethnic rivalry, 18, 44, 85
ethnic settlements, 13, 20, 21, 23, 40, 41, 43
ethnic soldiers: accused of plundering, 97, 109; at Gettysburg, 147; attitudes toward slavery, 131–32; criticize American soldiers and officers, 63, 92–93, 95–96, 143, 161; in artillery, 61–63, 106, 118;

ethnic soldiers (*cont.*)
    reenlist, 160; stereotypical views of, 158–59
ethnic tensions, 19, 20, 26, 42; overcome by war, 36
Ewell, Richard S., 110, 111, 144

Fair Oaks and Seven Pines, battle of, 113–15
famine, 2, 3, 4, 42
Farragut, David, 123
Fenians, 18, 19, 27, 36, 42, 48, 161
Ferdinand II, 6, 7
Fifteenth Corps, 62, 65, 148
Finland, 4, 5
First Corps, 112, 123, 124, 144, 145
Fischel, Arnold, 48, 60
foreign-born generals, 65–66
Forsse, Eric, 79
Fort Sumter, 22, 39, 51
forty-eighters, 7, 12–15, 18, 35, 38, 47, 85, 94; and 1860 election, 31; and Democratic Party, 31; and emancipation, 100, 131; and ethnic identity, 45, 67; and Republican Party, 24; and slavery, 22; backgrounds of, 14, 29; careers in US, 29, 64–67; command ethnic regiments, 49, 50, 56, 59, 64–67; critical of US, 29–30; criticized by fellow immigrants, 29, 30–31, 38; forced exile of, 12–14; in Civil War, 10, 15, 40; impact of, 28–31; motivations to enlist, 73–74; numbers, 13; postwar life, 161–62; regimental chaplains, 67
Fourteenth Corps, 150, 153
Fox, William F., 48, 52, 56, 59, 122, 159
France, 6, 11, 12, 13; emigrants from, 10
Frank, Paul, 59, 114–15
Fredericksburg, 53, 104, 105, 140, 141; battle of, 130–31, 157
Frémont, John Charles, 26, 64, 66, 99, 109, 110, 111, 123; proclaims emancipation, 100
French Americans, 20, 49, 56; in the South, 22; recruitment among, 43, 48, 53, 61
French regiments, 55

Freudenberg, Carl Gottfried, 13, 59, 114, 147
Frick, Adolph, 129, 155

Gaines's Mill, battle of, 116, 118
Garibaldi, Giuseppe, 9, 11, 14, 44, 58
Gerhardt, Joseph, 127
German Americans: and African Americans, 38; and Democratic Party, 31; and draft riots, 134–35; and Irish Americans, 18, 19; and postwar memory, 158; and Republican Party, 26, 27; attacked, 41, 69–70; attitudes towards slavery, 22, 30, 37–38, 39, 75–76; Catholics, 25, 28, 81, 82; Confederates' hatred of, 108; criticize United States, 34; diversity of, 17, 18, 30–31; drinking among, 104; Frémont and, 99; "Greys" and "Greens," 26, 36; in artillery, 61–62; in elections, 26, 28; in Irish regiments, 52, 54, 82, 83; in labor movement, 18–19; in the South, 22–23; join Confederacy, 76; patriotism of, 33, 34, 36, 39, 45, 46; reactions to war, 37; reject assimilation, 19, 21; stereotypes, 19
German regiments, 43, 44–64, 117–18, 138; accused of cowardice, 141–43
German-American press, 19, 22, 30, 31, 94; on emancipation, 129
Germany, 6, 17, 45, 64, 72, 81; emigration from, 11
Gerstein, Dietrich, 22, 25, 129
Gettysburg, 55, 59, 60, 62, 106, 135, 155; battle of, 144–47; nativism after, 159
Grant, Ulysses S., 62, 122, 123, 150, 154, 156, 157; at Shiloh, 118–21; at Vicksburg, 148–50; commander in chief, 155; on Union army, 161; president, 161
Gratz, Louis A., 72, 73
Griffiths, James, 93, 133
guerrillas, 41, 84
Guiney, Patrick R., 141

Halleck, Henry W., 100, 137, 147, 154, 157; and German-Americans, 101

Hammer, Adam, 39, 40

Harvey, Louis P., 49

Hassendeubel, Franz, 43, 49

Hecker, Friedrich, 14, 64, 74, 82, 131, 159; as Latin Farmer, 29; commands 24th Illinois Infantry, 45; commands 82nd Illinois Infantry, 46, 51, 67; in 1848 revolution, 6, 7, 12–13; in politics, 26; wounded at Chancellorsville, 139

Heg, Hans Christian, 24, 44, 48–49, 82, 122, 150, 151

Heine, Heinrich, 6, 9

Heine, Wilhelm, 60

Heinzen, Karl, 30

Hemlandet, 20, 23, 28, 44, 76, 80

Herold des Westens, 30

Heusinger, Otto, 93–94

Highland (Illinois), 21, 46, 108

Hill, A. P., 127, 144

Hoffmann, Ernst, 69, 70

Hooker, Joseph, 125, 137, 138, 140, 142, 148

Horstmann, August, 74, 82, 104, 110, 112, 148, 155, 160

Howard, Oliver O., 137–38, 139, 142, 143, 144, 145, 147

Hungarian Americans, 13, 18, 26, 38, 49, 56, 99; forty-eighers, 31; in 1860 election, 28; patriotism of, 33, 36, 39; recruitment among, 54, 79

Hungary, 5, 7, 9, 12, 25, 59, 61

hungry forties, 2, 3, 6, 10

Illinois Staats Zeitung, 34, 45, 79

Illinois, 21, 22, 24, 25, 27, 29, 30, 43, 78; ethnic regiments from, 45, 46, 49; 16th Cavalry, 46, 78; 6th Infantry, 74; 8th Infantry, 133; 9th Infantry, 45, 79, 101, 121; 19th Infantry, 36; 23rd Infantry "Irish Brigade," 46, 50; 24th "Hecker" Infantry, 45, 46, 74; 27th Infantry, 122; 43rd "Körner" Infantry, 46, 75, 80, 83, 119, 122; 44th Infantry, 46, 152; 46th Infantry, 79; 55th Infantry, 81, 119, 120;

57th Infantry, 79, 121; 65th Infantry, 57; 73rd Infantry, 152; 82nd "Second Hecker" Infantry, 46, 51, 67, 131, 139, 141, 160; 89th Infantry, 151; 90th Infantry "Irish Legion," 46, 105; 1st Light Artillery, 62; 2nd Light Artillery, 62, 122

immigrants, xii–xiii; and Democratic Party, 22, 23, 75; and emancipation, 129–31; and politics, 21–28; and Republican Party, 22–24, 25, 26; and slavery, 22; as slave owners, 23; in the South, 22–23, 76–78; join nonethnic regiments, 64, 69, 71; language barriers, 20; lured into army, 73; patriotism of, 31, 33–38; reactions to nativism, 25, 39, 41, 101, 142–43; reactions to war, 33,41–43; rural, 21; stereotypes, 19, 20, 23, 105; urban, 17, 18, 19, 20, 22–23, 33, 49, 82; violence against, 41, 76–77; visibility of, 18, 19, 23, 41, 76; war weariness among, 143. *See also under various ethnic groups*

immigration, 21; impact on US society, 19; numbers, 12, 17, 22; postwar, 161

Indiana, 40, 43, 75; ethnic regiments from, 47–48; 11th Infantry, 67, 120; 23rd Infantry, 75, 121; 32nd Infantry, 47–48, 103, 120, 151, 153, 159; 35th Infantry, 48, 78, 81; 79th Infantry, 67

Indianapolis *Freie Presse*, 100

industrialization, 1, 2, 11, 73

Iowa, 21, 40, 84

Ireland, 2, 3, 4, 45, 161

Irish Americans: and African Americans, 18, 23, 26–27, 28; and Democratic Party, 38; and draft riots, 134–35; and German Americans, 18, 19; and politics, 26–27; and slavery, 22–23; antiwar sentiment among, 54, 102, 130, 134; Catholics, 20, 25, 48, 78, 81; drinking among, 104; economic situation of, 17–18; ethnic identity, 18, 31, 44–45, 52, 143; in elections, 26, 28, 105; in German regiments, 51, 52; in the South, 22–23; join Confederate army, 34, 76, 105;

Irish Americans (*cont.*)
  join Union army, 34, 44–45, 50;
  motivations for enlistment, 70–71;
  nativism against, 43, 161; oppose
  emancipation, 129–30; stereotypical views
  of, 19–20, 105–6, 135, 157, 158; support
  McClellan, 130; unionism among, 33, 34,
  36, 39
Irish Brigade, 52, 53, 54, 58, 70, 90, 92,
  102, 125, 130, 155, 156, 157, 159; at
  Antietam, 125–26, 128; at
  Chancellorsville, 140, 141, 143; at Fair
  Oaks, 114–15; at Fredericksburg,
  130–31; at Gettysburg, 145–46; in Seven
  Days' Battles, 115–17
Irish News, 26
Irish regiments, 43, 44, 46–48, 52–54, 82,
  87, 117–18, 130; courage of, 52, 106,
  115–16, 128, 137, 143, 155; reputation
  for drinking and brawling, 47, 50, 105
Irish-American, 102
Iron Brigade, 71, 124, 144, 161
Italian Americans, 20, 33, 56; recruitment
  among, 43–44, 53, 54
Italy, 5, 6, 9; wars of unification, 11, 14

Jackson, Claiborne, 39, 40, 97
Jackson, Thomas "Stonewall," 88, 109, 123,
  124, 125, 137; at Chancellorsville,
  138–40; at Cross Keys, 110–11, 115
Jacobs, William H., 48, 139, 142
Jansson, Eric, 4, 21
Jews, 11, 14, 17, 23, 25, 46, 72, 73, 82; as
  regimental chaplains, 48, 60
Johnston, Albert S., 118, 120
Johnston, Joseph E., 113, 115, 148
Joliat, Francis J., 50, 107

Kansas, 14, 25, 38, 40; ethnic recruitment
  in, 49; border war in, 25, 26, 39; 1st
  Infantry, 49, 98; 2nd Infantry, 49, 98
Kansas-Nebraska Bill, 24, 39
Kapp, Friedrich, 58
Karberg, Peter, 36, 71–72, 132

Kaufmann, Wilhelm, xii, 46, 49, 51, 59, 62,
  66, 67, 77, 91, 150
Kautz, Valentin, 93, 94–95, 156
Kelly, James, 88–89
Kelly, Patrick D., 54, 140, 147
Kentucky, 30, 40, 84, 109, 118; ethnic
  recruitment in, 49; 6th Cavalry, 72; 5th
  Infantry, 49, 102, 160; 6th Infantry, 49,
  102, 121, 154, 160
Keppler, Gustav, 83–84
Keyes, Erasmus D., 113
Kinkel, Gottfried, 13, 18, 24, 64, 65
Kiolbassa, Peter, 78, 161
Kiolbassa, Stanislas, 10, 13, 21, 77
Kircher, Henry, 132
Kleinz, Christian, 52
Knefler, Frederick, 13, 14, 67
Knoebel, Cornelius, 124
Knoebel, Emil, 144–45, 147
Know-Nothings, 24, 37, 43, 52, 102
Koltes, John A., 51, 124
Körner, Gustav, 22, 24, 26, 100
Kossuth, Lajos, 7, 8, 9, 12, 13, 29, 36, 66;
  and Hungarian-American identity, 18
Kozlay, Eugen, 59–60, 110, 111
Kraus, Albert, 67
Krause, Albert, 63, 70, 83, 95, 131–32
Krez, Conrad, 48
Krumme, Friedrich, 79
Krzyzanowski, Wladimir, 10, 56, 60, 70, 74,
  80, 91, 103, 111, 129, 131, 138, 145,
  150, 160
Kuné, Julian, 45
labor movement, 14, 18–19, 30

Laiboldt, Bernhardt, 150, 152, 153
Landgräber, Klemens, 62, 150, 159
language, 19, 20–21, 83, 103; ethnic
  identifiaction and, 50, 80, 91
Latin Farmers, 22, 29, 40, 46, 49, 59, 65,
  76, 80
Lee, Robert E., 115, 116, 127, 130, 137,
  140, 144, 146, 147, 155, 156
Lieb, Hermann, 8, 10–11, 133

Lincoln, Abraham, 22, 27, 33, 40, 43, 56, 65, 67, 87, 88, 99, 112, 113, 131, 134, 137, 138, 143, 150, 155, 158, 162; and Frémont, 100, 109; and pacifists, 85; calls for volunteers, 34–35, 42, 70, 79; ethnic support for, 28, 31, 73; issues Emancipation Proclamation, 128–29; leadership criticized, 141; reinstates McClellan, 125; relieves McClellan, 123, 130

Lockman, John T., 60

Longstreet, James, 114, 124, 152

Lonn, Ella, xii, xiii, 59, 62, 85, 103, 147, 159

Lookout Mountain, battle of, 154

Louis Napoleon, 8, 9

Louisiana Tigers, 117

Louisville Anzeiger, 45

Lutherans, 22, 24, 75, 82

Lyon, Nathaniel, 40, 41, 97, 98, 99

Lytle, William Haines, 47

Mahler, Franz, 145

Maine, 52; 15th "Old Fifteenth" Infantry, 52

Malmborg, Oscar, 119, 120, 121

Malvern Hill, battle of, 116–17

Martens, Friedrich, 38, 74, 108

Marx, Karl, 7, 13, 128

Maryland, 49; 3rd Infantry, 49; 5th Infantry, 49, 126

Massachusetts, 18, 81; ethnic regiments from, 52, 53; 9th Infantry, 45, 53, 81, 115, 116, 117, 141, 159; 20th Infantry, 81; 28th "Faugh a Ballagh" Infantry, 53, 70, 128; 29th Infantry, 116; 54th Infantry, 132

Mattson, Hans, 21, 24, 44, 80, 82, 86, 102

Mazzini, Giuseppe, 6, 9

McCarter, William, 71, 103–4, 105; on McClellan, 130; on Sigel, 125

McClellan, George B., 55, 91, 92, 109, 110, 113, 115, 116, 117, 118, 123, 124, 125, 126, 127, 128, 130, 155

McClernand, John, 119, 122

McCook, Alexander McDowell, 150–51

McCook, Robert L., 46, 47, 153

McCulloch, Herny E., 77, 98

McCunn, John H., 54

McDowell, Irwin, 88, 124

McIvor, James P., 54

Meade, George G., 144, 145

Meagher, Thomas Francis, xii, 3, 52, 53, 80, 87, 90, 93, 97, 105, 116, 126, 128, 130, 143, 154, 159; and Democratic Party, 26, 34; and Irish Brigade, 44–45, 54, 102, 103; and Irish-American identity, 18, 67; at Fair Oaks, 113–15; at first Bull Run, 88–89; characterized, 90; criticized, 118; defends Corcoran, 42; drinking habits, 103–4, 157; exile, 9, 14–15; on Frémont's staff, 100; pro-southern attitude of, 22, 34; resigns, 140; staff of, 92; unionism of, 34

mercenaries, xi, 78, 160

Mersey, August, 45, 79, 101, 121

Mexican War, 46, 51, 58, 93, 102

Mexico, 60, 77

Michigan, 38, 61; 1st Cavalry, 73; 29th Infantry, 75

Mihalotzy, Geza, 45, 74, 79

Miles, D. S., 89

militias, 42, 43, 56, 77, 79, 88

Milliken's Bend, battle of, 133

Milroy, Robert H., 109, 123

Milwaukee, 17, 22, 29, 33, 42, 43, 82; ethnic regiments from, 48

Milwaukee *Seebote*, 24, 37, 104

Minnesota, 20, 21, 38; 3rd Infantry, 80, 82; 7th Infantry, 83

Minnesota *Press*, 80

Minnesota Staats Zeitung, 72, 129, 134

Missionary Ridge, 67, 154; battle of, 150, 154–55

Missouri, 21, 24, 25, 38, 48, 62, 67, 72, 97, 99, 100; ethnic regiments from, 49–50; guerrilla war in, 41; saved for Union, 108; 4th Cavalry, 37; 1st Infantry, 98;

Missouri (*cont.*)

1st Volunteer Infantry (three months),
39–40; 2nd Infantry, 107, 148, 152; 2nd
Volunteer Infantry (three months), 40,
65; 3rd Infantry, 80, 107, 148, 149; 3rd
Volunteer Infantry (three months), 40,
45, 50, 63, 65, 66, 82, 96, 97–98; 4th
Infantry "Schwarze Jäger," 40; 5th
Infantry, 97, 98; 5th Volunteer Infantry
(three months), 40; 7th Infantry "Wild
Irish," 50, 105; 8th Infantry, 69; 12th
Infantry, 49, 67, 107, 132, 149, 160; 15th
Infantry "Swiss Rifles," 49, 50, 61, 107,
148, 152, 154, 155, 160; 17th "Turner"
Infantry, 43, 49, 82, 101, 107, 108–9

Mitchel, John, 3, 9, 14, 18, 22, 26, 34

Monaghan, Jay, 107

Montieth, William, 53

Moor, August, 127

Morgan, John Hunt, 84

Morgenblatt für gebildete Leser, 94

Morton Oliver, 47, 83

Mulholland, St. Clair A., 52, 92, 140

Mullen, Bernard F., 48, 78, 81

Mulligan, James A., 46

music in ethnic units, 106–7, 138

mutinies, 96–97

Napoleonic Wars, xi, 1, 5, 35

Native Americans, 107

Nativism, 23–24, 30, 37, 39, 43, 49, 53,
102, 104, 147; postwar, 161. *See also*
prejudice

Naughton, Patrick, 50

Nelson, Bersven, 72, 73

Netherlands, emigration from, 11

Neustädter, Johann Albert, 62

New Hampshire, ethnic regiments from, 52,
53; 10th Infantry, 53, 83

New Jersey: 3rd Infantry, 71; 8th Infantry, 76

New Market, 66

New Orleans, 20, 22, 52, 76, 78, 123

New York, 9, 13, 14, 17, 18, 19, 24, 40, 42,
43, 62, 64, 84, 85, 92; ethnic regiments
from, 53–56, 73; 103rd Infantry "Third
German Rifles," 60; 1st Cavalry, 57; 4th
Cavalry, 57, 91; 14th Cavalry, 84;
Independent Battalion "Enfants Perdus,"
55; 5th Independent Battery, 62; 7th
Infantry "Steuben Rifles," 57, 86,
116–17, 126, 131; 8th Infantry "First
German Rifles," 57–58, 60, 66, 67,
87–90, 94, 104, 110, 112; 11th Infantry
"First Fire Zouaves," 54; 20th "United
Turner" Infantry, 43, 58, 72, 94, 106;
29th Infantry "Astor Rifles," 58, 59, 82,
88, 90, 139; 31st Infantry, 56, 58; 37th
Infantry "Irish Rifles," 54; 38th Infantry,
56, 63; 39th Infantry "Garibaldi Guard,"
44, 54–55, 58, 88, 91, 110, 146–47; 40th
Infantry, 81; 41st "DeKalb" Infantry
"Second Jäger," 59, 61, 67, 91, 94, 110,
111, 138; 45th "Platt Deutsch" Infantry
"Fifth German Rifles," 59, 74, 82, 110,
112, 138, 145; 46th Infantry "Frémont
Rifles," 59, 127; 52nd Infantry "Sigel
Rifles," 59, 114–15, 131, 160; 53rd
Infantry, 55; 54th Infantry "Schwarze
Jäger," 59–60, 90, 110, 138; 55th Infantry
"Gardes Lafayette," 55–56, 58, 63, 103;
58th Infantry "Polish Legion," 56, 60, 91,
111, 160; 63rd Infantry, 54, 90, 126; 68th
Infantry "Second German Rifles," 60, 90;
69th Infantry, 52, 54, 71, 90, 114–15,
117, 118, 126; 79th Infantry "Cameron's
Highlanders," 56, 58, 88, 89, 96–97, 160;
88th "Mrs. Meagher's Own" Infantry, 54,
90, 114, 117, 140; 105th Infantry, 54;
116th Infantry, 63, 70, 131; 119th
Infantry, 60, 145; 155th "Wild Irish"
Infantry, 54; 164th "Corcoran Guard"
Infantry "Phoenix Regiment," 54, 155,
159; 170th "Fourth Corcoran Legion"
Infantry, 54, 155, 159; 175th Infantry, 54;
182nd Infantry, 54; 1st Light Artillery,
118; 30th Light Artillery, 73; 34th Light
Artillery, 63; 20th Militia "Ulster Guard,"
54; 69th Militia, 42, 44, 88–90

New York City, 20, 29, 33, 37, 54, 55, 81, 84, 87
New York Herald, 141
New York Times, 94, 141
New Yorker Staats Zeitung, 29, 37
Nicholas I, 9
Nordhoff, Charles, 85
Norway, 4
Norwegian Americans, 21, 104; and Republican Party, 24; recruitment among, 44, 62
Nugent, Robert, 54, 115, 117, 155

O'Kane, Owen, 146
O'Meara, Timothy, 46
Ohio, 37, 40, 62, 74; ethnic regiments from, 46–47; 3rd Cavalry, 47; 9th "Turner" Infantry "Die Neuner," 45, 46–47, 153; 10th "Montgomery" Infantry, 47, 50, 105; 15th Infantry, 151; 18th Infantry, 74; 22nd Infantry, 74; 28th "Second German" Infantry, 47, 127; 37th "Third German" Infantry, 47, 82; 49th Infantry, 151; 56th Infantry, 83; 61st Infantry, 123; 67th Infantry, 105, 131; 106th "Fourth German" Infantry, 47; 107th "Fifth German" Infantry, 47; 108th "Sixth German" Infantry, 47; 120th Infantry, 131; 15th Light Artillery, 84
Ohlenburger, Ferdinand, 77
Olustee, 55
Oregon, 27
Osterhaus, Peter Joseph, 49, 65, 67, 150; at Pea Ridge, 107
Owen, Joshua T., 52, 126

pacifists, 84–85
Palatine, 51, 57
parliaments, German and Prussian, 7, 8
patriotism, 106, 160; as motivation to enlist, 70–72, 85
Pea Ridge, 50, 63; battle of, 107–8
Pemberton, John C., 148, 149, 150
Pennsylvania Dutch, 51

Pennsylvania, 85, ethnic regiments from, 50–52; 5th Cavalry, 48, 52, 60; 9th Cavalry, 72; 24th Infantry (three months), 52; 27th Infantry "Washington Brigade," 51, 82, 88, 110, 111, 139; 35th Infantry, 51; 48th Infantry, 52; 69th Infantry "Philadelphia Brigade," 52, 126–27, 146, 159; 73rd Infantry, 51, 90, 139; 74th Infantry, 51, 91, 110, 123, 124, 138–39, 144–45; 75th Infantry, 51, 91, 110, 139, 145; 98th Infantry, 52; 116th Infantry, 52, 71, 92, 105, 125, 128, 140; 153rd Infantry, 138
Petasch, Paul, 80, 120
Pfänder, Wilhelm, 119
Philadelphia, 23, 51, 52, 82
Pickett's Charge, 146–47
Pittsburgh, 22, 51, 86
Poland, 5, 6, 7, 9–10, 25, 61, 70, 73
Polish Americans, 19, 23, 26, 38, 41, 49, 56, 99; forty-eighters, 31; patriotism of, 33, 39; recruitment among, 53
political officers, 94, 102
Pope, John, 122, 123, 124
Porter, David Dixon, 148, 149
Porter, Fitz-John, 116, 124
prejudice, 19, 24, 81, 87, 99, 102, 104, 159, 160. *See also* nativism
Prentiss, Benjamin M., 118, 119
Price, Sterling, 41, 97, 98, 107, 133
Prussia, 5, 7, 14, 17, 36, 49, 57, 64, 92
public memory, 157–58
Puritanism, 24

Quakers (Society of Friends), 4, 85
Quinlan, James, 117

racism, 38, 132
Raith, Julius, 46, 119, 122
reform movements, 22, 23
regimental chaplains, 48, 67, 81, 82
regular army, 43; Germans and Irish in, 34, 42
Reichhelm, Eduard, 72, 132

Reichhelm, Julius, 14, 29, 67, 72

Reistle, Eugen, 83

Rentschler, Gottfried, 102–3, 106, 132

Revolutions: American, 33–34, 35, 42; French (1789), 5, 35, 36, 47; of 1830, 5

Revolution of 1848/49, 2, 3, 5–12, 14, 22, 25, 26, 36, 51, 58, 75; American reactions to, 9; political refugees from, 9–11. *See also* forty-eighters

Rhode Island, 3rd Heavy Artillery, 63

Richmond, 22, 81, 86, 113, 117, 118, 156

Roberts, Humphrey, 74

Rosecrans, William S., 109, 148, 150, 152, 153, 154

Rossi, Robert, 104

Rudberg, J. B., 75

Russian Americans, 56

Salm-Salm, Felix, 60, 79, 93, 94

Salomon, Carl Eberhard, 14, 40, 48, 96, 98

Salomon, Eduard, 14

Salomon, Edward S., 46

Salomon, Friedrich, 14, 64, 66, 96

San Antonio, 23

Sarner, Leopold, 60

Saxony, 79

Scandinavians, 24, 26, 154, 158; and abolition, 75; patriotism of, 33, 35; recruitment among, 43, 44, 46, 48, 80; vote for Lincoln, 28. *See also under* Swedish Americans, Norwegian Americans, Danish Americans

Schadt, Otto, 49

Scheller-de Buol, Ulysses, 12, 29–30

Schenck, Robert C., 123

Schirmer, Louis, 62, 110, 111

Schlüter, Wilhelmine, 37, 73

Schmalzried, Friedrich, 73, 75

Schofield, John M., 98, 99

Schurz, Carl, 30, 37, 48, 51, 56, 103, 123, 129, 138, 147; and German ethnic identity, 18; appointed general, 65; at

Chancellorsville, 139; at Gettysburg, 144–45; attacked by German Americans, 31; blamed after Chancellorsville, 141–43; campaigns for Republicans, 24, 26, 73; in 1848 revolution, 13; on Blenker, 57–58, 93; on elections, 27; on emancipation, 100, 128; on forty-eighters, 29; on outbreak of war, 35; on slavery, 24; postwar career, 161; recruits ethnic regiments, 57, 64, 78

Schüttner, Nikolaus, 40

Schweizer, Adrian, 133–34

Scotland, 2, 3, 4

Scottish Americans, 21, 28, 33, 41; argue for emancipation, 22; recruitment among, 53, 56

Scottish regiments, 56, 58

Seasongood, Emily, 31

secession, 28, 31, 33, 40, 76, 128

Second Corps, 90, 125, 145, 146

Sedgwick, John, 126

Seven Days' Battles, 86, 115–18

Shakers, 84, 85

Shenandoah Valley, 88, 109, 110

Sheridan, Phil, 148, 152

Sherman, William T., 62, 88, 89, 118, 119, 121, 155

Shields, James, 102, 110, 111

Shiloh, 62, 67, 78, 86, 123; battle of, 118–21

Sigel, Franz, xii, 14, 43, 45, 50, 51, 67, 72, 80, 82, 137, 150; ability of, as commander, 99; and Halleck, 100–101; as ethnic idol, 66, 67, 98, 109, 124; at Carthage, 97–98; at Pea Ridge, 107–8; at Second Bull Run, 123–25; at Wilson's Creek, 98–99; career in US, 29; characterized, 65–66, 125; criticized, 98, 99, 101; in 1848 revolution, 12; in St. Louis, 39–40; on African-Americans, 132–33; postwar career, 161

Silfversparre, Axel, 44, 62

slavery, xiii, 21–24, 27, 29, 30, 48, 56, 76, 79, 99, 100, 128, 130, 131, 132, 155;

abolition of, as motivation to enlist, 69,
  74; as cause of war, 37–38, 70
Smith, Peter, 69–70
Smith, William F., 127
South Carolina, 28, 147
Spanish Americans, recruitment among, 55
Sparrestrom, Frederick, 122
Spiegel, Marcus, 131
St. Louis, 14, 17, 18, 19, 29, 30, 33, 35, 38,
  43, 63, 69, 99, 100; ethnic recruitment
  in, 49, 50, 64, 72; saved for Union, 39–41
Stahel, Julius, xii, 66, 88–89, 90, 110, 161
Stanton, Edwin M., 132, 135, 137, 142, 143
Steele, Frederick, 148, 149
Stevens, Isaac, 97
Stohlbrand, Charles J., 62, 80, 122
Stones River, 67, 81, 148, 159
Struve, Gustav, 6, 8, 13, 26, 29, 94
Stuart, David, 119
Stuart, J. E. B., 140
Sullivan, James Patrick, 71, 106–7, 124,
  141, 144, 161; on Eleventh Corps, 145
Sumner, Edwin V., 113–14, 125, 126–27
Sweden, 2, 4, 5, 61, 109
Swedish Americans, 20, 104; and Republican
  Party, 24, 26; and slavery, 23; in the
  South, 22–23; recruitment among, 44, 62
Swiss Americans, 21, 33; recruitment
  among, 46, 49, 50, 61
Switzerland, 9, 10, 12, 13, 30, 38, 61, 81, 84

Tafel, Gustav, 36, 47, 158
Tägliche Metropole, 36, 39
Taylor, Zachary, 9
Tegner, Fritz, 77
Tennessee, 22, 81, 92, 109, 147
Texas, 10, 13, 76; immigrants in, 17, 21, 22,
  23, 77
The Citizen, 26
Thielemann, Christian, 46, 78
Thomas, George H., 150, 152–53
Tiedemann, Dietrich, 79
Tipperary Advocate, 34
Trepp, Caspar, 61, 147

Tully, Joseph, 71
Turchaninov, Ivan Vasiljevich, *see* Turchin,
  Basil
Turchin, Basil, 36, 153
Turkey, 29, 66
Turners, 19, 36, 58, 64, 80, 98, 106, 127;
  raise ethnic regiments, 43, 82

Underground Railroad, 24
Union army, 137, 160–61; at First Bull Run,
  88; democratic structure, 95;
  discrimination in, 101–2, 124; drinking
  in, 103–4; ethnic tensions in, 48, 52, 73,
  81, 92, 103; ethnic visibility in, 43, 64,
  82, 87, 89, 91–92, 94, 150; immigrants
  in, xii, 34, 36, 64, 83, 85, 97, 156, 162;
  morale, 97, 130, 141; promotions in, 93;
  southerners in, 76–78; under McClellan,
  91
United States Colored Troops, 128, 134;
  immigrants in, 129, 132, 133; 5th
  Colored Heavy Artillery, 133; 6th Colored
  Heavy Artillery, 133; 4th Colored
  Infantry, 129; 82nd Colored Infantry, 132
United States Sharpshooters, 61, 147
Uterhard, Carl, 79, 95, 101, 103, 104, 132

Van Derveer, Ferdinand, 153
Van Dorn, Earl, 107, 108
Vicksburg, 105, 150, 155; Grant's campaign
  against, 148–50
Virginia, 75, 88, 97, 99, 109, 127, 147
von Amsberg, Georg, 59, 74, 110, 112, 145
von Bechtold, Wilhelm, 78
von Egloffstein, Fred W., 60
von Gilsa, Leopold, 59, 66–67, 91, 111,
  138, 145
von Hartung, Adolph, 138–39
von Knobelsdorff, Carl, 46
von Rosa, Rudolf, 59
von Schack, Georg, 57, 117
von Schimmelfennig, Alexander, 51, 123,
  142, 143, 144, 145, 147, 156
von Steinhausen, Albert, 60

von Steinwehr, Adolf, 58, 82, 88, 90, 123, 138, 139, 144, 147
von Vegesack, Ernst Mathias Peter, 36, 127
von Wangelin, Hugo, 49–50, 51, 149, 150

Wales, 3
Wallace, Lew, 67, 121
Warberg, Adolf C., 109, 111, 131
Washington, DC, 47, 56, 64, 88
Washingtoner Intelligenzblatt, 33
Weber, Max, 58, 72, 94, 126, 127
Weinmann, Philipp, 71
Weinrich, Conrad, 41
Welsh Americans, 21, 28, 74; recruitment among, 60–61
Welsh, Peter, 70
Wesslau, Karl, 135
Westbote, 37
Westliche Post, 35, 41, 101
Weydemeyer, Joseph, 13, 30
Wiedrich, Michael, 62, 91, 111, 144, 147
Wiley, Bell I., 158–59
Wilhelmi, Franz, 72, 101
Willich, August, 14, 47, 48, 51, 66, 103, 150, 159; adored by troops, 122; at

Chickamauga, 151–54; at Missionary Ridge, 154; at Shiloh, 120; cares for soldiers, 153–54
Wilson's Creek, battle of, 98–99
Wisconsin Banner, 29
Wisconsin, 14, 21, 24, 40, 44, 64, 71, 74; ethnic regiments from, 48–49; 6th Infantry, 71, 106, 144; 9th Infantry "Salomon Guards," 48, 95, 96, 133; 11th Infantry, 48; 15th Infantry "Scandinavian Regiment," 48–49, 72, 82, 122, 151; 17th Infantry, 48; 26th Infantry, 48, 105, 139, 142, 160; 27th Infantry, 48; 34th Infantry, 48
Wöchentliches Belleviller Volksblatt, 129
Württemberg, 42, 51, 73, 84
Wutschel, Franz, 110, 112

Y Drych (Welsh newspaper), 22
Yates, Richard, 79
Young Ireland, 3, 14

Zagonyi, Charles, 13, 29, 109
Zimmer, Georg Michael, 95–96, 133
Zsulavszky, Ladislas, 13, 71, 132

About the Author

MARTIN W. ÖFELE has taught history at the Universities of Leipzig and Munich. He is the author of several publications on the Civil War Era in Germany.